Management for Professionals

More information about this series at http://www.springer.com/series/10101

Ralf T. Kreutzer

Toolbox for Marketing and Management

Creative Concepts, Forecasting Methods, and Analytical Instruments

Ralf T. Kreutzer
Berlin School of Economics and Law
Königswinter, Germany

ISSN 2192-8096   ISSN 2192-810X (electronic)
Management for Professionals
ISBN 978-3-030-13822-6   ISBN 978-3-030-13823-3 (eBook)
https://doi.org/10.1007/978-3-030-13823-3

© Springer Nature Switzerland AG 2019
Original German edition published by Springer Fachmedien Wiesbaden GmbH, Wiesbaden, Germany, 2018
This work is subject to copyright. All rights are reserved by the Publisher, whether the whole or part of the material is concerned, specifically the rights of translation, reprinting, reuse of illustrations, recitation, broadcasting, reproduction on microfilms or in any other physical way, and transmission or information storage and retrieval, electronic adaptation, computer software, or by similar or dissimilar methodology now known or hereafter developed.
The use of general descriptive names, registered names, trademarks, service marks, etc. in this publication does not imply, even in the absence of a specific statement, that such names are exempt from the relevant protective laws and regulations and therefore free for general use.
The publisher, the authors and the editors are safe to assume that the advice and information in this book are believed to be true and accurate at the date of publication. Neither the publisher nor the authors or the editors give a warranty, express or implied, with respect to the material contained herein or for any errors or omissions that may have been made. The publisher remains neutral with regard to jurisdictional claims in published maps and institutional affiliations.

This Springer imprint is published by the registered company Springer Nature Switzerland AG.
The registered company address is: Gewerbestrasse 11, 6330 Cham, Switzerland

The main idea
Simplify!
Simplify!
Simplify!

Introductory Words

Dear Reader,

The first heading should already indicate one thing:

Clarity!

By now this is one of the most important concepts in management and life for me, besides **valuing our interactions with one another**!

This book is intended to help you become (even more) successful in marketing and management. Keeping it short and sweet, I will present helpful tools that support your work and how they should be implemented. When coaching and consulting, as well as in training and lectures, I realise time and again how uncertain people are when it comes to **the goal-oriented implementation of different tools**.

This creates a problem which *Paul Watzlawick* has expressed so nicely:

> Those who only have one hammer as a tool see only one nail in every problem.

Therefore, I would like to introduce you to many different tools, thereby ideally providing the perfect tool for every problem!

Additionally, before introducing the individual tools, I will explain how to give a good **presentation** nowadays (Chap. 1). We have all seen presentations which were (perhaps) filled with good content but presented terribly. Generally, the way we present determines how the (fascinating) content is perceived.

Seeing as we must give presentations more frequently these days, including in online conferences and webinars, I would like to share key **communication success factors** with you.

It is very important that you read this first chapter. You should then skim over the rest of this book to familiarise yourself with the methods and in which situations to use them. Afterwards you can always take a closer look to discover which tools you need to implement individual methods.

I not only wish you success with this, but also lots of fun, because I firmly believe that learning and working should always be fun.

On that note, all the best!

Königswinter, Germany Ralf T. Kreutzer
March 2019

Contents

1 Presentations: Conveyer Belt of Your Success 1
   1.1   Meaning of Presentations for Personal Success 1
   1.2   Success Factors of Presentation Styles 4
   1.3   Success Factors of Presentation Content 13
   1.4   Success Factors of Respectful Communication 21
   References 31

2 Vision, Mission and Goals 33
   2.1   Development of Vision and Mission 33
   2.2   Definition of Goals 36
   2.3   Pyramid of Goals 43
   2.4   Balanced Scorecard 44
   References 48

3 Concepts for the Development of Strategies 49
   3.1   Preliminary Remark: Variety of Strategic Concepts 49
   3.2   Concept of Customer-Oriented Strategies 49
       3.2.1   Market Field Strategy 50
       3.2.2   Market Stimulation Strategy 53
       3.2.3   Market Segmentation Strategy 56
       3.2.4   Market Area Strategy 66
   3.3   Canvas Concepts 68
   3.4   Kano Concept 72
   3.5   3 Horizons Framework 74
   3.6   Brand Management Concepts 79
   References 85

4 Tools for the Strategic Analysis 89
   4.1   Preliminary Remark: Planning the Implementation of Analytical
       Tools 89
   4.2   PEST or PESTEL Analysis 97
   4.3   SWOT Analysis 99
   4.4   Scoring Model 114
   4.5   Portfolio Analysis 116

	4.6	Benchmarking	123
	4.7	Value Chain Analysis	127
	4.8	Gap Analysis	133
	4.9	Customer Journey Map	134
	4.10	Digital Maturity Analysis	137
	References		141
5	**Forecasting Methods**		143
	5.1	Trend Extrapolation	143
	5.2	Scenario Analysis	145
	5.3	Analogy Forecast	147
	5.4	Delphi Method	148
	5.5	Predictive Analytics	150
	5.6	A/B Testing	152
	References		155
6	**Customer Value Models**		157
	6.1	Fundamentals of the Customer Value Concept	157
	6.2	Methods to Determine Customer Value	160
	6.3	Net Promoter Score	170
	References		172
7	**Methods to Create New Products, Services and Business Models**		175
	7.1	Brainstorming and Brainwriting	175
	7.2	Attribute Listing	176
	7.3	Design Thinking	177
	7.4	*Lego* Serious Play	184
	7.5	Mind Map	186
	7.6	World Café	189
	References		193
8	**Innovative Project Management Tools**		195
	8.1	Scrum	195
	8.2	Lean Startup	211
	References		220
9	**Budgeting Concepts**		221
	9.1	Percentage of Sales Method	221
	9.2	Competitive Parity Method	221
	9.3	All You Can Afford Method	222
	9.4	Objective Task Method	222
10	**Strategic and Operational Marketing Plan**		225
	10.1	Creating a Strategic Marketing Plan	225
	10.2	Creating an Operational Marketing Plan	226
	References		229

11 Change Management Tools................................ 231
    11.1   Designing the Change Management Process................ 231
    11.2   Phases and Tools of the Change Management Process......... 234
    References... 250

Index.. 253

List of Abbreviations

B2B	Business to business
B2C	Business to consumer
BCG	Boston Consulting Group
BtB	Business to business
BtC	Business to consumer
cf.	confer
CLV	Customer lifetime value
CPI	Cost per interest
CPO	Cost per order
CRM	Customer relationship management
CRV	Customer reference value
EBIT	Earnings before interest, tax
EBT	Earnings before tax
EBITDA	Earnings before interest, tax, depreciation and amortisation
e.g.	exempli gratia (for example)
i.e.	id est (in other words)
KPI	Key performance indicator
MVP	Minimum viable product
NOMS	National one-man sample
NPS	Net promoter score
R&D	Research and development
ROCE	Return on capital employed
ROI	Return on investment
ROS	Return on sales
PR	Public relations
SBU	Strategic business unit
SBF	Strategic business field
SoA	Share of advertising
SoV	Share of voice
SUV	Sport utility vehicle
WIP	Work in progress

List of Figures

Fig. 1.1	Slide from a presentation for German guests in South Korea. Author's own figure	10
Fig. 1.2	How convincing can an advertisement with capital letters be? Source: Adapted from an ad from *Ralph Lauren*, 2018	17
Fig. 1.3	Negations in headlines	22
Fig. 1.4	Emotional map—basic concept. Author's own figure	23
Fig. 1.5	Emotional map to position words. Author's own figure	23
Fig. 1.6	Mechanism of speech. Author's own figure	24
Fig. 1.7	Speakers are positioned on an emotional map. Author's own figure	25
Fig. 1.8	Problem-focused vs. problem-solving questions. Author's own figure	25
Fig. 1.9	Successful course of a problem-solving conversation. Author's own figure	28
Fig. 1.10	Personal dialogue assessment. Author's own figure	28
Fig. 2.1	Hierarchical target system of a company. Author's own figure	35
Fig. 2.2	Visualisation of goal relationships (in millions of euros). Author's own figure	43
Fig. 2.3	Basic concept of the balanced scorecard for a company. Author's own figure	45
Fig. 2.4	Marketing scorecard for customer relationship management. Author's own figure	47
Fig. 3.1	Concept of customer-oriented strategies. Author's own figure	50
Fig. 3.2	Product/market matrix—Ansoff Matrix. Source: Adapted from Ansoff (1979)	51
Fig. 3.3	Traditional market layer model. Author's own figure	53
Fig. 3.4	Framework for designing the market stimulation strategy. Author's own figure	54
Fig. 3.5	Positioning model—example for the furniture market in Germany. Author's own figure	55
Fig. 3.6	Positioning model highlighting a positioning gap. Author's own figure	55

Fig. 3.7	Types of market segmentation. Author's own figure	57
Fig. 3.8	Selected criteria for market segmentation in the BtC market. Author's own figure	58
Fig. 3.9	Selected criteria of market segmentation in the BtB market. Author's own figure	59
Fig. 3.10	Persona foundation document. Source: Adapted from Pruitt and Adlin (2006, pp. 230–234)	61
Fig. 3.11	Concept of the customer relationship life cycle. Source: Adapted from Stauss (2000, p. 16)	62
Fig. 3.12	Triad of customer service. Author's own figure	63
Fig. 3.13	Selected features to describe your prospects and customers in the BtC market. Author's own figure	64
Fig. 3.14	Decision fields of the market area strategy. Author's own figure	66
Fig. 3.15	Strategies for international expansion. Author's own figure	67
Fig. 3.16	Concept of the business model canvas. Source: Adapted from Osterwalder and Pigneur (2010, p. 44)	68
Fig. 3.17	Concept of the platform canvas. Author's own figure	71
Fig. 3.18	Concept of the lean change canvas. Source: Adapted from Canvanizer (2018)	72
Fig. 3.19	Kano model of customer satisfaction. Source: Adapted from Berger et al. (1993, p. 26)	73
Fig. 3.20	Basic concept of the 3 horizons framework. Source: Adapted from Baghai et al. (2000, p. 5) and Blank (2015)	74
Fig. 3.21	3 horizons framework for strategic analysis. Author's own figure	75
Fig. 3.22	Creation of dualism in the transformation process. Author's own figure	78
Fig. 3.23	Definition of the brand identity by internal stakeholders. Source: Adapted from Burmann et al. (2015, p. 43)	80
Fig. 3.24	Brand identity approach. Source: Adapted from Esch et al. (2005, p. 211)	81
Fig. 3.25	Development of the brand image in the minds of target groups. Source: Adapted from Burmann et al. (2015, p. 57)	81
Fig. 3.26	Holistic brand management in the digital age. Author's own figure	82
Fig. 3.27	*Alphabet* as an example of a brand-product lines matrix. Author's own figure	83
Fig. 3.28	Concept for services development. Author's own figure	84
Fig. 4.1	5D concept of marketing research. Author's own figure	90
Fig. 4.2	Macro- and microenvironment of the company. Author's own figure	98
Fig. 4.3	Basic concept of the SWOT analysis. Author's own figure	100

Fig. 4.4	Result of the analysis of strengths and weaknesses in a competitive comparison. Author's own figure	103
Fig. 4.5	Johari Window for self- and company analysis. Author's own figure	104
Fig. 4.6	Selected questions used in marketing tool audit. Author's own figure	105
Fig. 4.7	Extended product life cycle as an analysis concept. Source: Adapted from Fritz and Oelsnitz (2006, S. 174)	106
Fig. 4.8	Basic concept of *Porter*'s 5 Forces analysis. Author's own figure	109
Fig. 4.9	SWOT matrix—synthesis of the external and internal perspectives within the SWOT analysis. Author's own figure	112
Fig. 4.10	Example of a SWOT synthesis from the consumer goods market. Author's own figure	113
Fig. 4.11	Scoring model for evaluating a new product. Author's own figure	116
Fig. 4.12	Basic concept of BCG portfolio analysis. Author's own figure	118
Fig. 4.13	Different product portfolios as triggers of corporate development. Author's own figure	119
Fig. 4.14	Market attractiveness-competitive advantage portfolio. Author's own figure	120
Fig. 4.15	Technology portfolio. Author's own figure	123
Fig. 4.16	Step-by-step concept of benchmarking. Author's own figure	125
Fig. 4.17	Basic concept of a value chain. Source: Adapted from Porter (2004b)	128
Fig. 4.18	System of value chains. Author's own figure	129
Fig. 4.19	Physical and digital value chain. Author's own figure	132
Fig. 4.20	Gap analysis. Author's own figure	133
Fig. 4.21	Touch points of a customer journey. Author's own figure	135
Fig. 4.22	Basic concept of a customer journey map. Source: Adapted from Kaplan (2016)	136
Fig. 4.23	Digital maturity model. Source: Adapted from Peyman et al. (2014, p. 38)	138
Fig. 4.24	Analysis grid to determine digital maturity. Author's own figure	140
Fig. 5.1	Trend extrapolation. Author's own figure	144
Fig. 5.2	Scenario analysis. Author's own figure	145
Fig. 5.3	Analogy forecast. Author's own figure	147
Fig. 5.4	Delphi method. Author's own figure	149
Fig. 5.5	Basic concept of A/B testing—example website optimisation. Author's own figure	154
Fig. 6.1	Task and approaches of value-oriented customer management. Author's own figure	159
Fig. 6.2	ABC analysis of the customer base. Author's own figure	161

Fig. 6.3	Definition of "good customers" ($n = 78$; multiple answers possible). Source: Verint (2014, p. 1)	162
Fig. 6.4	Error sources in the customer management. Source: Adapted from Helm et al. (2017, pp. 20–24)	162
Fig. 6.5	Criteria to determine customer value. Author's own figure	164
Fig. 6.6	Confidence in various forms of advertising in Germany ($n = 1037$ respondents; German-speaking population ages 18 and over). Source: Statista (2018a)	166
Fig. 6.7	Scoring model to determine customer values in a travel agency. Author's own figure	166
Fig. 6.8	Approaches used to determine customer value ($n = 197$ managers; multiple answers possible). Source: Statista (2018b)	167
Fig. 6.9	Competence pyramid for determining customer value. Author's own figure	168
Fig. 6.10	Individual model for determining the (customer-) reference value. Author's own figure	169
Fig. 6.11	Continuum of social influencers. Author's own figure	169
Fig. 6.12	Concept of the net promoter score. Author's own figure	171
Fig. 6.13	Use of the net promoter score in the hotel sector. Author's own figure	172
Fig. 7.1	Attribute listing for the development of a textbook. Author's own figure	177
Fig. 7.2	Phases of the design thinking process. Author's own figure	180
Fig. 7.3	Empathy map for a persona. Author's own figure	181
Fig. 7.4	*Lego* Serious Play—material and results. Author's own figure	185
Fig. 7.5	Mind map concept (created with webgreat.de). Author's own figure	187
Fig. 8.1	Differences between classic and agile project management. Source: Adapted from Preußig (2015, pp. 41f)	196
Fig. 8.2	Significant changes in the competence map. Author's own figure	196
Fig. 8.3	Scrum team and other players. Author's own figure	198
Fig. 8.4	Overall flow of Scrum process. Author's own figure	202
Fig. 8.5	Scrum burndown chart. Author's own figure	203
Fig. 8.6	Scrum Kanban board. Author's own figure	210
Fig. 8.7	Analysis grid for innovations. Source: Adapted from Gourville (2006, p. 54)	212
Fig. 8.8	Time to market. Author's own figure	213
Fig. 8.9	Theory of the minimum viable product (MVP). Author's own figure	214

Fig. 8.10	Time to value. Author's own figure	214
Fig. 8.11	Lean startup model. Author's own figure	216
Fig. 8.12	Types of price differentiation as input for the lean startup process. Author's own figure	218
Fig. 8.13	Basic forms of distribution. Author's own figure	218
Fig. 8.14	Tasks that business partners can take on. Author's own figure	219
Fig. 10.1	Rough structure of a strategic marketing plan. Author's own figure	226
Fig. 10.2	Rough structure of an operational marketing plan. Author's own figure	227
Fig. 10.3	Ideal-typical assignment of action modules of a marketing plan as a function of the respective phases of the product life cycle achieved. Author's own figure	228
Fig. 11.1	Change management steps. Author's own figure	232
Fig. 11.2	Matrix of effect: typology of perceived changes. Author's own figure	233
Fig. 11.3	Classification of different change triggers in the matrix of effect. Author's own figure	234
Fig. 11.4	Segmentation of employees in change processes. Author's own figure	236
Fig. 11.5	Classic course of a change management process. Author's own figure	237
Fig. 11.6	Four-room concept of change management. Source: Adapted from Human Change (2018)	239
Fig. 11.7	Challenge in the change process. Source: Adopted from Lewin (1947, p. 28)	240
Fig. 11.8	Influencing factors of the change process. Author's own figure	241
Fig. 11.9	Prerequisites for successful change management. Author's own figure	243
Fig. 11.10	Team development clock. Author's own figure	244
Fig. 11.11	House of digital transformation. Author's own figure	248

Presentations: Conveyer Belt of Your Success

1.1 Meaning of Presentations for Personal Success

What sets a **successful manager** apart nowadays?
Communication, communication, communication!
Communication is the prerequisite for you to be successful in and with your team. This increases your team's performance in the long run through a **transparent and prompt exchange of information**. Communication is also needed to define goals, expectations and tasks. Furthermore, identifying and ideally eliminating uncertainties along the way requires feedback and continuous communication. Keep in mind that it is important to *recognise* relevant stakeholders, who play a critical role in your own career and/or in the success of your responsibilities, at an early stage.

Only communication enables **teamwork and cooperation**. It is necessary to define the responsibilities of the team and its members.

Feedback highlights accomplishments or pinpoints areas that need improvement. Through honest, prompt and constructive communication, you will create an atmosphere of trust and respect, which is essential for long-lasting success within a company (and in life)!

In addition to communication within a team, **personal face-to-face communication** is very important. While praise and recognition in front of others can have positive effects, corrective communication, as in **constructive feedback**, should rather be done in private.

I am purposely avoiding the term "negative feedback", which merely points out mistakes without providing ideas for improvement. Saying "that was a bad presentation" is never helpful. People receiving such criticism are left to guess what the feedback provider did not like. And with this guessing game, the receiver can be right or wrong, something you should not leave to chance.

It is equally important to note that the feedback process should not be designed as a one-way road. Even you, as the manager or project leader, should be open to (constructive) feedback from your team, because they generally talk quite openly (amongst themselves) about what is going well or badly. Therefore, it is essential that you know this as well. Only then can you react and act appropriately (cf. Fig. 4.5 "blind spot" as well).

> **Remember Box**
> Feedback is like a present. Whether you unpack it or not is up to you. It is still a present! A present which can help you learn and develop.
> Keep in mind that feedback that you initially reject with deepest conviction often points out opportunities for you to grow the most. Opportunities that you just don't want to see at first because perhaps they are outside your comfort zone.

A **comfort zone** is the area of a person in which he or she feels comfortable and at ease, which is defined by habits. These are familiar things, including activities done "hundreds" of times (keyword "routines") and people in our everyday lives. Every person has a different comfort zone, because people have their own, different habits. Those people who have mostly worked in the background and not stood on the stage themselves have a different comfort zone than someone who "hogs the limelight" and loves nothing more than performing in front of an audience.

On the other hand, someone who must give a speech for the first time, thereby leaving their comfort zone, is forced to overcome personal limitations to increase their own comfort zone. Understandably, this leads to **growth pains**, just like with all other development processes! These arise when expanding one's own comfort zone through fear, stress, struggles and internal battles and trying to push us to simply give up on something new!

Indeed, the challenges that allow people to grow are found in the so-called **growth areas**. It is discovered when a person leaves their own comfort zone and takes on a challenge which is still deemed as unsafe. Here actions are more difficult and require more energy, because entering a "terra incognita" demands "adjustment".

> **Remember Box**
> Growth begins beyond the limits!

However, we should avoid the **panic zone**. We enter this zone when taking on tasks which are so far from our previous experience and habits that failure is highly probable. Thus, to develop new habits and a sense of security, it is recommended to learn by gradually passing from the comfort zone to the growth area. This not only applies to you but also your colleagues, whose growth you must foster as a manager.

How did *Dale Carnegie* put it so nicely? Learn to swim, but in lukewarm water.

1.1 Meaning of Presentations for Personal Success

During feedback processes, but also in general, it is necessary to be mindful of the **form of communication** and **every single word**.

> **Remember Box**
> Thoughtless words, an arrow that is released and a missed opportunity cannot be brought back.

Those who continue to see management training as "brainwashing" will always put a negative spin on the content that is presented there for themselves and their audience. Even if words are meant to be ironic, often only the negative term "brainwash" is remembered. If a leading paper states that countries try to "wrangle money" out of companies through taxes, the word choice misleads its readers. It only seems natural that companies pay taxes to finance the hard and soft infrastructure of countries which supports their business model.

Instead of a "semester break", I also always call it an "outside of term working time", because the latter term better describes the actual activities. Therefore, we should also avoid using supposedly funny terms for our clients, such as "fuzzys" (I heard this once at a telephone marketing training course). Also, shortening the term passenger to "paxe" in the tourism industry does not make it clear that these are valued clients.

Those who call their IT colleagues "nerds", their marketing colleagues "cash burners" and their accounting colleagues "bean counters" should not be surprised that there is little cooperation. It is not much better when managers consider the "morning meeting" as a time for a "morning scolding". Such words have negative effects that quickly determine our actions.

> **Remember Box**
> Be mindful of your thoughts, because they become your words!
> Be mindful of your words, because they become your actions!
> Be mindful of your actions, because they become your habits!
> Be mindful of your habits, because they become your character!
> Be mindful of your character, because it becomes your fate!
> Jewish Talmud

For many managers **presentations** are another important form of communication. Regardless of their level in the hierarchy and range of responsibilities, they must always demonstrate their results through presentations to either persuade others and win them over as a follower, to gain customers or to simply to present the status quo or findings of studies.

> **Remember Box**
> Keep in mind that every presenter is a salesperson. They sell themselves first and foremost because whether the content, suggestions, ideas, concepts and results are accepted depend entirely on the (perceived) personality of the presenter. Only then is the content of the presentation considered.

At this point I would like to refer to the quote "the medium is the message" by *Marshall McLuhan*. It means that the **medium** combines with the message itself and is therefore perceived as one. This creates the symbiotic relationship between the sender and receiver, which significantly impacts whether the message itself is perceived. In a presentation the presenter is the medium. The presenter should be fully aware of their own impact on the outcome of the communication.

It is often said that 70–80% of what is remembered relates to the **way it is presented** (body language and tone), whereas the content only accounts for 20–30%. This proportion should give all of us something to think about. Why? Because in my career, I have never met anybody who plans their preparation time according to these percentages:

- 80% of the time spent on the method to present the content
- 20% for the content

We usually use 99% of the time to prepare our content! The good news is:
You can change this very easily. After all, you are your own time manager!

> **Remember Box**
> In addition to preparing the content of your presentation, you should pay special attention to the way you present. You should particularly pay attention to how you yourself act in front of the audience (verbal and nonverbal).

1.2 Success Factors of Presentation Styles

You have all experienced it yourself. Presenters at conferences, you have not only had to pay to participate but also make time for, begin with the following statements:

- "I quickly made the presentation last night in my hotel room".
- "My slides are in German and English. Unfortunately, I did not have time to translate them".
- "I was actually supposed to talk about XY, as indicated in the programme. However, I have changed the title and content again".

1.2 Success Factors of Presentation Styles

How are you supposed to take somebody like that seriously? Somebody gets up in front of the audience and says that they don't take it seriously. Otherwise they would have come prepared and delivered what they had promised! Thanks for that!

> **Remember Box**
> You forget what it was about, but you don't forget how you were treated.

On the other hand, imagine how much more sophisticated you as a presenter appear by mentioning that you are thankful for the invitation during your introduction. You can also let the audience know how happy you are to share your knowledge, experience, etc. that you have gathered over the past weeks, months or even years.

Appreciation in its purest form!

At the same time, in this way you address emotions, which are much more important than figures, data and facts when it comes to establishing a relationship with the audience.

The opening words already largely determine the success of your presentation. These words should enable your target audience to easily assess your speech. After all, the audience would quickly like to know whether you have something relevant to offer. This simply means that you need to start off by selling the content of your presentation in the best possible way. This should involve answering the following **unspoken questions** of the audience:

- Why is it so important to listen specifically to you?
- What can the audience learn from your talk?
- What will the audience learn from you that they did not know before?
- Why is your speech useful for the audience?

Give them hints without giving too much away, since you must keep them in suspense. However, then you must deliver during your speech!

Also, don't forget:

You never have a second chance to make a first impression!

Therefore, when preparing a presentation, you should not only carefully consider the impact of the first words but also to how you communicate them. If you rush on stage and are not really with it yet, you will not have a successful start. The same applies when your first (defining) sentences are lost in the murmur of the audience, because you have not been able to gain their full attention.

I will give you a **recommendation** that I learnt from my marketing professor and have used thousands of times. Once you have finished your preparations in the room for the speech or lecture you are about to give, stand in front of the group where everyone can see you and do nothing else but wait for the conversations in the room to come to an end. At the same time, you can appreciatively look around the auditorium.

You might have to silently wait for 30 s, maybe even 1 min. I have never had to wait longer than 2 min until there was absolute silence, even with an audience of several hundred people. Then wait another 10 s before you begin your speech. **A successful start to a presentation** could look like this. The first time you do this, it will be strange to silently wait, seeing as you are now leaving your comfort zone! Nevertheless, you will get used to it and eventually really enjoy it. You will smile at those who continue to fight to get the audience's attention by yelling at them. Yelling certainly very rarely scores first sympathy points!

To grab the audience's attention from the beginning, you must also start the presentation with a bam. To do so you can make or ask the following statements or questions when beginning your presentation:

- What do we have to do to stand up to competitor XY from China, who continues to get stronger?
- How can you decrease the acquisition cost of new clients by 30%?
- Which surprising discoveries did we make through our recent competitor analysis?
- How start-ups are attacking us and why we haven't noticed it until now?
- Which companies in our industry have already become victims of digital Darwinism, and what we can do against it, so that we don't become victims ourselves?
- Why brand management is done differently in the digital age than in the past, and how we can accommodate to it?
- Why we must review our human resource strategies, so that we still have and can find enough employees in the future?
- Others

An introduction with a comprehensive (promotional) company presentation is not recommended when participating at (paid) conferences. It is completely understandable that the audience would much rather know if you have something to say about this topic. This should become apparent quickly!

It is said that the **introduction** can account for up to 50% of presentation success. Even if it were only 20 or 30%, it is important to focus on the introduction. Same goes for the **conclusion**. Have you ever not noticed that a presentation was already over? There is an awkward pause, until the presenter relieves the audience by saying, "that was the end of my presentation". This is also not very convincing! In the final part, you should again explain to the audience what the key points of your presentation were and what they should ideally remember:

- What should be remembered, in other words, the key message?
- What should the audience be talking about on their way home?
- What are the golden nuggets that the audience should remember?
- What must be done?
- What are the next steps?

Thus, you should not only write, "Thank you for your attention" on your last slide. Instead, you can write, "More exciting ideas can be found here..." and refer to relevant books that you recommend about your subject. A call for action can also be very effective at the end of your presentation.

The psychology of learning can be used to explain the relevance of the beginning and end of a presentation. In this field, the term **serial-position effect** is used to describe the tendency of being able to recall the first content (**primacy effect**) as well as the last-mentioned content (**recency effect**) the best in a learning cycle (cf. Stangl 2017). That is why not only well-worded closing words but also a **confident exit** is so important.

Time and again I see presenters wanting to rush off the stage after their last words. This doesn't communicate confidence! Firstly, you can enjoy the (hopefully deserved) applause. Calmly accepting this is also a sign of appreciation. Then you should take questions from the audience. After opening the floor to questions, you must also wait to see if there are any.

Waiting is also a sign of sovereignty and appreciation, because, depending on the audience, the initial shyness to ask questions must be overcome. At this point you must also give the audience time!

It is said that the **concluding part of a presentation** accounts for 30% of the success of presentation, meaning that the middle part merely contributes 20%.

> **Remember Box**
> A successful start and end are crucial for a favourable outcome of a presentation.

Aside from the content, you should pay close attention to body language, as well as voice pitch and modulation during the presentation. Regarding **body language**, you should be aware of how confidently you are standing in front of the audience. Are you hiding behind a podium, holding it and not daring to step forward? Or can you leave the lectern in a poised manner or even walk back and forth on the stage? Keep in mind that you shouldn't walk back and forth on the podium like a hungry tiger, although we often see US-American speakers doing this. For me this rather seems like a show, which (often) is used to distract from the weak content.

Furthermore, slowly walking through the audience during the presentation is particularly challenging. When you do this for the first time, you will feel a special energy from your audience and, at the same time, notice the strong forces trying to pull you back into your comfort zone (behind the lectern).

Your **posture** also plays a significant role **when presenting**. It tells your audience how comfortable you are with the topic. Therefore, it is important that you already step on to the stage with confidence. Personally, during presentations given by women, I always wonder how a confident and secure entrance can be ensured in high heels!

Moreover, your **gestures** are equally of great importance **when presenting**. For instance, are you holding on to a board marker or clicking a pen because you are nervous? It is best to have nothing in your hands, except a clicker if necessary. With your hands, you can underline your achievements, make accentuations clear or announce actions. However, make sure that your words and gestures fit together and tell the same story.

Even though some believe it gives an easy-going and confident impression, in my opinion your hands should not be in your pockets during a presentation. Some speakers leave them there until the end of the speech and are in no way convincing but rather rude! By bending your arms and positioning your hands at the height of your belt, you will have the ideal starting position to emphasise information with your right or left hand. Regardless of which gestures you use, they must fit to you and the content that you are presenting.

The face is often described as a mirror of the soul. Your **facial expression** reflects your current feelings, and therefore, you should pay close attention to it. If you begin a presentation with a bad feeling or lack of conviction, the audience will notice it. On the other hand, if you have dedicated your heart and soul to the topic, then your audience will be able to feel your enthusiasm.

> **Remember Box**
> How did *Augustinus* express it so well?
> *Only those who burn themselves, can ignite fire in others.*

To do this and step to the podium full of energy and happiness, you should prepare your body for success and not say to yourself, "This is probably not going to go well (again)". We are all familiar with the phenomenon of the **self-fulfilling prophecy**. We should refrain from doing this because such sentences set ourselves up for failure. Instead, why don't we say, "I have spent my entire (professional) life preparing for this particular presentation"? Now that is a statement that must, can and will provide certainty.

And seeing as we are already describing the **face as a mirror of the soul**, we should take the following quote from *Teresa von Ávila* to heart:

Do something good for your body, so that your soul may desire to dwell in it.

And we should do this especially, but not only, before presentations, so that we can step up to the task in a good mood and loaded with energy!

Giving a confident impression also involves a good amount of **eye contact** with the audience. But what does this mean? You should slowly glance over the entire audience to equally (personally) address everyone. When people of a higher rank are present in the room, some presenters tend to focus on making continual and often over-the-top amounts of eye contact with them. The other participants notice this, of course, and could therefore feel neglected by the speaker. Sometimes it is also important to continuously let your eyes wander over the audience to catch the first reactions (body language) towards the content being presented. When doing this we should avoid the following trap: people in the audience who are nodding and thereby naturally seem especially nice. Unexperienced speakers tend to then say, "more of the same" to continue getting approval. This makes us easy to manipulate. We should be aware of this risk!

Furthermore, you should avoid another common mistake of **speaking to the wall** where your wonderful slides are projected. Although "a beautiful rear can also endear", in this case it is seldom true, because we would rather see the speaker's face. Therefore, the speaker should present the content using either a screen in front of him/her or printouts of the presentation while looking at the audience.

It is also important to pay attention to **pitch** and **voice modulation**. The more nervous a presenter is, the higher his voice gets. When you speak without periods or commas, you not only indicate your nervousness to the audience but also a lack of appreciation. Monotone speakers even put the most interested listeners to sleep. On the other hand, speaking in a powerful, loud, clear and slow manner is easy to understand. You can participate in valuable **phonation courses** for this reason. When something is particularly important, you can also lower your voice, because this sends a strong message and encourages attentiveness.

> **Remember Box**
> The best way to reduce nervousness is practice, practice, practice, not with beta blockers!

To present skilfully, you should give your audience time to think and understand important content. You can do this by asking rhetorical questions, which they can answer themselves. Small dramatic pauses can also lead to an increased understanding, because they separate pieces of information. Besides, this creates variety in a speech, which prevents acoustic boredom and holds your audience's attention.

Making sure that the audience can understand you seems natural, but unfortunately it only seems this way. Some speakers want to appear extremely competent by using words that only highly qualified specialists understand. Rather than showing your audience that you value them, this behaviour builds a wall between you and them.

Simply reading out a speech instead of presenting also does not indicate much appreciation. It is particularly bad when the text is written to be read rather than presented. Then the sentences are too long and convoluted and thereby too complex to be properly understood only through listening. This does not work at all!

Besides, in a business context, most speakers do not do themselves any favours by **writing their speech out** in advance. They lose the connection to the audience by frequently looking at their notes (really, who has a teleprompter). Seeing as the speaker must concentrate so much not losing his/her place in the notes, there are little to no gestures—which line am I at? Not to mention, if you get confused, you can't get the sentences straight, lose the main idea and can't get back into the speech.

I tell most speakers that, "if you have mastered your topic, then you don't need to write out your speech and use it as a crutch to be able to get up in front of the audience". And everyone that takes the stage should master their topic; otherwise they should just leave it be!

> **Remember Box**
> Speaking freely is a sign of competence. In the field of business, it is expected to give a speech without a script. And you can learn it!
>
> A script becomes a corset, making it impossible for you to move freely. Additionally, it strongly reduces the speech's impact and is therefore also rarely valued by the audience.

"Speaking the language of the audience" during a presentation also means translating charts accordingly. This seems to go without saying, but apparently not. While on a study trip in South Korea, many speakers used slides with Korean characters (cf. Fig. 1.1). For me this is an imposition. After all every speaker had to assume that none of the participants from the German group would understand these documents.

I already briefly spoke about the relevance of every single word. Of course, this applies to speeches and presentations as well. You should avoid **exaggerations** that make you look like a (supposed) superstar. **Leading questions** or **assumptions** are also not well received by audiences. The audience doesn't want to feel stupid when

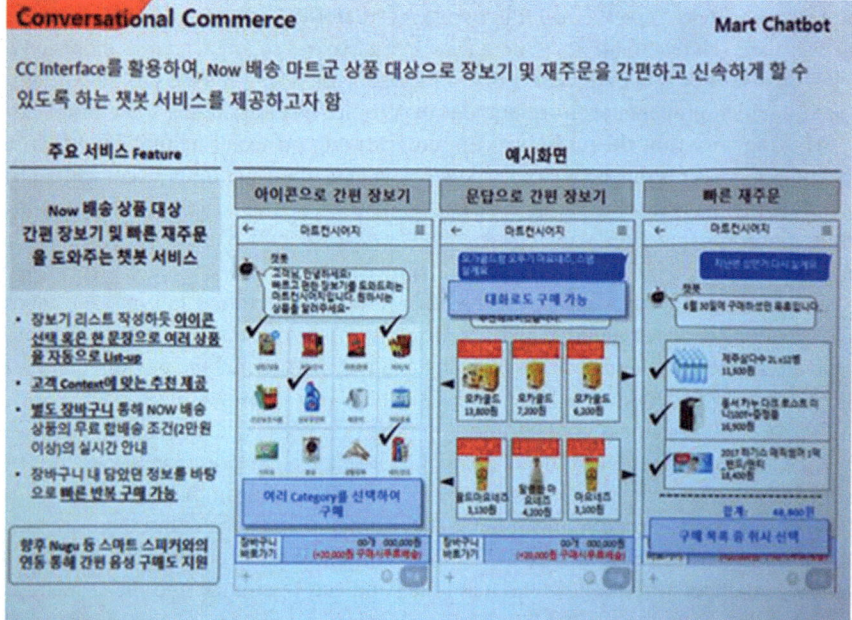

Fig. 1.1 Slide from a presentation for German guests in South Korea. Author's own figure

1.2 Success Factors of Presentation Styles

the speaker says, "I will gladly explain it again for you"! If you want to convince them, you should avoid softer terms such as "perhaps", "actually" and "possibly". Making consolidations and generalisations, including "as always" or "has never worked", will also not help you make friends, because such statements do not account for the complex structure of reality.

> **Remember Box**
> Clear messages also need clear concepts! Therefore, you should express yourself concretely rather than abstractly.

The reasons for this are as simple as they are convincing; our brain can't properly store content that it can't understand. When you communicate in an incomprehensible manner, "confusion" is remembered instead of "content". This can't be our goal. Therefore, we should make our content user-friendly by structuring it concretely as possible, rather than abstractly. Then they will understand and remember it.

"Our engines guarantee a mileage of 800,000 km" would be considered **abstract**. On the contrary, "You can go to the moon and back with our motors, a total of 800,000 km" is **concrete** and indeed much easier to imagine.

Clarity also means refraining from using (incomprehensible) **technical terms** as much as possible. Should they be important and unavoidable, you must clearly explain what they mean. If not, you should avoid these technical terms. We rarely give speeches to an audience that gets more enthusiastic the more incomprehensible our statements are. However, some speakers do not seem to know this!

> **Remember Box**
> You seem more unfriendly, unapproachable and arrogant, the more technical terms you use.

Additionally, clarity means directly addressing **uncomfortable truths**. The audience often already expects this when talking about personnel cutbacks or relocating production facilities. If you say that 1500 employees will lose their jobs and that thereby 1500 people will now have the possibility to lead a more "self-determined life", those affected will feel like you are pulling their leg. Instead "don't sugar-coat something that already doesn't smell or taste good. You must be open and transparent and most importantly explain why this step is necessary at this point in time" (Kantowsky 2017, p. 24).

On the other hand, you can make your speech more entertaining, exciting and informative by using a presentation style that involves occasional **storytelling**. We can all remember stories much better than mere facts and figures. Therefore, we should consider tying key messages into little stories. To do so you can talk about specific conversations with clients, colleagues, opinion leaders, etc. who further clarify certain points. Expressive pictures, convincing **comparisons** and **metaphors** also contribute to a successful presentation.

Antoine de Saint-Exupéry already made it clear that if you want to build a ship, then don't gather the people to collect wood, divide the tasks and organise the work. Instead, you should teach them to desire the big, blue ocean.

How does the saying go? "Repetitio est mater studiorum" or in English "practice makes perfect!" This is especially true for speeches when the audience can't simply go back to reread something interesting. Thus, you can repeat important things. I sometimes do this by creating a **golden nugget list**, which contains the most important information of the speech. This prevents your audience from forgetting them and provides a summary of the most important points at the end. It also serves as a takeaway for the audience.

> **Remember Box**
> The number of charts you have should fit to your speaking time to ensure a good presentation. It is not very convincing when a C-Level speaker prepares 295 charts for a 45-min speech and effectively clicks through all of them (repeating "that is not so important" or "that is a bit too much now" 25 times in a row).
>
> It is much better to just reduce your number of charts based on the allotted speaking time!

To ensure a successful presentation, the **technology** must work as well. I have seen leading (media) agencies drastically fail at big congresses, because they were not able to properly use the technology. And yet, if you arrive on time, it is so easy to test everything beforehand, without an audience. I also find it a pity that women often must have men help them when the technology does not work. I have seen this hundreds of times. On the other hand, how competent does a speaker seem who can handle the technology by herself? And another tip, based on painful experiences as an event organiser, if you are using an *Apple* product, you should always have the essential adapters with you and not assume that the organiser has these in stock.

You can only see how you yourself act in front of an audience through **video training sessions**. In many training sessions that I have led, I discovered that the participants can dramatically improve their performance through little alterations and that they already have the resources to do so! They simply need to be brought to light, by expanding one's comfort zone (cf. Sect. 1.1).

I would also like to point out that again, and again I come across speakers that discourage the audience from taking notes, because they will make the slides available later. In my opinion this is not helpful. I could also say, "That is complete nonsense!" When I take notes during speeches, I very rarely copy the slide word for word. Nowadays it is much easier to take a picture of them! Instead, many times I write down ideas that come to mind based on the speech, if I have a different point of view and which studies I should also analyse. That is why I often start a to-do list while listening to a speech, where I jot down such tasks immediately. We should encourage these types of activities!

One of my speakers once said at the beginning of his speech: "Now lean back and enjoy!" I corrected him by saying to the audience: "Much better: Lean forward and take notes!"

I am amazed again and again how few people in the audience do in fact take notes at congresses. My only explanation is that everyone, except me, is brilliant enough to remember all the presented material, including possible links to further content, exciting figures and informative quotes. Only I must jot down things to use them in my own speeches, publications or daily work later. After all, that is why I go to these events and invest my time and money. I have never understood why many people don't do the same.

1.3 Success Factors of Presentation Content

A **good story** is most important to your presentation. It can start with an anecdote, an exciting analytical finding or something similar. It is important to awaken the audience's curiosity for the upcoming content. A **cover image** which ideally illustrates the key message of the whole presentation can also help you do this.

When formulating a story or choosing a cover image, it is important to **have a good idea of your audience**:

- Who will be sitting in the audience?
- What previous knowledge does the audience have?
- What are the expectations?
- What resistance to my ideas, suggestions, concepts, etc. can be expected?
- Which hierarchies will be present?

A (positive) hook that the audience considers exciting should therefore be at the start and be revisited, analysed and expanded upon in the middle. It is important to support your own arguments, ideally with citations from (recognised) third parties or studies, etc. Here you notice time and again that even "professional" speakers are unable to properly **cite studies**.

When citing a study, the source should be noted on the appropriate presentation slide. Otherwise interested people or enemies can ask where to find this study during the presentation. Presenters who then start search and panic because they do have the answer readily accessible have (partially) lost. On the other hand, a much more confident response would be, "Those who can read clearly have an advantage! You can find the source at the bottom of my slide!"

However, that is not enough to properly cite a study. Even these, possibly unasked, questions must be coherently answered (cf. also Sect. 4.1):

- **Who conducted the study? Can we trust this institution?**
  This information is important to determine the possibility of a **pro domo effect**. This is referring to the phenomenon when companies like to speak positively about their own services. If the German postal service, *Deutsche Post*, declares

that mailing advertisements are the best way to win customers, they could also have the goal of making their services look good. Even though doing so is legitimate, an impartial speaker should avoid uncritically using such statements. "Pro domo" means positively accentuating one's own activities, by definition "for one's own house". A **hidden agenda** can be referred to because underlying "ulterior motives" or "hidden motives" prevent the objectivity of presentation of results.

On the contrary, if the findings come from well-respected market research firms or consultancies, it can be assumed that the results are more objective. And, the perceived credibility of the speaker increases.

- **How many people, companies, etc. were interviewed?**

To communicate the value of a study, it helps to provide concrete details about the **sample size** (e.g. $n = 1200$) and clarify if it is representative. In this case you can expect the same results for the whole population (therefore "representative") as in the study itself. This information is important to indicate quality.

If you can't find this information in the study, you can assume that it is not **representative**. Thus, you are unable to apply these results collectively. We must then be careful when using the findings.

Sometimes studies explicitly state that the findings are "only" exploratory. This means that the study went into "unchartered territory" and aimed to collect first experiences. This can be equally important and good. You should just mention this so that you are not vulnerable in your presentation.

- **When was the study conducted?**

The most recent studies often contain the most relevant findings. Therefore, when dealing with very dynamic developments, **topicality** becomes another indication of quality. If a study is a bit older, it should be explained whether the phenomena being presented have increased or decreased since then. Otherwise the audience may be led to question if the "old" information still apply. You should, however, be prepared to answer these questions.

- **Where was the study conducted?**

Findings from studies that do not clarify whether US citizens or Europeans or Germans were surveyed can't be used in presentations. When citing a study from the USA in China, it must be made clear why and what exactly is interesting from this study for a Chinese audience. Often the response is only that this is an "international" study. However, what does "international" mean? Does this only include the USA, France, Germany, Great Britain, China and Japan? Or were indeed people in 200 countries surveyed?

> **Remember Box**
> You should always start by analysing where specific data is coming from (the sender, how it was collected, the sample size, the time of the data collection) before "trusting" it and possibly using it to predict future developments or developing strategies based on these data.

1.3 Success Factors of Presentation Content

It is my goal to prevent you from making yourself vulnerable by **incorporating studies** in the wrong way in any future presentation. The reason being is that sometimes rivals for the next promotion or competition for the next assignment are sitting in the audience. Don't allow this to happen!

> **Remember Box**
> Beware of mono-casual explanations in two different ways. Avoid trying to trace complex changes back to a single cause, even if studies seem to support them. Additionally, don't believe any mono-causal explanations of yourself that others (often politicians) present to you.
> Today's world is too complex for simple solutions!

A successful presentation also means being able to explain every single term in your presentation, as well as every image that you have taken from literature. During oral examinations in the past, I have repeatedly observed the inability to explain graphics used in Bachelor's and Master's theses. Stating that, "I actually didn't look at it that closely!" is particularly "helpful" in this case. There are no bonus points for an answer like this! This also applies when using graphics or charts in a presentation and being unable to explain them.

> **Remember Box**
> You must be able to explain everything that is written on your slides in depth!

It is always "nice" when a speaker admits that this slide is a **strain on the eyes**, in other words, not legible for anyone. This is when you ask yourself what the point is. If the presenter already knows that you can't read the content on the slide, it should not even be presented in the first place. You should rather say, "Seeing as this overview is unfortunately difficult to read, I will show you the relevant pieces of data".

It is also helpful if you have prepared ample backup slides of calculations for very interested members of the audience. Nobody should bore the audience with detailed analyses. In most cases the **big picture** is enough. However, if there are questions about exact calculations, you can easily jump to the **backup pages** and show the detailed calculations.

Nonetheless, you should not click through the entire (animated) presentation to get to the backup slides. This is something I have observed on numerous occasions, and there is an easy way to avoid it. When in the presentation mode in *PowerPoint* presentations, you must simply type the desired page number, for instance, 29, and press Enter, and then you are immediately on page 29. You do the same to get back. I have seen countless presentations where the presenter goes back and forth through the slides click by click. This is dreadful, particularly in very animated presentations!

Additionally, if nobody asks to see your meticulously prepared backup slides and you still want to show them because of the time invested in their creation, you can include relevant rhetorical questions. For example, "I am sure you have asked yourself how exactly we came to these figures. You can find results in the appendix". You can then quickly pull up the backup page and return to the original slide. Or, "If you are asking yourself which specific experts we interviewed, you can find the answer here on our backup slide". In this way it is up to you whether important backups are shown or not!

To do this elegantly, it is, however, necessary that you have a printout of your presentation in front of you, so that you know the relevant page numbers, because most people don't memorise them. Or, the important page numbers are visible to the presenter while in presentation mode.

Another important topic is the **use of majuscules** (capital letters) in presentations, as well as advertisements, flyers, mailings, posters and online. There are compelling findings about the influence of majuscules on communication activities (cf. Teuber 2017).

- **How do we read?**
  Our eyes only scan the top of letters. This means we don't read words letter by letter but rather see a word as a whole.
- **Therefore, what are the effects of majuscules?**
  Legibility and reading speed are reduced!
- **Why?**
  In general majuscules have a significantly more continuous flow than upper- and lowercase letters, seeing as there is a lack of visual structure in CAPITAL LETTERS. Since everything looks the same and there are no extensions to the top or bottom, it is more difficult to recognise the word.
- **What is the result?**
  The reader must put more effort into spelling out the texts and therefore often avoids reading it altogether.

Therefore, since majuscules are considerably harder to read than upper- and lowercase letters, we should not use majuscules in longer texts, including on slides! A little test can highlight the relevance of these conclusions. Please read the following text (translated from German; Brandl 2010, p. 29).

"Aorccdnig to a sutdy at an Elngsih uvinertisy, the odrer of the ltetres is uminoprtnat. It olny mtaters taht the frist and lsat ltetres are in the rgilıt pcale..."

And now please read this:

"THE FSRIT CAN BE A CPMOLTLEEY OUT OF OEDRR AND YOU CAN SLITL RAED IT WTIHUOT A PBROELM".

I am sure that you realised that it was much more difficult to read the second text than the first. As in the first text, it is usually easy to correctly read the content, despite the mixed-up letters.

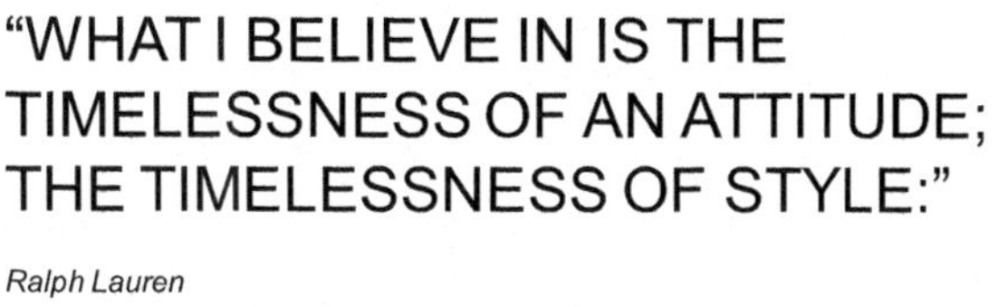

1.3 Success Factors of Presentation Content

Fig. 1.2 How convincing can an advertisement with capital letters be? Source: Adapted from an ad from *Ralph Lauren*, 2018

"WHAT I BELIEVE IN IS THE TIMELESSNESS OF AN ATTITUDE; THE TIMELESSNESS OF STYLE:"

Ralph Lauren

In the future, if you want to limit the use of majuscules in general and not only in presentations, conflicts with agencies will be inevitable, because many agencies love majuscules. That is why you should consider the following recommendation:

THE NEXT TIME YOUR AGENCIES PROPOSE TO WRITE LONG HEADLINES OR EVEN THE BODY OF THE TEXT IN CAPITAL LETTERS, JUST ASK THE AGENCY WHAT THE GOAL IS—SUPPOSED BEAUTY OR LEGIBILITY, SO THAT THE MESSAGE CAN BE UNDERSTOOD AND LEARNT.

Based on this knowledge, I am always surprised to see advertisements such as in Fig. 1.2. This advertisement launched in 2018 by Ralph Lauren only has majuscules in the body of the text and in a font that is difficult to read. Is nobody supposed to read this? Then why do I place such an advertisement?

Seemingly implicit, but again only seemingly, you should refrain from using **long sentences** and **texts** in your slides. Unless you are giving definitions (use sparingly) or showing analysed texts. This is because the presenter can't read out the text at the same speed as the audience. Therefore, you should only present keywords and structures or meaningful images and explain the exciting content related to them. Clearly and briefly describing the content of slide with one sentence in the heading can be very helpful as well. Throughout the presentation, you can then support this initial message on every single slide. On the other hand, writing all the content on the slides makes oneself useless as presenter, because you don't need a reading buddy anymore!

> **Remember Box**
> A good presentation is one that is <u>not</u> self-explanatory.

Hence, you can design your own slides so that the audience wonders what they even mean. This is how you generate curiosity and thereby attentiveness. And this enables you to win the audience's favour when competing against the endless alternatives of smartphones, laptops and tablet computers.

Good presentations are supported by (few) **animations**. You can attract the audience's attention to a certain extent with animations, since as the presenter, you decide which content you will show and at what time. Those who present a slide that is rich in content in one go leave the audience to decide what to do with it. When the presenter is only explaining the second point, the audience might already be considering points 7–12. Not really the point!

This particularly applies to questions that you would like to discuss at the end of your presentation. If you show these all at once, then everyone can concentrate on a different one. At this time the presenter should and must guide as well; otherwise the interest of the audience will be lost!

It is important to use **suitable animation**. Animations are meant to help the audience understand through processes, etc., not irritate them. Every animation has a subtext with an unspoken but still communicated message. If certain content is lost due to the animation, this indicates low relevance. The time between making something appear and disappear is also influential. These should be fitting with the content of the presentation.

> **Remember Box**
> Animations help direct the audience to the content just discussed. For this, the presentation and animation must be consistently coordinated.

Long lists still appear in far too many presentation slides today. Although it is true that "people like lists", they should be primarily used to read content both online and offline. However, **infographics** are much more exciting and entertaining in a speech. Lists rarely show the connections between individual elements, whereas graphics can do this much more easily. In addition, innovative graphics also generate more attention. Ideally, your audience then tries to connect the verbally presented content with your graphics to understand. That is exactly what we want!

I should also mention that you must not forget the **page numbers** on your slides; otherwise the audience cannot ask precise questions about your slides. Then you hear, "On a slide more forward with a red box you have ...", and then the wild search for the slide starts, often clicking through from start to finish. Additionally, specifying page numbers is simply good craftsmanship, yet it is still forgotten again and again!

A classic in presentations is also **pointing out mistakes** that the presenter has just noticed in their presentation. This makes me also feel like saying, "Oh, here's a spelling mistake". The stupid thing is that I then draw the attention of the entire audience to this mistake, which 50, 70 or even 90% might have otherwise not noticed. Remember that you should not focus on individual mistakes, unless they could lead to wrong conclusions. Then it is necessary to correct them.

> **Remember Box**
> In presentations and articles, you should make sure that you do not exceptionally use the so-called greengrocer's apostrophe. You will find it regularly in presentations by third parties, in articles, on posters and in retail stores. Then you read about CEO's, KPI's or CD's, when in fact only CEOs, KPIs and CDs were meant.

Mistakes also occur frequently when German authors use the word "lose" in English presentations. Instead of "losing" something, they start "loosing" items. Educated listeners are bound to be confused.

A particularly bad example was when a journalist referred to a win-win and loose-loose situation in an article. The mind starts to wonder what was loose here....

You should also avoid the common mistake of naming a subsection 1.1 without having a subsection 1.2. In this case, the content of Section 1 would be identical to that of subsection 1.1. Even though you can't do this, you often find it in scientific textbooks. However, at least as of today, you will never make this mistake again!

Timing must also be taken into consideration in presentations. I have already experienced speakers who had prepared 280 charts for 45-min of presentation. A speaker once said, "In the next 2 hours I have to get through these 180 slides, then we can discuss your questions!" Great!

Many people, including myself, tend to prepare too much because we worry that there will not be enough content. This has never been the case for me, but I still prepare too much. When we present particularly exciting content about slides, we often can't show more than two to three slides per minute. That means that for a 45-min presentation, approximately 15–25 slides are enough! These can then be presented calmly and confidently.

If you can't limit yourself to a few slides in advance and notice that you are running out of time, you should skip certain ones. However, again, please do not click through and say, "I wanted to show you this, but there is not enough time", or "Unfortunately, I can't present this exciting case anymore!" I have witnessed both scenarios.

The best thing you can do is skip ahead to a later slide jump by specifying the target page number. Hardly anyone will notice this, and will you gain valuable time while staying in the timeframe of your presentation. Additionally, you avoid giving the audience the impression that they missed out on something exciting because you have lost control over the time.

In **group presentations** it is also "wonderful" when the first group members take too much time and then together force the last presenter to talk faster because time is running out. Furthermore, I often notice that some group members are unaware of **when it is their turn to present**, which irritates other members. This always leads to awkward pauses, because nobody knows who is next. Additionally, if there are several presenters, they should not switch off between themselves too often. On the one hand, it seems very restless for the listeners. On the other hand, it can lead to the already mentioned irritations of not knowing when it is one's turn to speak.

The following checklist shows you how you can increase your success when presenting. **The questions** in it help you **create a convincing presentation**.

▶ **Implementation Tips**
Preparation of the Presenter

- How much time do I spend preparing the contents of my presentation?
- How much time do I spend preparing my personal appearance for this presentation (voice, gestures, rhetorical questions, etc.)?

Preparation of the Presentation Style

- Do I have a verbally and visually strong introduction to my presentation?
- Does my introduction make it clear that I have something important to say?
- Do I make it clear that I am just the right person to talk about this here and now?
- Am I consciously not giving a (boring) company presentation?
- Am I prepared to wait in front of the audience until I get their full attention?
- Have I thought about what my audience should remember about my presentation from the very beginning? (keyword "takeaway" or rather "golden nuggets")?
- Have I considered the serial-position effect by putting important content at the beginning (primacy effect) or at the end (recency effect)?
- Can I use my body language and especially my gestures to get certain points across?
- What attitude do I want to have in my presentation?
- Which facial expression do I want to have?
- How much eye contact do I want to have with the audience?
- Have I prepared enough to be able to speak to the audience and not the screen?
- Can I use my voice pitch and voice modulation to highlight certain points?
- Do I use words that my listeners understand?
- Have I forgone writing out my speech in full?
- Do I deliberately avoid exaggerations, suggestive questions and assumptions?
- Do I use storytelling, images, comparisons and metaphors to make my content more easily understandable?
- Have I check in advance that the technology is working, or can I do so before my presentation?

Preparation of the Presentation Content

- Can I tell a good story?
- Does the beginning of my story help generate curiosity about my presentation?
- Have I considered who will be in the audience so that I can create a presentation tailored to the target group?
- Have I chosen studies carefully to support key statements?
- Can all relevant information about the study be found on the respective slide?
  - Who conducted the study?
  - Can we believe this institution?
  - How many people, companies, etc. were surveyed?
  - When was the study conducted?
  - Where was the study conducted?
- Is the content of my slides readable (not a strain on the eyes)?
- Do I refrain from using capitals, except for proper names and, if necessary, short texts?
- Have I prepared backup slides for the interested listeners?
- Can I jump back and forth in my presentation to get to specific slides?
- Have I removed longer sentences and texts on my slides?
- Do I use animations specifically to facilitate understanding and guide the listeners?
- Do I use information graphics rather than boring lists?
- Have I thought about page numbers on the slides?
- Am I aware that I should not point out errors in my slides while I am presenting?
- Am I keeping an eye on the time and not preparing a presentation that will take two or three times longer than my time slot?
- Is a precise order defined and a time manager determined for group presentations?

If you use these questions to guide you while preparing your next presentations, you will gain more sovereignty and at the same time greater confidence for the presentation.

1.4 Success Factors of Respectful Communication

Negations are an interesting topic in lectures, presentations and meetings. Speakers try to take away fear by saying:

- "Company XY will not be crushed".
- "This loss of customers is not a disaster".
- "We don't have lousy IT".

- "We will not dismiss 1000 employees after the merger".
- "Our company is not a swamp of donations".
- "No problem!" (often used by employees in the service sector).

The speakers forget that nobody can think in negative. Would you like an example? Don't think of pink elephants now! Have you noticed, we cannot "not" think of something said. What remains in the minds of the listeners of the above statements? "Crushed", "disaster", "lousy IT", "1000 employees dismissed", "swamp of donations" and "problem".

You can avoid such negative recollections by simply saying:

- "The company XY will continue to be a single entity".
- "We can compensate for this loss of customers through other projects".
- "Even after the merger, we will keep the current workforce".
- "We have properly accounted for the donations".
- "We will gladly do it for you" (Doesn't that sound much nicer than the "No problem" we've heard too often in response to a customer's or guest's wish?)

Not so difficult, is it? Nevertheless, headlines that neglect this important aspect of human communication are often found in newspapers and on presentation slides (see Fig. 1.3). Additionally, such statements are heard in everyday life and tend to be taken out of context.

There are other reasons why you should refrain from sending such negative messages:

- **Negative statements** are always noticed first and focused on nine times more frequently than positive ones. Hence the media slogan: "Bad news is good news!"
- At the same time, **negative statements** have a much stronger impact, up to ten times stronger than positive statements.

Therefore, it is understandable why journalists prefer using statements such as those shown in Fig. 1.3 in the headlines of their contributions to the corresponding events.

Let us bear in mind that when hearing the term "**alternative facts**", a frequently used expression these days, many readers and listeners tend to associate the term

Fig. 1.3 Negations in headlines

"I am not arrogant!"

"The company isn't in a crisis!"

"This law is not a coup de main, not a coup d'état…"

"We don't want to destroy company XYZ!"

1.4 Success Factors of Respectful Communication

"facts" with positive connotations. Therefore, we should state clearly what the truth is; "alternative facts" are nothing more than lies, false reports, etc.

Knowing this we should really choose our words wisely. It's worth it. Most of the words we use are linked to emotions in our conversational partners and therefore located on an **emotional map**. Such a map is depicted in Fig. 1.4.

In Fig. 1.5 various terms are arranged in this emotional map. These almost always trigger the same positive or negative emotions in the audience. This means that, through our word choice, we can have a lasting influence on the mood of our audience. With the terms found in the upper section of Fig. 1.5, we spark a positive mood. On the other hand, terms such as "project" or "task" have a neutral sound for many people. The feelings that are triggered by this depend on the individual's respective associations.

On the contrary, in the lower part of Fig. 1.5, there are terms that generate highly negative emotions. It also illustrates that a word like "challenge" can mean the new challenge a person is looking for, whereas the same term can trigger fear in someone else because they must leave their own comfort zone. Hence, it is important for us to use our intuition to show empathy as a speaker or discussion partner so that we communicate what the word truly means.

Fig. 1.4 Emotional map—basic concept. Author's own figure

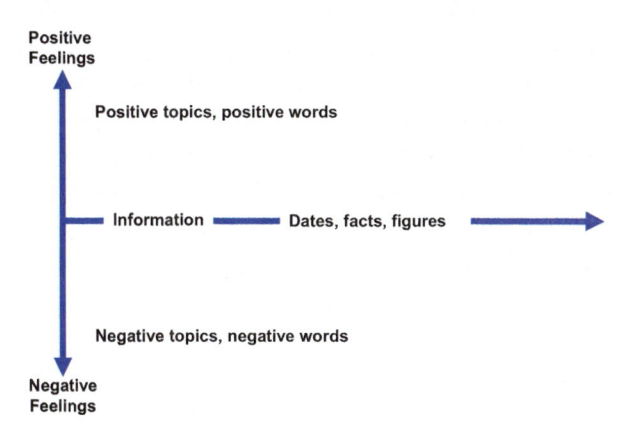

Fig. 1.5 Emotional map to position words. Author's own figure

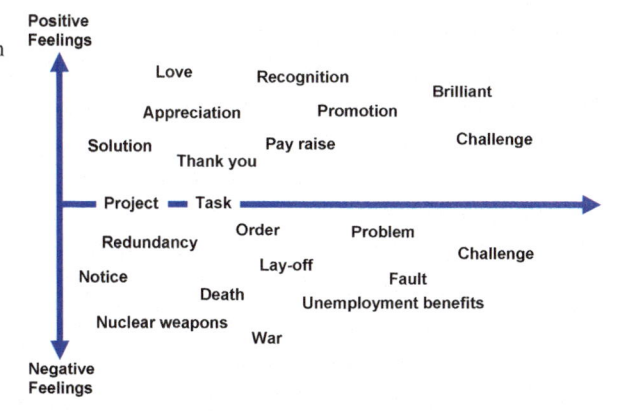

Fig. 1.6 Mechanism of speech. Author's own figure

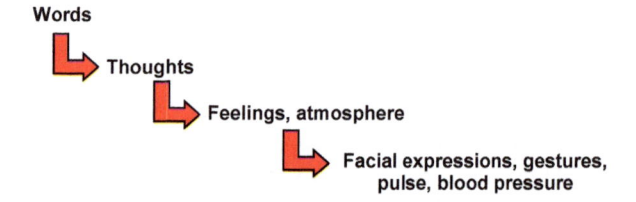

Words
↳ Thoughts
 ↳ Feelings, atmosphere
  ↳ Facial expressions, gestures, pulse, blood pressure

The underlying **mechanism of speech** is shown in Fig. 1.6. Clearly our choice of words triggers thoughts for the members of the audience. These thoughts, in turn, trigger certain feelings and thus affect the atmosphere. This can even have a direct effect on facial expressions, gestures, pulse and blood pressure. We should know that words automatically invoke the brain to identify "associated links" as well as the data that goes along with it, combined with positive or negative associations.

> Remember Box
> We always bring about emotions through language! Words are strong emotional triggers!

However, speakers themselves, not just their words and explanations, are also positioned on an emotional map. That means that everything that applies to words is also true for the sender. As a result, other people store my **"file" with an emotional account** in their minds as both a speaker and a **person** in general. You don't believe me? Do you remember a time when you saw a person for the first time in many years? And, do you also remember that you spontaneously had an emotional feeling about this person? It might have been "positive" or "I am not quite sure" or "negative", in the sense of "something went wrong here". That's exactly what I mean! The people we interact with unconsciously store us as humans on an emotional map, as shown in Fig. 1.7.

> Remember Box
> We forget what it was about.
> But we don't forget how we were treated.

Even if we don't know exactly how we came to our conclusion in the first place, our intuition can clearly tell us that with a person "is best not to mess with".

The way we ask questions is another important field of discussion, both in professional and private settings. When we were raised and educated, we were taught to ask **questions about problems**. You will find these problem-focused questions in Fig. 1.8. The question "why" comes up if projects are not won, errors occur or there are other losses. It is said that **those who ask lead**! And in this case, through our questions we "force" our interlocutors to justify their behaviour or

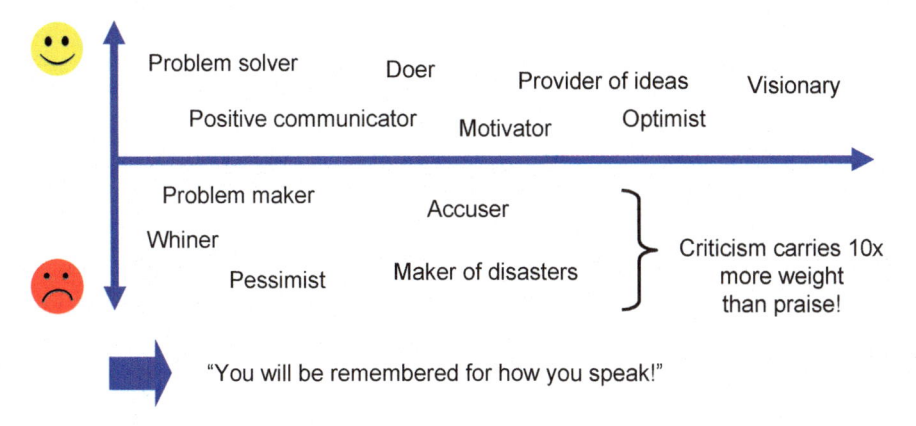

1.4 Success Factors of Respectful Communication

| Problem solver | Doer | Provider of ideas | Visionary |
| Positive communicator | Motivator | Optimist | |

Problem maker	Accuser	
Whiner		Criticism carries 10x
Pessimist	Maker of disasters	more weight than praise!

"You will be remembered for how you speak!"

Fig. 1.7 Speakers are positioned on an emotional map. Author's own figure

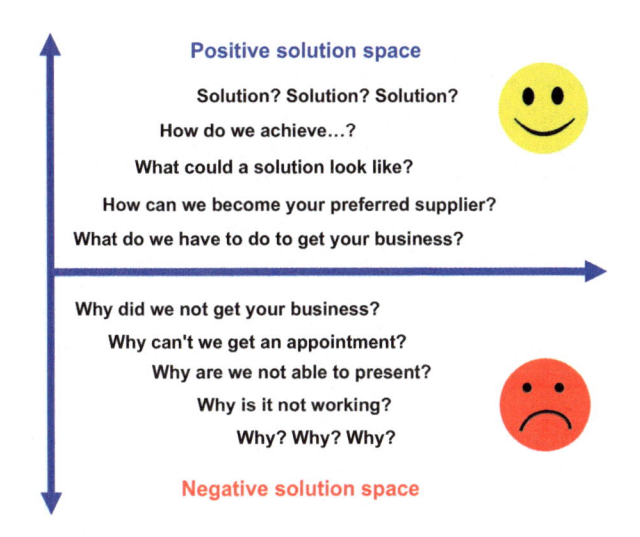

Positive solution space

Solution? Solution? Solution?
How do we achieve…?
What could a solution look like?
How can we become your preferred supplier?
What do we have to do to get your business?

Why did we not get your business?
Why can't we get an appointment?
Why are we not able to present?
Why is it not working?
Why? Why? Why?

Negative solution space

Fig. 1.8 Problem-focused vs. problem-solving questions. Author's own figure

explain their mistakes, one by one. Afterwards, we are often smarter but still do not know how to avoid a similar result in the future.

We can come to completely different conclusions by asking **problem-solving questions**. These can be found in the upper part of Fig. 1.8. Through them we motivate our discussion partners to think about possible improvements and solutions. However, keep in mind that since our counterparts often do not expect this kind of question, we must give them time to think. This means you shouldn't just keep talking during pauses allowing for silence. My personal motto is "**endure the silence**"! There is no way around this waiting time, because your conversation partner is now thinking about solutions and no longer just about what went wrong and why, which they would have been fully prepared for!

> **Remember Box**
> If you have the strength to ask the right questions, you can use your counterpart's creative potential to find solutions.
> Therefore, you should consistently ask problem-solving questions and avoid problem-focusing questions!

Similarly, these guiding ideas apply to **meetings** and even to small talk. You can set the (emotional) direction by **the way you start the discussion**. Below are two ways to start a discussion with which you will achieve two very different discussion balances.

Introduction 1

- Your last press conference was not so great.
- Are you also suffering from the effects of increasing protectionism?
- Did you also believe that the Euro will fall?
- Do you also feel threatened by China?
- Do you also have so many employees who are sick?
- Have your sales also gone down?
- Which products of your products are doing particularly bad?
- Who will disrupt your business model?

Introduction 2

- Your presentation yesterday was very convincing.
- I heard that you won XY as a major client.
- What is currently going particularly well for you?
- What ideas do you have to increase sales of product A?
- What are your plans for the next few months?
- What can be improved in your opinion?
- By when do you want to reach XY?
- What went particularly well in your digital transformation?

You can assume that it will be rather difficult to get the first conversation started, because we immediately pull our counterpart to the negative side. In the second case, a positive relationship and thereby trust is first built up, a prerequisite for people to open in conversations. Therefore, I think it is an exciting idea to start a team meeting with a **report about solutions and accomplishments**. To do so, the following questions can be used as an introduction on a regular basis for all normal meetings:

- What are the good news?
- What has been finished?
- Where did you/we get further?

- What is developing well?
- Where are you moving forward?
- What went well?
- What can be improved?

I myself started many meetings by reporting solutions and accomplishments, and it has made an amazing impact. Even though problems, difficulties, lost customers, etc. had always been the focus, it now became clear to everyone that (despite all the difficulties) a lot of positive things had been achieved. This made those who were present proud of what had been achieved and released energy to find solutions for the tasks that had not been completed.

I also think it is important to remember that it's not about seeing the world through rose-coloured spectacles, because it's not only rainbows and butterflies. It is a matter of not focusing only on the problems but also of acknowledging what has been achieved, despite all the difficulties, in the last month, in the last week or in the last few days. The reason being that we all want to be proud of our achievements and not have the impression (which is often also not true) that nothing is going well!

> **Remember Box**
> Meetings that only focus on problems and what caused them rarely lead to the energy needed to solve them. It is therefore much more convincing to proceed as follows:
>
> - We ask open W-questions (Who? How? When? With what? For what?).
> - We say what we like.
> - We solve instead of getting angry.

Figure 1.9 shows what a successful, problem-solving discussion could ideally look like. You start off with solutions and achievements. Then, with a positive energy, you can focus on the current tasks. Ideally, the meeting is concluded with ideas and concrete proposals for a solution.

If you want to improve in this field, you should conduct a **personal dialogue assessment** after very important discussions. This also applies to written dialogues (e.g. by e-mail). The following questions can help:

- Was I able to make a valuable contribution?
- Have I spoken in a way that my counterpart can understand?
- Were there sympathy fields that connected us?
- Were problems solved quickly?
- Were there good results?
- Have we learned anything that will let us advance?
- Have we reached a consensus?

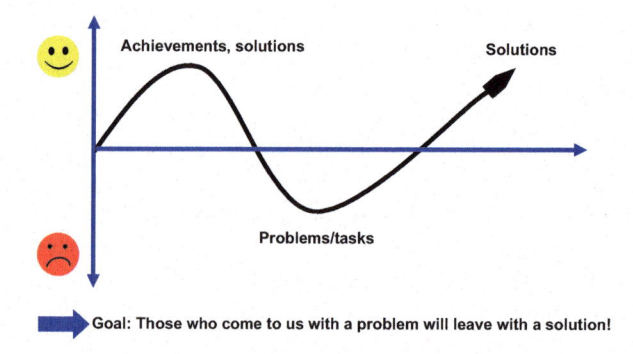

Fig. 1.9 Successful course of a problem-solving conversation. Author's own figure

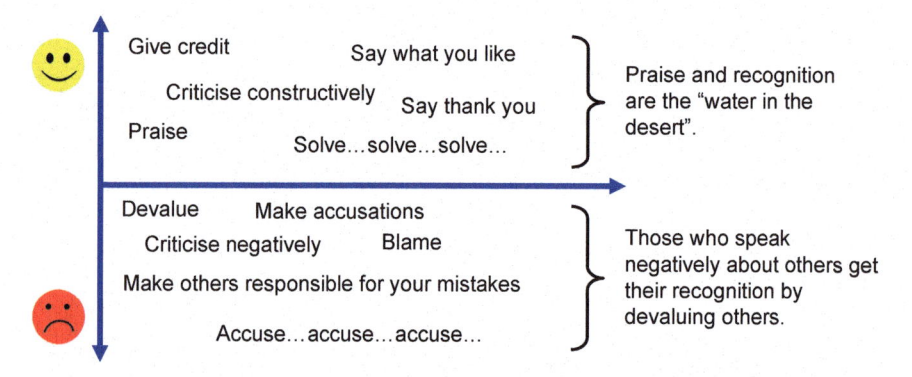

Fig. 1.10 Personal dialogue assessment. Author's own figure

If this personal assessment has many "no" answers, then you should not ask "why?". Here it is also much better to approach the topic in a problem-solving manner with the question, "How can I achieve that...?

Fig. 1.10 shows possible results of such a dialogue assessment

> **Remember Box**
> - Communication is a decisive value-adding factor in every situation.
> - Therefore, the way we communicate is always of utmost importance!

So why do so many people still speak in a very negative, destructive way and destroy value day after day in their private lives, in companies and in society? Many people believe that the **advantages of speaking in a negative way** include acquiring power, influence, attention and authority. Unfortunately, based on what we hear nowadays, especially in social media, these people are partially right. At the same time, some people try to increase their own self-esteem by devaluing others. Moreover, we all know the saying "attack is the best defence". Managers who strike back immediately to every ounce of criticism are approached less about undesirable developments, even though this is not only a disadvantage for them as a person but also for the team and the company.

However, what **disadvantages of speaking in a negative way** that people who decide to do so must accept? Speaking in such a way leads to more conflicts, arguments, stress, anger and confrontation because often no solutions are found. After all, one often does not get to the causes and cannot work out solutions together. Furthermore, the devaluation of third parties can lead to escalating conflicts and put the relationship into question. In addition, such behaviour patterns negatively impact the quality of life and well-being of most of those involved.

Part of your credibility as a speaker also comes from your ability to use **the power of two-sided reasoning**. In presentations, in direct sales talks as well as the design process of advertising materials, it must be determined whether to use a one- or two-sided argumentation. The **one-sided reasoning** lists only the advantages of your own solution, your own offer, etc. On the contrary, a **two-sided reasoning** not only identifies its own advantages but also possible disadvantages (such as a higher price, a greater complexity).

Studies show that a two-sided argument can lead to greater credibility and influence attitudes more. After all, there are rarely solutions without any disadvantages. If you address these dark sides or counterarguments yourself and perhaps already point out how to deal with them, (almost) nothing more stands in the way of a successful conversation. Sometimes a two-sided reasoning even results in an **immunisation effect** because it is difficult to refute the overall message afterwards. This in turn has a positive effect on the speaker and his/her content (cf. Fuchs and Unger 2014, pp. 505–508).

▶ **Implementation Tips: Guidelines for Respectful Communication**
In summary, the following guidelines **illustrate how to communicate in a valuable way**:

- Speaking in an appreciative way means consciously and intentionally upgrading other people!
  - Positive reasons valorise
  - Constructive questions signal appreciation and interest
- Using emotionally positive words creates a solution-oriented discussion atmosphere!
  - Key question: Based on what I say, will the other person feel good or bad?
  - Not only what you say is decisive but the feeling you evoke in the other person.
- Problems are addressed to solve them, not only to find culprits!
- Ask questions that lead to a positive solution space!

> **Remember Box**
> Language has power! Language is power!
> Every second we can decide how we want to use it!
> In my opinion, the **guiding principle "with appreciation to success"** is also helpful and goal-oriented, because people of all ages, genders and cultures are largely guided by the following attitudes:
>
> - I want my job to be fun.
> - I want to solve tasks.
> - I want to have positive emotions.
>
> If a Mr. X or a Mrs. Y <u>always</u> ruins my mood, <u>never</u> has a solution and <u>always</u> looks for someone to blame, then that <u>always</u> makes me angry, and I will think about consequences beforehand.
> The success factors listed here provide a good basis for more successful communication in the future.

▶ **Implementation Tips: Communicate More Successfully**

- First select an aspect from the different points that have been discussed and try to implement it as soon as possible, e.g. the "problem-solving questions".
- It is important that you use the new behaviour model as often as possible, ideally with good results.
- This behaviour will only gradually become part of your routine.
- It requires one thing—repetition.
- Once you have newly established a behaviour pattern, you can start with the next item on your to-do list.
- In this way you expand your comfort zone step by step in a playful way and hopefully have good results.
- You can also reward yourself for expanding your comfort zone. Every time you cross a "red line" on your way to personal growth, you can reward yourself by putting another 5 US Dollars in a special piggy bank. After 1 or 2 months, you can use the money you saved to take your loved one out to dinner and buy a nice bottle of wine or a great book.
- You will notice that such motivational instruments also work for you.

In addition to the knowledge about the format of presentations, a successful appearance itself and an appreciative and problem-solving style of communication, it is also of course about the relevant contents. Managers need powerful tools to gain exciting insights that they can use in presentations and further communication. These are presented in the following chapters.

References

Brandl, P. K. (2010). *Crash-Kommunikation: Warum Piloten versagen und Manager Fehler machen*. Offenbach: GABAL.

Fuchs, W., & Unger, F. (2014). *Management der Marketing-Kommunikation* (5th ed.). Wiesbaden: Springer Gabler.

Kantowsky, J. (2017). Fachjargon macht unsympathisch. *Frankfurter Allgemeine Zeitung, 23*(9), 24.

Stangl, W. (2017). *Stichwort: 'serieller Positionseffekt', Online Lexikon für Psychologie und Pädagogik*. Accessed September 25, 2017, from http://lexikon.stangl.eu/4881/serieller-positionseffekt

Teuber, M. (2017). *Kriterien für die Lesbarkeit von Texten*. Accessed September 29, 2017, from http://www.medien.ifi.lddmu.de/fileadmin/mimuc/mmi_ws0304/exercise/aufsaetze/Mathias_Teuber.html

2 Vision, Mission and Goals

2.1 Development of Vision and Mission

Every company should have a **vision** and **mission** that have a greater importance than the quantitative company goals and thus ideally have a meaningful effect. The vision and mission are often based on **core values** of the company (cf. Kreutzer 2017; Kreutzer et al. 2018).

The **company vision** broadly defines an ambitious plan that describes what the company wants to achieve in the long term.

- Audi (2018) formulates its vision as follows, "Our promise is to stay ahead. We inspire through sustainable and individual premium mobility. Our "premium vehicles" continue to be the basis".
- Facebook (2018) defines its vision as follows, "Bringing the world closer together".
- IKEA (2017) sums up its vision and business idea as follows, "IKEA's vision is creating a better life for many people every day. Our business idea is to offer a wide range of beautifully designed and functional furnishings at prices that are affordable for most people".
- SpaceX (2018) says: "SpaceX designs, manufactures and launches advanced rockets and spacecraft. The company was founded in 2002 to revolutionise space technology, with the ultimate goal of enabling people to live on other planets".
- Tesla (2018): "Our goal when we created Tesla a decade ago was the same as it is today: to accelerate the advent of sustainable transport by bringing compelling mass market electric cars to market as soon as possible".
- Uber (2018) states, "Uber is evolving the way the world moves. By seamlessly connecting riders to drivers through our apps, we make cities more accessible, opening up more possibilities for riders and more business for drivers". The

vision statement is: "Make transportation as reliable as running water, everywhere, for everyone".
- Wikipedia (2018) has described its vision for an online encyclopaedia as follows, "The aim is to make the entire knowledge of humanity freely accessible to everyone".

When formulating visions, you should focus on customer benefits and the benefits the company provides to society. Such visions, together with the current state of the company, can create a **creative tension** that motivates managers and employees alike to work towards achieving the vision. Convincing company visions can have an **action-directing role** in the following ways (cf. Hungenberg 2014, p. 419):

- **Identity role**
  The vision contains the trend-setting goals, which can guide the employees of a company in the long term.
- **Identification role**
  The vision conveys the overriding meaning to employees, as well as the purpose of their actions. This enables the feeling of belonging to the company to be strengthened. In this context, nowadays the "purpose" or the "purpose quest" (otherwise known as the "quest for meaning") of the company is often mentioned.
- **Mobilisation role**
  The vision motivates employees to work towards the defined vision of the future of the company.

To enable your vision to play these roles, you should not outsource the task of developing it to external consultants or agencies. While they can, and should, accompany and moderate this process, the central content for the company's vision must come from the personnel itself. Otherwise, the visions decorate boardrooms and management floors, while the employees simply smirk at them.

When it comes to working on a vision, the following **triple jump**, also known as the "**golden circle**", has proven to be successful (cf. Sinek 2011).

1. **Why?—The core of the vision**
2. **How?—Possible ways to implement it**
3. **What?—Defining the planned products and services**

The decisive factor is the order in which these questions are answered in the company! Traditionally, many companies start with the "what?" and thus come up with a narrow product and service perspective that often allows only a few possibilities for identity and identification. Instead, you should start working on the vision by asking "why?" to address the increasing search for meaning and orientation in business and society. Nowadays, companies are required to do this in particular because of Generation Y, i.e. the employees born between 1980 and 2000 (see in depth Lischka 2016; Hurrelmann and Albrecht 2016; Kreutzer and Land 2017).

2.1 Development of Vision and Mission

Extensive employee involvement is also required when the company's vision is put into concrete terms. Using the questions above, the previously mentioned **company mission**, or through so-called **mission statements**, can be a good starting point to do so. Important activities or core competencies of the company are identified which are used as a basis for creating the vision. The mission, in combination with the vision, gives the company both a framework, as well as a direction, of action. Thus, a mission and vision represent the starting point of all corporate and marketing planning. This idea of "defining the business" also makes sense at the beginning of any business start-up.

It is often a good idea to also define the **key values of a company**, otherwise known as the corporate core values, during this process. If these corporate values are indeed taken seriously by the management, then all business activities are based on them.

However, the work also is not completed with printing the posters and brochures for employees and making it available on the company intranet. At this point it is rather a matter of motivating the entire workforce to implement the vision and mission and to take the values in the company into account daily. To do this, you must facilitate **management training**. Each of the managers should ensure that the information is communicated across the different hierarchical levels, using the train-the-trainer concept. Furthermore, you should also initiate concrete measures to ensure that **daily actions reflect the vision and mission, as well as the company values**. As already mentioned, managers set an example of reflecting these values when communicating with their employees. Incidentally, the necessary communication is a process that will never end, if you take your vision, mission and values seriously and don't just give them an alibi function in the company.

To sum it up, the corporate vision and mission are described as a **corporate purpose** that is based on **corporate values**. The vision and mission are subordinate to the definition of **the general expectations for success** in business activities (cf. Fig. 2.1). Terms mentioned in Fig. 2.1 will be explained later.

Fig. 2.1 Hierarchical target system of a company. Author's own figure

▶ **Implementation Tips**

- Vision, mission and corporate values should be developed within your company if you want them to have a real impact on the behaviour of your employees.
- During the development process, you can rely on external support, but you must develop the content within the company.
- To ensure that the vision and mission have an impact in the company, you should first educate the managers about them. It is necessary to clarify that this is not a joke, but rather a real concern of the management team, and above all, that the top executives support this completely.
- You should assign managers the task of discussing the implementation of vision, mission and values in their respective areas of responsibility with their own employees. This ensures that concrete measures for implementation will be derived.
- At the end of a fiscal year, you should check whether the company and the team's behaviours have moved in the desired direction.
- There must be consequences, if the defined goals were not achieved, otherwise no one takes the guidelines seriously, and they disappear.

2.2 Definition of Goals

Many companies can easily agree on a vision and mission statements, as well as on core values, because they often remain relatively general and therefore not very concrete. On the other hand, **goals** can and must **concretely describe future situations** to clarify what exactly should be achieved (cf. Fig. 2.1). Thus, they provide the **central points of orientation for actions**, both in a professional and personal setting.

When defining goals, you should consider the following **roles goals play**.

- **Orientation and guidance**

    Defining goals; "where the journey should go". Resource allocation decisions can only be made based on objectives. In the distribution of scarce resources, be it employees, capital, plants, etc., the defined goals provide the mandatory framework of orientation.

    Ideally, you will encourage "concerted action" of all employees and managers through powerful goals. Then everyone is not only pulling on the same rope but also in the same **direction**! Only if the captain and the entire crew know where the voyage is going can all those involved align their strategies and measures with these goals.

2.2 Definition of Goals

> **Remember Box**
> Without concrete objectives, it is not possible to properly allocate resources because what needs to be achieved is unknown.
> This is equally true in both professional and personal settings.

- **Control**

    You are only able to evaluate the success of your company by setting and putting goals in writing, e.g. per month, quarter or at the end of a financial year. Only the comparison of the goals and the actual results will show you the un- and successful areas of your company.

> **Remember Box**
> Without objectives, you cannot monitor success!
> That's why they say, "You can't manage what you don't measure!"

- **Motivation**

    With goals you can and should equally motivate employees and managers. You achieve this primarily by linking non-monetary incentives (such as promotion opportunities) or monetary rewards (such as commissions, royalties or profit sharing) to the achievement of certain goals. You make it clear to those involved that their own behaviour has a direct influence on their own development in the company, beyond the pure annual salary. The higher the position of employees in the company hierarchy, the higher the variable portion of the salary. This share can amount to 40–80% of the annual salary for executives. If the bonus is linked to the share price, it is possible to earn a multiple fold of the annual salary.

> **Remember Box**
> However, goals only play a motivational role if they are deemed realistic from the point of view of employees and managers. If not, they do exactly the opposite, because it is assumed that it will be impossible to achieve goals even with the highest level of commitment. It is essential that the incentives are aimed at long-term successful corporate development, and do not promote short-term profit maximisation.

For the goals you have defined to be a form of control, monitoring and motivation, several **requirements** must be considered when **formulating the goals**. Time and again an analysis of goals, whether they be personal or professional, shows that they are often insufficiently specified and thus also do not have a comprehensively binding character. The following four requirements should always be considered when defining goals, if they are to have the previously described positive effects:

- **Content of a goal: What do you want to achieve?**
    First, the goal you are striving to reach must be specified in terms of content. It is certainly easy to agree on a goal of **customer satisfaction** in a company.
    - However, what exactly does this mean, and how can you measure whether the goals have been met?
    - Are you going to measure the proportion of "multiple offenders" by taking loyal customers who have remained loyal to the company for 2 or 3 years?
    - Or, measure the amount of complaints by tracking the number of returned products or calls to the customer service centre?
    - Are there any plans to carry out a special customer satisfaction study in which a concrete question is asked about "satisfaction"?
    - Is it possible to measure the satisfaction of your own customers in comparison to important competitors?

    As you can see, a goal such as "customer satisfaction" requires an exact definition to play a role in both controlling and motivating.

    The same applies to a goal of **increasing competitiveness**. Within the company you can certainly quickly agree on the importance of this type of goal. However, the key factor is how to measure competitiveness. To do so, there is a wide range of key performance indicators (KPIs), from core criteria to measuring corporate performance (cf. Krause 2016; Krause and Arora 2010). Some examples are listed below:
    - Absolute or relative market share
    - Turnover
    - Return on sales, investment and equity
    - Profit
    - EBIT/EBITDA
    - Cash flow
    - Production costs per unit
    - Lead time, e.g. to produce a car or to develop an innovative product or service

    You can compare these calculations with those of your competitors to determine your own competitiveness. This is the only way to determine your own competitiveness.

    In this context, you should distinguish between "effectiveness" and "efficiency". When talking about **effectiveness**, you should ask yourself, "are we doing the right things?" It is important to ensure that an action leads to the desired result. This means the "degree of effectiveness" in terms of achieving a certain goal. For example, one could spend a long time debating whether *Volkswagen*'s construction of the *Phaeton* vehicle was one of the "right things", since the company never made any profit by selling this vehicle. Even if the production of the *Phaeton* in the *Transparent Factory* in Dresden was perfectly organised, meeting the **efficiency** goal addresses the question, "are we doing the things right?"

    Efficiency focuses on the principle of economic efficiency ("degree of efficiency") and thus on the input-output relation. Regardless of whether the result of this process helps the business achieve its goals. When considering effectiveness,

however, it is examined whether an action or an interim goal contributes positively to an overriding goal (profit or EBIT at *Volkswagen*).
- **Extent of a goal: How much do you want to achieve?**

  You should emphasise a clean **operationalisation** of every goal. The objective is to make the content of the goal measurable. Only when a goal is "measurably" formulated can you be sure that you can control and monitor it. You should ask yourself the following questions:
  - **How much** turnover or profit should you make?
  - **How many** customers (in percentage) should be "very satisfied or satisfied" with the company?
  - **How high** should the "relative market share" be?

  When defining how high goals should be, a distinction must be made between maximisation or minimisation, as well as the satisfaction, goals. With **maximisation goals** it is important to achieve a maximum high market share or profit. On the other hand, **minimisation goals** strive to have "minimum production costs" or build a vehicle in "the shortest possible time".

  The problem with developing this kind of goals is that "at the end of the day", nobody can determine whether they have been achieved. How can you know if you really have the lowest production costs? Even if a company can produce its products cheaper than all its competitors, this does not mean that it has already achieved the lowest possible costs. And who can decide in day-to-day business whether you are making the "maximum profit"? As a result, you cannot control and monitor with maximisation or minimisation goals. Therefore, the motivation of the employees who are evaluated in this way decreases. Consequently, you should refrain from defining maximisation or minimisation goals.

  Instead, it is a much better idea to formulate **satisfaction goals**. This means that the sales target is 650 million euros or the production costs for the basic version of an e-car model are set at 22,000 €. At university, the satisfaction goal can be to aim for an overall average of 1.2 (roughly corresponding to a first in the English university system). When you formulate goals in this way, you can check exactly whether they have been achieved. You will also be able to more effectively determine which actions have contributed to the achievement of a goal.
- **Time frame of a goal: Until when do you have to achieve it?**

  Often goals, even operational ones, are not precisely defined within a time frame. This means the important information of when you want to achieve a certain goal is missing. **Strategic goals** (e.g. setting up a *Bayer* production site in China) often have a time frame of 3–5 years, by which point, in this example, the product plant is meant to be running.

  It is necessary to break strategic goals down into **operational goals** to achieve them. This is usually based on the company's financial year. The interim targets must be met to achieve the strategic goal within the next 12 months. Additionally, other goals can be assigned a shorter time span.

  The relevance of such a time specification results from the controlling role of goals. If a time frame is not defined for a goal, then the participants do not know by when to achieve the goal. Therefore, it is also not sufficient to set a goal of attaining an overall average of 1.3 (roughly corresponding to a first in the English university system) in a bachelor's programme without specifying whether this goal is to be achieved within the standard period of study, or in eight or ten semesters.

It is therefore recommended that you not only break down strategic targets into operational targets for a year but define them further as quarterly targets, in both your private and professional lives. When it comes to important intermediate goals, they are also often referred to as **milestones** which must be achieved. These must be specified on a monthly, weekly and/or daily basis to ensure the most effective procedure possible.

- **Scope of a goal: Where is it to be achieved?**

  If your company is aiming for market leadership, then ambitiousness of this goal varies depending on whether this position is to be achieved in Texas, in Germany, in the EU or in the world market. The goal also differs if you are aiming for this market leadership for the entire company and not only in a defined business area (e.g. for confectionery in the premium market). Thus, when defining goals, you must also determine their scope.

> **Remember Box**
> To successfully define goals, you must ensure that they precisely outline the content and extent, as well as the spatial and temporal scope.
> Only goals that equally consider all these requirements can play the essential orientation, control and motivation roles of goals.

Sometimes, the requirements for defining goals are also referred to as **SMART goals**. This acronym (special case of an abbreviation) is made up of the first letters of the following words:

- **Specific** (in the sense of an exact indication of the desired result) or **stated** (meaning a concrete target)
- **Measurable** (in the sense of the ability to exactly measure whether a target is achieved)
- **Achievable** (in the sense of the reachability of the target altitude)
- **Relevant** (meaning the relevance of the objective for the respective context) or **Realistic** (in the sense of if the projects can be done in reality)
- **Targeted** (meaning a factual specification) or **Time-oriented** (in the sense of a temporal specification)

I have already covered all the aspects with the previous requirement criteria, except for **achievable, realistic** and **relevant**. These three terms are on a different logical level. With these criteria it is not about formulating goals as precisely as possible but rather about **assessing the goals** themselves. This raises the question of who should assess the reachability and relevance of goals. After all, goals represent

2.2 Definition of Goals

targeted conditions in the future. The achievement of these goals cannot be predicted, even with the best forecasting instruments, nor can their significance be conclusively assessed. You can easily imagine that in target agreement discussions between a superior and an employee, a consensus about how realistic a target is cannot easily be reached if, for example, 40% of the employee's annual salary depends on achieving this target! You should take this into account when using the SMART criteria.

Important goals are specified below so that you can use them properly for corporate management (cf. Krause and Arora 2010).

- **EBITDA** (earnings before interest, tax, depreciation and amortisation)
  EBITDA measures the profitability of a company. You calculate it as follows:

  Net income or loss (result of ordinary activities)
  +Taxes on income and earnings (−tax refund)
  = EBT (earnings before taxes)
  +Interest expenses
  = EBIT (earnings before interest and taxes)
  +Amortisation of intangible assets (including goodwill)
  = EBITA (earnings before interest, tax and amortisation)
  +Depreciation of property, plant and equipment
  = EBITDA (earnings before interest, tax, depreciation and amortisation)

This calculation allows companies to be compared internationally. Since "earnings before taxes" (EBT) are calculated, country-specific tax laws have no influence on the calculated value. By calculating "earnings before interest" (EBIT), the financing structure of the company is not taken into consideration. The calculation of "profit before depreciation of property, plant and equipment" and "profit before amortisation of intangible assets" removes company- and/or country-specific depreciation modalities from the equation.

EBIT (earnings before interest and tax)
  This allows the influences of funding and taxes to be deducted from the results.

EBT (earnings before tax)
  This means the net profit is calculated before taxes are applied.

Profit

Turnover

Sales (expressed in quantity not value)

Market share
- Absolute market share (own share of turnover or sales of a defined total market in %)
- Relative market share (own market share divided by the market share of the largest competitor; the result has no percentage or value)

Return on investment (ROI)

ROI measures the amount of interest paid on invested capital. ROI is therefore a measure of return (profit) on capital. To calculate this the profit is divided by the invested capital and multiplied by 100.

Return on capital employed (ROCE)

ROCE measures the extent to which the capital employed bears interest and is therefore a measure of the return on total capital employed. The profit is divided by the capital employed and multiplied by 100.

Return on sales (ROS)

ROS measures the profitability of the generated turnover. To calculate the profit is divided by turnover and multiplied by 100.

Market capitalisation (market cap)

Market capitalisation (also called stock exchange capitalisation or market value) is the total value of the shares of a listed company. It is calculated by multiplying the market value of the corresponding shares by the number of shares of the company in circulation. Treasury shares are not included in this calculation.

This selection represents some of the most important financial key figures that you should use to manage your company.

▶ **Implementation Tips**

- No company can survive in the long term without a precise formulation of goals.
- Even though the age of agile management demands a high degree of flexibility, this does not mean that you can sacrifice clear goals. On the contrary, you must define exactly which goals you want to manage in an agile way in which business areas.
- The call for agility therefore only seems to contradict precise goals!
- Goals only develop their desired effects of orientation, motivation and control if you formulate them precisely.
- To this end, you must specify the goals in terms of content, extent, temporal and spatial relation.
- Of course, at the end of the target time frame, you need to check to what extent the goals have been achieved. Then, if necessary, you must take countermeasures and/or reward the team for its performance.
- You should combine the achievement of goals with your company's bonus scheme, so that it pays off for your employees to get involved in the achievement of goals.
- However, as a manager you can't delegate the core task of supporting your own employees in achieving their goals.

2.3 Pyramid of Goals

Companies often present all their goals in a hierarchy of goals as shown in Fig. 2.1. Based on the corporate purpose and overarching corporate goals, divisional goals are defined on the following level. These goals can be developed in different areas, including human resources, production, marketing, sales and procurement. You can then further specify the goals in marketing, on a strategic and instrumental basis.

When designing such a **system of goals**, you must consider that there is a **middle-purpose relationship** between goals on different hierarchical levels. This means that the achievement of a certain market share for a product or service should help to achieve the overall goals of the marketing department. The achievement of the marketing goals, as well as the goals of the other functional areas, should in turn contribute to the achievement of the overriding corporate goals. The same applies to the goals in the areas of production, procurement, sales, etc.

When defining goals, you should make sure that goals which are in a hierarchical relationship complement each other. This means that the achievement of the marketing goals contributes to the fulfilment of the company goals. Ideally, this **goal complementarity** (also called **goal harmony**) should also be ensured within and between the goals of the individual functional areas (see Fig. 2.2, left). For instance, such a goal harmony is seen between the "reduction of production costs" on the one hand and "reduction of sales prices" on the other, as well as between "increase in advertising expenses" and "achievement of sales growth".

However, sometimes **goal conflicts** exist on purpose in corporate goal systems (also referred to as **goal competition**, see Fig. 2.2, middle). This is done deliberately in some cases. Such a goal competition appears, for example, when you have a goal of "reducing costs in the customer service centre" and "increasing the service level towards customers". There is also a conflict of goals when trying to "reduce advertising expenditures" and "increase the customer base". You can define such contradictions in the goal system so that employees think about new ways of providing services and think outside the box.

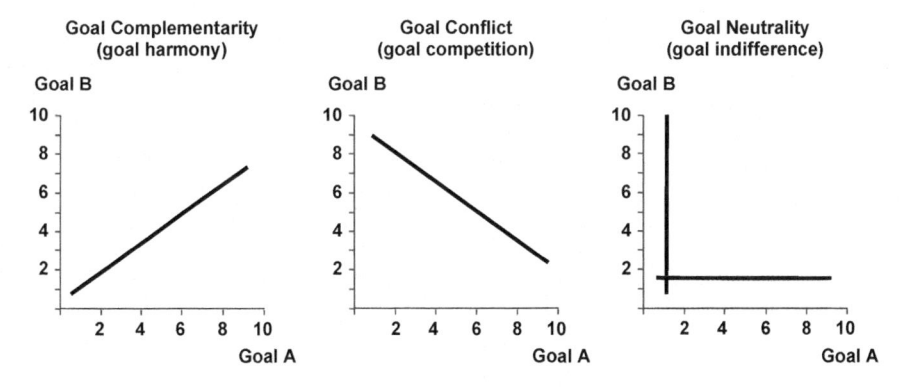

Fig. 2.2 Visualisation of goal relationships (in millions of euros). Author's own figure

> **Remember Box**
> You can use conflicting goals in a targeted manner in companies to initiate change processes and overcome thought blockades.
> In this way you can avoid a permanent "more of the same".

Goal neutrality (also called **goal indifference**) is given if the achievement of one goal has no influence on the achievement of other goals (see Fig. 2.2, right). An example of this would be the global goal of "introducing English as a corporate language". However, a more detailed analysis of this goal reveals that using English as a corporate language could make it easier to enter other countries or to start relationships with foreign partners. This would possibly benefit the achievable market share. Therefore, you can assume that all goals of your company have a positive or negative relationship to each other, whether it be directly or indirectly.

▶ **Implementation Tips**

- You should combine the goals of your company in a goal pyramid.
- You can then systematically check how these are related to each other in a target-means relationship.
- In doing so, you should tend to avoid conflicting goals and focus on achieving gaol harmony.
- However, you can "plan in" specific goal conflicts when formulating your goals to break up existing patterns of thought and behaviour and promote innovation.

2.4 Balanced Scorecard

Nowadays, on a company level, the focus increasingly lies on a planning and control instrument, the **balanced scorecard**, which overrides the pyramid form described in Sect. 2.3 (cf. fundamentally Kaplan and Norton 1996; Müller 2017, pp. 71–75). The balanced scorecard is a combination of different perspectives and layers of corporate and/or divisional goals. This leads to a **multidimensional goal framework**. This can be referred to as a **control cockpit of the company**. In addition to corporate finance goals, process-, customer- and employee-related goals are defined at the same hierarchical level. The goals defined must be achieved at the same time. This will often lead to conflicting goals.

With a balanced scorecard, you ensure that several strategic perspectives that are important for a company's performance are taken into consideration at the same time. After all, corporate management based solely on financial ratios is no longer sufficient today.

2.4 Balanced Scorecard

> **Remember Box**
> How did *Jack Welch*, a very successful former CEO of *General Electric* and promoter of shareholder value for many decades, describe his one-sided focus on financial ratios? As "the dumbest idea in the world!" (Büschemann 2010).

The word "balanced" in the phrase "balanced scorecard" is used to express that a company will only be successful in the long term if it ensures a "balanced" achievement of objectives in the various performance areas. With the balanced scorecard, you transform the classic goal pyramid (see Fig. 2.1) into a **goal cockpit**. In this way, you also keep the needs of the stakeholders in mind. Using the stakeholder concept means that your company will only achieve its overall goal if all the fields defined in the scorecard are achieved in a balanced way.

By using the balanced scorecard concept, you can avoid optimising subareas of the company (e.g. the financial key figures) at the expense of other areas (such as the personnel sector or customers). The achievement of a "balanced" result is promoted if the variable components of the remuneration of broad groups of employees, not only of top and middle management, are linked to the achievement of the goals defined on the scorecard.

The starting point for the **development** of a **balanced scorecard** is the vision or mission of the company (see Sect. 2.1). From this the four areas defined in Fig. 2.3, goals, key figures and guidelines, are derived based on the following questions:

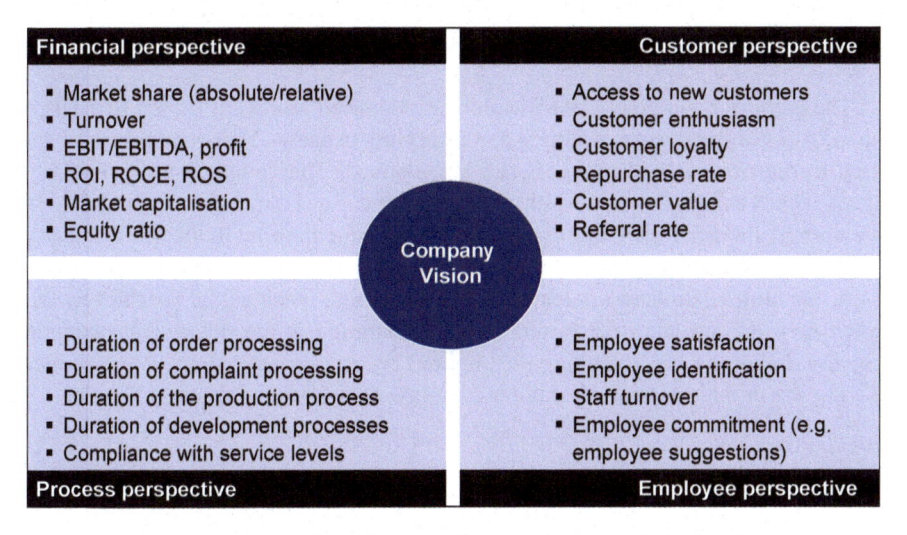

Financial perspective	Customer perspective
• Market share (absolute/relative) • Turnover • EBIT/EBITDA, profit • ROI, ROCE, ROS • Market capitalisation • Equity ratio	• Access to new customers • Customer enthusiasm • Customer loyalty • Repurchase rate • Customer value • Referral rate
• Duration of order processing • Duration of complaint processing • Duration of the production process • Duration of development processes • Compliance with service levels	• Employee satisfaction • Employee identification • Staff turnover • Employee commitment (e.g. employee suggestions)
Process perspective	Employee perspective

(Centre: Company Vision)

Fig. 2.3 Basic concept of the balanced scorecard for a company. Author's own figure

- **Financial perspective**
  How do we intend to document our financial success for our shareholders?
- **Customer perspective**
  How do we want to measure the extent to which we convince customers of our products and services?
- **Process perspective**
  How do we want to determine which processes are efficient and effective?
- **Employee perspective**
  How do we intend to determine whether we are convincing our employees of our vision and whether they are actively and successfully involved in its implementation?

With this type of a balanced scorecard, you define the central corporate goals for a fiscal year. Through the underlying **goal-setting process**, you can ensure that several company-relevant perspectives, such as the customer and employee perspectives, are considered simultaneously at the highest company level. Quarterly or at the end of the fiscal year, you can check which areas are on track and what action is needed based on the goals you defined.

> **Remember Box**
> When a balanced scorecard is used, there is always a conflict of goals between the different areas. The balanced scorecard helps to make these conflicts visible at the highest company level. You must address and resolve these conflicts.

The company sub-goals shown within the balanced scorecard should be backed up with action programmes during the **planning process**. These programmes are used to determine whether a goal can be achieved. The company must regularly check if each sub-goal is achievable. Additional measures may have to be initiated in the current financial year to ensure this. By documenting goals in the scorecard, possible interdependencies with other goals can be detected at an early stage.

A **learning organisation** identifies the causes both when a goal is achieved and when it is not and takes the results into consideration in the subsequent planning process. In some cases, planning assumptions were incorrect, competitor activities were over- or underestimated or the market potential was misjudged.

> **Remember Box**
> Only by regularly determining and documenting the **causes of success and failure** and integrating them into new planning processes you can improve the results achieved from one planning session to another. This is how you can build up **closed action cycles**.

2.4 Balanced Scorecard

Focus on acquisition	Focus on customers

• Cost-per-Interest (CPI per channel/action)
• Cost-per-Order (CPO per channel/action)
• Customer value based on contact method
	• Access to new customers
	• Distribution of customer base according to:
	  – repeat customers
	  – referrals
	  – customer value

• Usage rates of information offers
• Conversion rates by type/time of initiation
• Potential interested parties (by channel)
	• Distribution of clients according to:
	  – inactivity
	  – decreasing sales
	• Switcher rate

Focus on prospects	**Focus on winning customers back**

(Centre: **Marketing**)

Fig. 2.4 Marketing scorecard for customer relationship management. Author's own figure

You should break the balanced scorecard of the company down further to the key areas, since several goals must be considered simultaneously in all areas, in marketing, for example. Based on the overarching corporate and marketing goals, you can use a **balanced scorecard in marketing** to indicate the key performance figures listed in Fig. 2.4 for CRM (customer relationship management). The associated goals must also be backed up with appropriate action programmes. Sometimes specific **brand scorecards** are also used in marketing.

Using balanced scorecards to control companies or individual functional areas is only just gaining ground. The increased use of such **integrated planning and control elements** allows for a holistic view of the relevant stakeholders of the company and helps to keep an eye on various criteria of different departments simultaneously. This allows you to overcome the frequently criticised silo mentality. Often employees still try to optimise their own area, even at the expense of other departments. However, you can minimise this behaviour by measuring the success of the (entire) workforce based on whether the goals of a balanced scorecard were achieved.

▶ **Implementation Tips**

- By using balanced scorecards at company and departmental level, you can counteract the silo mentality that is still frequently encountered. This mentality manifests itself when individual areas want to achieve their departmental goals at the expense of the whole company.
- To achieve a cross-departmental cooperation, it is important that you combine personal incentives with the achievement of all goals found on the balanced scorecard.

- To ensure the full commitment of your employees, you should clearly communicate what the company is aiming to achieve when first introducing a balanced scorecard.
- To foster this change process, you can use tools that will be presented in Chap. 11.

References

Audi. (2018). *Unternehmensstrategie*. Accessed October 20, 2018, from http://www.audi.com/corporate/de/unternehmen/unternehmensstrategie.html
Büschemann, K.-H. (2010). *Die blödeste Idee der Welt*. Accessed April 1, 2018, from http://www.sueddeutsche.de/wirtschaft/shareholder-value-lehre-die-bloedeste-idee-der-welt-1.405826
Facebook. (2018). *Facebook*. Accessed March 15, 2018, from https://www.facebook.com/pg/facebook/about
Hungenberg, H. (2014). *Strategisches Management im Unternehmen*. Wiesbaden: Springer Gabler
Hurrelmann, K., & Albrecht, E. (2016). *Die heimlichen Revolutionäre: Wie die Generation Y unsere Welt verändert*. Beltz Verlag:Weinheim and Basel
IKEA. (2017). *Vision und Geschäftsidee*. Accessed October 2, 2017, from http://www.ikea.com/ms/de_DE/this-is-ikea/about-the-ikea-group/index.html
Kaplan, R. S., & Norton, D. P. (1996). *The balanced scorecard: Translating strategy into action*. New York: McGraw-Hill.
Krause, H.-U. (2016). *Controlling-Kennzahlen für ein nachhaltiges Management: Ein umfassendes Kompendium kompakt erklärter Key Performance Indicators*. Munich: De Gruyter.
Krause, H.-U., & Arora, D. (2010). *Controlling-Kennzahlen – Key performance indicators* (2nd ed.). Munich: De Gruyter.
Kreutzer, R. (2017). *Praxisorientiertes Marketing, Grundlagen – Instrumente – Fallbeispiele* (5th ed.). Wiesbaden: Springer Gabler.
Kreutzer, R., & Land, K.-H. (2017). *Digital Branding – Konzeption einer holistischen Markenführung*. Wiesbaden: Springer Gabler.
Kreutzer, R., Neugebauer, T., & Pattloch, A. (2018). *Digital business leadership – Digital transformation – Business model innovation – Agile organization – Change-management, Wiesbaden*. Springer Gabler.
Lischka, C. (2016). *Wie sich auch Marken auf die Generation Y einstellen*. Accessed March 28, 2018, from http://page-online.de/branche-karriere/wie-sich-auch-marken-auf-die-generation-y-einstellen (Erstellt: January 13 2016)
Müller, H.-E. (2017). *Unternehmensführung, Strategie – Management – Praxis* (3rd ed.). Munich: De Gruyter.
Sinek, S. (2011). *Start with why: How great leaders inspire everyone to take action*. New York: Portfolio.
SpaceX. (2018). *Company*. Accessed March 31, 2018, from http://www.spacex.com/about
Tesla. (2018). *Tesla Mission*. Accessed March 31, 2018, from https://www.tesla.com/de_DE/blog/mission-tesla
Uber. (2018). *About*. Accessed October 14, 2018, from https://www.uber.com/about
Wikipedia. (2018). *Wikipedia*. Accessed November 26, 2018, from https://de.wikipedia.org/wiki/Wikipedia#Name_und_Logo

Concepts for the Development of Strategies 3

3.1 Preliminary Remark: Variety of Strategic Concepts

You can find **many strategic concepts** in management literature. Particularly important authors of such concepts include Porter (2004a, b), Kotler and Keller (2015) and Becker (2013). However, instead of showing you many different approaches, I will now present an approach that has proven itself in research, teaching and business practice.

The concept of **customer-oriented strategies** put forth by Becker (2013) can be used to both **plan a startup** and **analyse the business models of established companies**. You can also use this concept to develop **growth strategies for your company**. Best of all, the contributions of the other authors mentioned above can be integrated seamlessly into *Becker*'s concept. You won't miss anything if you "get your teeth" into this one concept!

Furthermore, this chapter introduces the **business canvas** concept, which is perfect for designing the content of customer-oriented strategies. The **Kano concept** can also help to sharpen strategic positioning and shape implementation in terms of content.

The special challenges you must meet in your strategy work nowadays are presented to you using the **3 horizons model**. Additionally, exciting **concepts for (digital) brand management** will be presented.

3.2 Concept of Customer-Oriented Strategies

To achieve strategic corporate and marketing goals, it is necessary to break them down in various steps and make them more concrete. In many cases, ambitious goals can only be achieved through **programmes** that are **designed for the long term** and thus define a **basic orientation of the company's activities**. Often such

```
┌─────────────────────┐                    ┌─────────────────────┐
│   Market field      │                    │  Market stimulation │
│   strategy          │                    │   strategy          │
│   "What?"           │                    │   "How?"            │
└─────────────────────┘                    └─────────────────────┘
                         Customer-
                         oriented
                         strategies
┌─────────────────────┐                    ┌─────────────────────┐
│ Market segmentation │                    │   Market area       │
│   strategy          │                    │   strategy          │
│   "Who?"            │                    │   "Where?"          │
└─────────────────────┘                    └─────────────────────┘
```

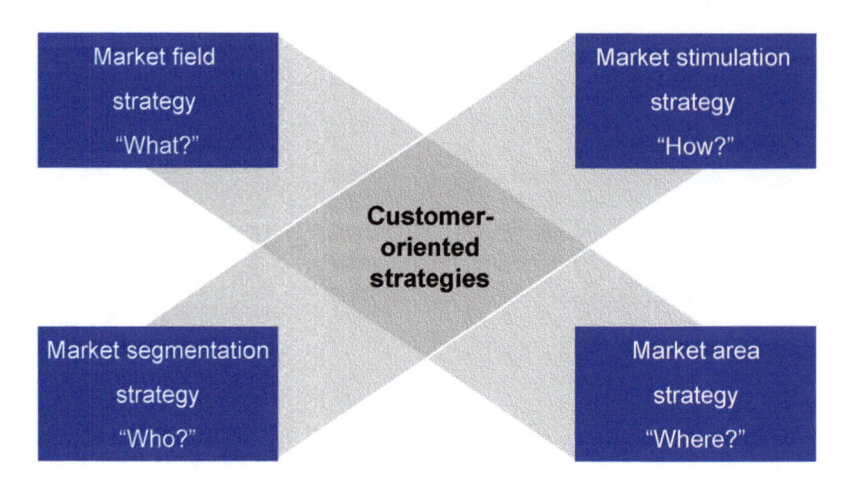

Fig. 3.1 Concept of customer-oriented strategies. Author's own figure

programmes, which are called **strategies**, have a duration of several years. Strategies are developed and defined within the framework of strategic planning.

With Becker's (2013) **customer-oriented strategy approach**, the focus of your strategic concept is not on your competitors but on your customers. This ensures a consistent market-oriented style of corporate management! This approach involves four interwoven decision levels, all of which require you must make decisions regarding the desired strategic position (see Fig. 3.1). When developing the **market field strategy**, the first question is **"what"** your company should offer. As part of the **market segmentation strategy**, you define the **"who"** as the target group of your activities. The **market stimulation strategy** determines **"how"** the targeted people should be motivated to purchase your services. Lastly, the **market area strategy** allows you to determine **"where"** your company wants to be active.

3.2.1 Market Field Strategy

The **product/market matrix** (also called **Ansoff Matrix**; see Fig. 3.2) developed by Ansoff (1979) is the basis of the **market field strategy**. Based on the criteria "products" (this also includes service offers) and "markets" both "existing" and "new", four operational fields can be identified for a company. You can use this to define in which **market fields** your company would like to operate. You should use the field "existing products/markets" as a starting point for strategy development. The arrows in Fig. 3.2 indicate the possible directions of your expansion strategy.

With the **market penetration strategy** seen in Fig. 3.2, you aim to penetrate **a market that is already served** even more strongly with the **existing product range**. There are different ways to start doing this:

3.2 Concept of Customer-Oriented Strategies

Fig. 3.2 Product/market matrix—Ansoff Matrix. Source: Adapted from Ansoff (1979)

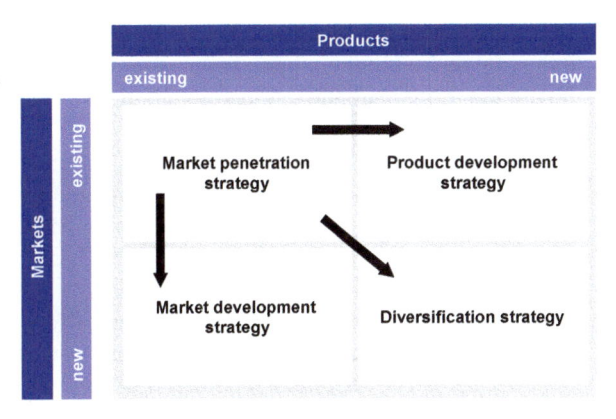

	Products	
	existing	new
Markets existing	Market penetration strategy	Product development strategy
Markets new	Market development strategy	Diversification strategy

- Increasing in the usage rate of the products or services
- Promoting (with caution) the artificial obsolescence or obsolescence of products by installing predetermined breaking points (consider the impact on trust and reputation)
- Making sales units larger to increase the turnover per purchase
- Winning over customers of competitors/acquisition of previous non-users

All types of advertising and sales promotion that intend to strengthen the presence of existing products and services more firmly in an existing market also contribute to the goal of increasing profits, turnover, sales and/or market share.

For this you do not need any additional resources for research and development (R&D), as only existing products and services are to be marketed more strongly.

The purpose of a **product development strategy** is to expand the existing product range in a market that is already being served. **Further developing existing products/services** and **expanding the range of products and services** are some of the techniques you can use to implement this strategy. This often requires additional resources for marketing research, R&D, production facilities, etc. Many of the methods described in Chap. 4 can be used here and for the other starting points of the market field strategies.

As part of your **market development strategy**, you can identify two central starting points to **enter new markets with your existing products**:

- **Acquisition of previously uncovered sales areas in the core sales area**
  Among other actions, this includes **closing white spots**, i.e. regions in the previous core sales area that have not yet been reached due to the existing density of sales outlets. For this purpose, additional sales investments are necessary.
- **Development of additional functional markets ("functional expansions")**
  To gain access to new markets, you can also expand the product suitability. This can be achieved by marketing a product developed for a certain target group to other customer groups (e.g. *Kinderschokolade*, chocolate bars for children). *HARIBO*'s positioning "*HARIBO* makes children happy" developed in the 1930s

was changed in the mid-1960s by adding "and adults as well" to tap into this target market with the existing product range (see Haribo 2018). In addition to investments in marketing research, additional communication campaigns are essential for functional expansions.

With a **diversification strategy**, your company enters new markets with new products/services. You can do so in the following ways:

- **Horizontal diversification**

    This strategy requires you to add **related offers** to existing product/service programmes which are on the **same economic performance level** (therefore it is "horizontal"). The **customer base tends to remain the same**. As a result, your company continues to operate at the same economic level. In my opinion this strategy is often not really diversification, but rather an expansion of the product range (i.e. the product development strategy described above).

    On the other hand, a true horizontal diversification is when a men's outfitter, for example, also includes women's clothing in its range, or when a midrange car manufacturer offers additional models in the premium segment. This means the company remains active at the same economic level (trade or manufacturer) but also covers new customer segments.

- **Vertical diversification**

    This type of diversification strategy involves the **integration of upstream or downstream production and/or marketing stages**, thus expanding a company's value chain. From a customer's perspective, **downstream integration** means integrating an activity back into the company's production process. An example of this is when a chemical company starts producing the raw material that was previously purchased from a supplier. **Forward integration** occurs when an economic level towards the customer is integrated. If you as a production company set up your own stationary sales outlets or online shops, you are implementing this strategy.

- **Lateral diversification**

    This is a more of a true diversification because you are aiming to **break fresh ground with completely new product and market areas**. There is no connection between the new activities and your previous focus. This option is usually associated with the greatest risks for your company, because you cannot fall back on existing experience in the new field of activity. Even though 10–20 years ago it was still "fashionable" to expand far beyond the borders of their own fields of competence, today companies concentrate more on their core business and sell the activities that do not fit to it.

▶ **Implementation Tips**

- The product/market matrix is a perfect tool for systematically considering various strategic options to further develop your company's offers.

- You can use the concept for both products and services.
- Even if the concept looks very "simple", it is well suited for strategy work and should be used by you regularly to stimulate your thoughts.

3.2.2 Market Stimulation Strategy

While the market field strategy defines which product-market combinations your company wants to operate in, the **market stimulation strategy** determines how to influence and control the market, thus the "stimulating of the target group to make purchases". To define this targeted positioning in the market, it is necessary to look at the general division of markets. You can usually do this by using the layer model shown in Fig. 3.3 as a basis. This model enables you to distinguish the **premium** and **brand buyers**, as well as the **promotional, brand, no-name** and **"price buyers"**.

The next question is which of these segments your product range should serve. This is a strategic decision because it impacts many other areas of the company's activities. You can choose from a wide range of strategies including the **dominant preference strategy** (also known as a **premium strategy**), the **midrange strategy** and the **dominant price-volume strategy**. Your "relative" position that you want to achieve in the market is decisive for positioning. With this strategy you define the **price- and quality-related positioning in the competitive environment** (see Fig. 3.4). Remember that when defining the "relative quality", you need to not only evaluate the product or service quality alone but the entire appearance of your offer, e.g. the design of the online and offline presences, as well as the service quality.

With the combination of a "relatively high quality and relatively low price", you are not exploiting the existing market potential (see Fig. 3.4). However, this

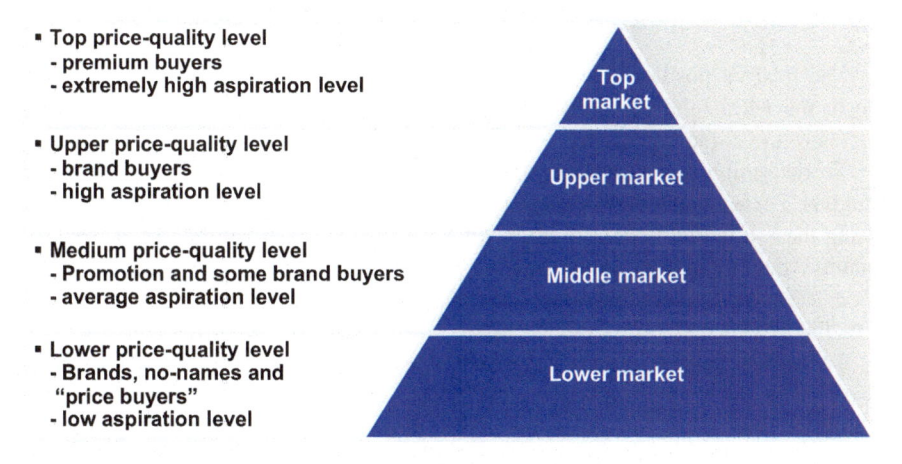

- Top price-quality level
  - premium buyers
  - extremely high aspiration level

- Upper price-quality level
  - brand buyers
  - high aspiration level

- Medium price-quality level
  - Promotion and some brand buyers
  - average aspiration level

- Lower price-quality level
  - Brands, no-names and "price buyers"
  - low aspiration level

(Pyramid: Top market / Upper market / Middle market / Lower market)

Fig. 3.3 Traditional market layer model. Author's own figure

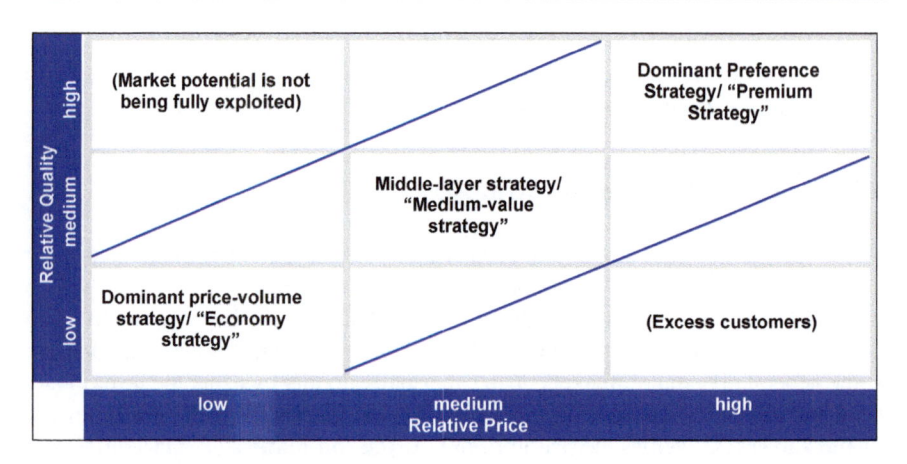

Fig. 3.4 Framework for designing the market stimulation strategy. Author's own figure

approach can be a transitional strategy for entering a new market if your company or offer does not benefit from a positive reputation yet. The opposite position of competing with a "relatively low quality and relatively high price" cannot ensure the long-term success of your company in competitive markets and should therefore be avoided.

In each industry, you can determine the relative positions of suppliers using the framework shown in Fig. 3.4.

- An **economy strategy** is implemented by certain food and fashion discounters (*Aldi, Lidl; Primark*). The low-cost carriers (*Ryanair, Easyjet, Eurowings*) also use this strategy.
- You can find a **medium-value strategy** at *Tesco*, as well as *Lufthansa*.
- A **premium strategy** is implemented by luxury fashion brands. *Audi, BMW, Lexus, Mercedes* and *Porsche* also plan their actions using this strategy.

The relative position that you aim for in the market is the result of strategic decisions within the company and is fundamentally derived from the company vision or the company mission (see Chap. 2).

To determine this desired strategic position, you can use various **positioning models**. These models do not only apply on company but also a product level. When using these it is often better to go beyond the criteria "relative price" and "relative quality" defined in Fig. 3.4 and define market-specific criteria for the positioning model. The selected criteria should be relevant from the customer's point of view (see Fig. 3.5).

This model enables you to **analyse the status quo of a certain market**. It makes it easier to understand the relative position of different companies or brands in a chosen market. This also helps you to better understand the success or failure of different companies and brands. Additionally, it may be possible to identify previously uncovered market segments. In conclusion, a positioning model is a good

3.2 Concept of Customer-Oriented Strategies

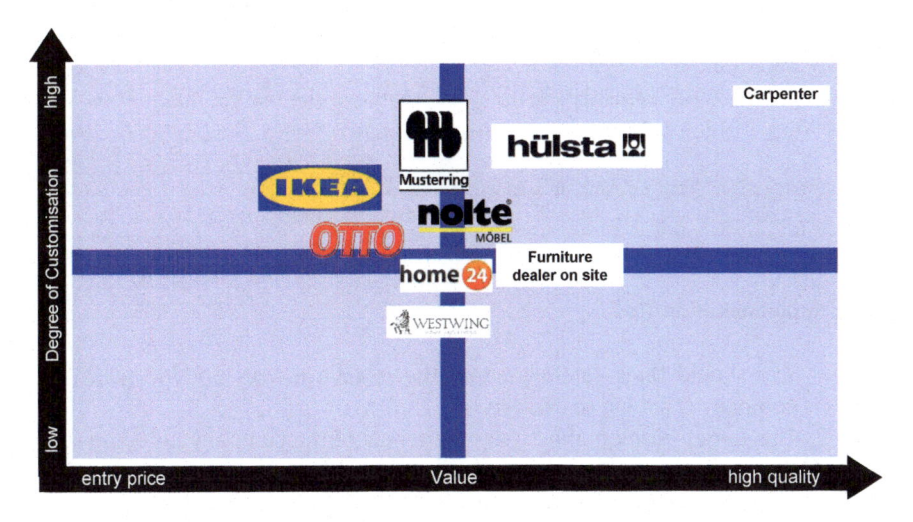

Fig. 3.5 Positioning model—example for the furniture market in Germany. Author's own figure

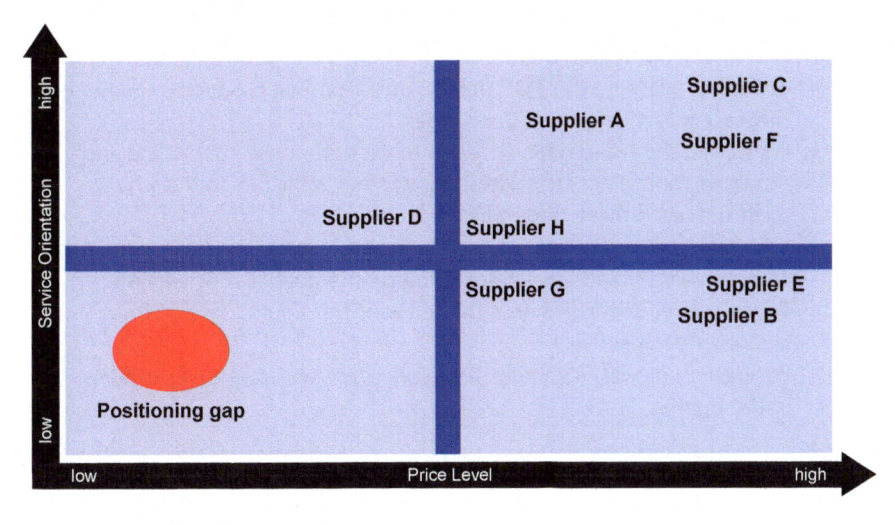

Fig. 3.6 Positioning model highlighting a positioning gap. Author's own figure

starting point to define a desired market positioning (**target position**) while taking into consideration the companies or brands in the environment that are already established.

An additional positioning model is shown in Fig. 3.6, which uses other criteria to analyse the market. This example clearly illustrates that such a model can also help you to find **positioning gaps** that have not yet been filled by any competitor.

> **Remember Box**
>
> Your concrete decisions determine your actions in the market. Keep Porter's (1996, p. 70) important statement below in mind:
>
> Strategy is making trade-offs in competing. The essence of strategy is choosing what not to do.

▶ **Implementation Tips**

- You should think carefully about the relative market position your company is aiming to achieve.
- This target position affects all other areas of the company including the personnel selection that is given the responsibility to achieve a desired position (qualified service personnel for a premium positioning vs. low-cost staff to reach the cost leaders in an economy strategy).
- When making this decision, you must accept trade-offs. This means that with a premium strategy, you inevitably must do without many customers from the "middle of the market". If you implement an economy strategy, the ROS (return on sales) per product is low; in this case you must attract the masses.
- If you, like the failed *AirBerlin*, want to be both a low-cost airline and attractive for business travellers, you will inevitably fail. That is why we must deal with these trade-offs.
- You can use positioning models separately when analysing on a company and brand level, depending on the goal of your analysis.
- To do this, you should select the relevant positioning criteria from a customer perspective.
- Positioning models also help you to visualise well-targeted positions in the market.

3.2.3 Market Segmentation Strategy

When **segmenting the market,** you divide the market into individual segments (meaning clearly defined subgroups of target objects, e.g. people or companies). You can then view each of these as a **separate target market** and process them differently. The division of the market is called **taxonomic market segmentation** ("taxonomy" is concerned with "classification"). You must define based on which criteria and into which segments the market will be divided. **Management-oriented market segmentation** involves deciding which of the segments you want to address with your offer. You must also specify whether you want to address only one or

3.2 Concept of Customer-Oriented Strategies

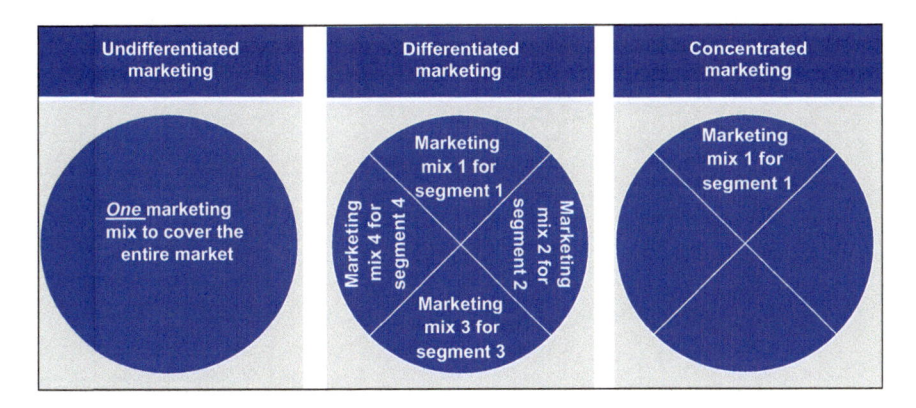

Fig. 3.7 Types of market segmentation. Author's own figure

several segments with different offers. Figure 3.7 shows the basic decision options that exist within the framework of market segmentation.

In **undifferentiated marketing** the **entire** market is covered by a specifically designed marketing diamond. This **marketing diamond** is made up of the following activities (cf. Kreutzer 2017):

- Product and programme policy
- Communication policy
- Distribution policy
- Pricing and conditions policy
- Staffing policy

Designing the marketing diamond for the entire market calls for a **mass market strategy**. Usually, only companies who benefit from a monopolistic situation in the market, thanks to the absence of competitors or to a dominant market position, can "afford" to implement this strategy. In today's highly competitive industries, it is rare to encounter this approach.

Differentiated marketing means using different marketing approaches for **all** or **many** of the defined segments of the market. You direct your activities to different market segments (e.g. individuals and companies as customers). To do so the marketing diamond is also designed differently. The *Accor* hotel group uses this approach by providing a variety of different offers and brands for different segments.

Concentrated marketing involves selecting only one of the identified market segments. *Montblanc* is an example of this because its products and services focus solely on the luxury segment.

To structure your acquisition measures in a target-oriented manner, you should use the **acquisition-oriented segmentation** first. You define which customer or market segments you will focus on acquiring. In online marketing, this is referred to as **targeting** (cf. Kreutzer 2018a).

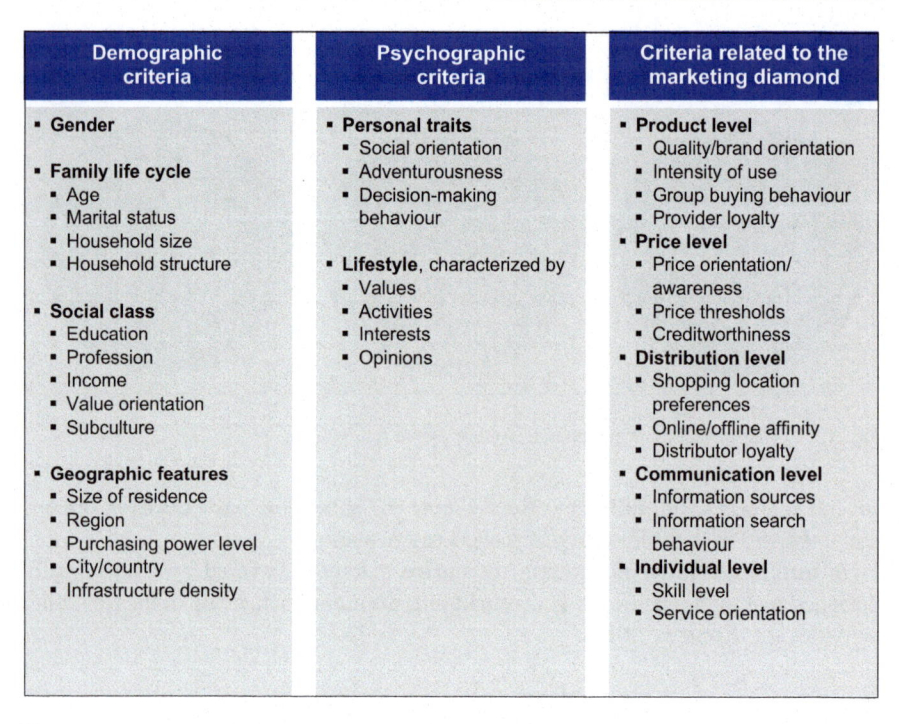

Demographic criteria	Psychographic criteria	Criteria related to the marketing diamond

• **Gender**
 	
• **Family life cycle**
  • Age
  • Marital status
  • Household size
  • Household structure
 	
• **Social class**
  • Education
  • Profession
  • Income
  • Value orientation
  • Subculture
 	
• **Geographic features**
  • Size of residence
  • Region
  • Purchasing power level
  • City/country
  • Infrastructure density
	• **Personal traits**
	  • Social orientation
	  • Adventurousness
	  • Decision-making behaviour
	
	• **Lifestyle**, characterized by
	  • Values
	  • Activities
	  • Interests
	  • Opinions
		• **Product level**
		  • Quality/brand orientation
		  • Intensity of use
		  • Group buying behaviour
		  • Provider loyalty
		• **Price level**
		  • Price orientation/awareness
		  • Price thresholds
		  • Creditworthiness
		• **Distribution level**
		  • Shopping location preferences
		  • Online/offline affinity
		  • Distributor loyalty
		• **Communication level**
		  • Information sources
		  • Information search behaviour
		• **Individual level**
		  • Skill level
		  • Service orientation

Fig. 3.8 Selected criteria for market segmentation in the BtC market. Author's own figure

Regarding segmenting the **BtC market**, there are various **groups of criteria** that you can use in different combinations to describe your target customers (see Fig. 3.8). Demographic and psychographic characteristics describe the general life situation and factors influencing behaviour. Additionally, you can determine which criteria provide clues as to how the marketing instruments for customer acquisition should be designed. Therefore, a combined application of these criteria is usually best.

When carrying out acquisition-oriented segmentation in the BtB market, you can first select target companies according to **macro criteria**, focusing on the core product of the other companies. You can refine this classification in the following step by taking **micro criteria** into account. It is important to specify the relevance of the offer provided by each company. The marketing diamond criteria are used in the same way as in the BtC market (see Fig. 3.9).

After **defining a target group**, you can select magazines, newspapers, billboards and online platforms that are relevant for them, as well as TV and radio stations for advertising messages.

> **Remember Box**
> When using an acquisition-oriented segmentation strategy, you define the "prey" for your acquisition measures.

3.2 Concept of Customer-Oriented Strategies

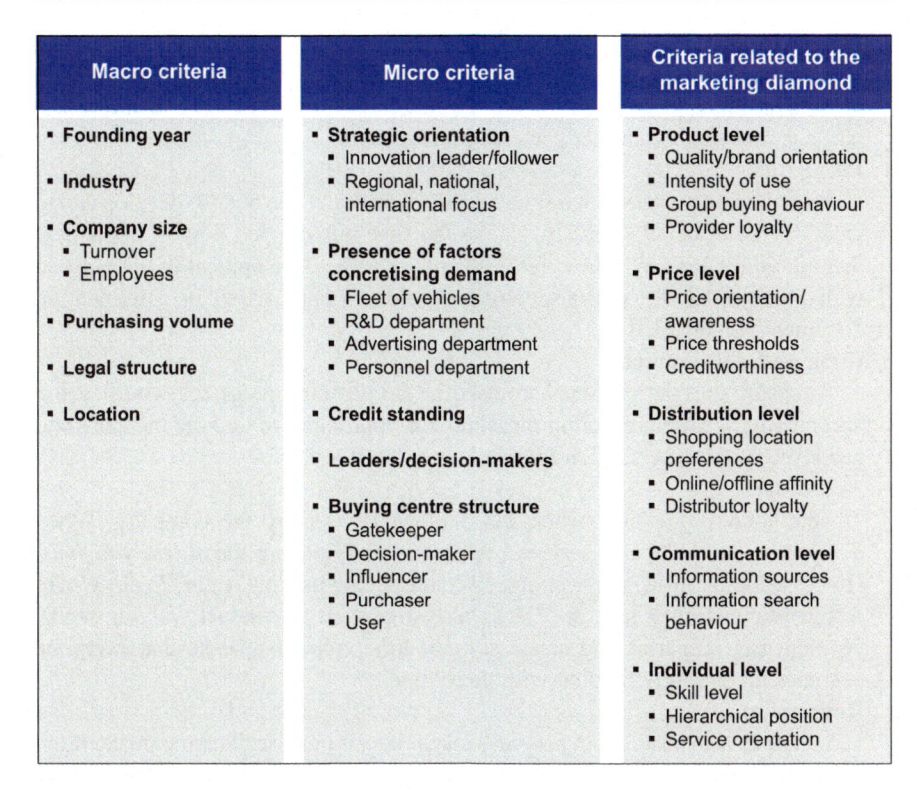

Macro criteria	Micro criteria	Criteria related to the marketing diamond

• **Founding year**
• **Industry**
• **Company size**
  • Turnover
  • Employees
• **Purchasing volume**
• **Legal structure**
• **Location**
	• **Strategic orientation**
	  • Innovation leader/follower
	  • Regional, national, international focus
	• **Presence of factors concretising demand**
	  • Fleet of vehicles
	  • R&D department
	  • Advertising department
	  • Personnel department
	• **Credit standing**
	• **Leaders/decision-makers**
	• **Buying centre structure**
	  • Gatekeeper
	  • Decision-maker
	  • Influencer
	  • Purchaser
	  • User
		• **Product level**
		  • Quality/brand orientation
		  • Intensity of use
		  • Group buying behaviour
		  • Provider loyalty
		• **Price level**
		  • Price orientation/awareness
		  • Price thresholds
		  • Creditworthiness
		• **Distribution level**
		  • Shopping location preferences
		  • Online/offline affinity
		  • Distributor loyalty
		• **Communication level**
		  • Information sources
		  • Information search behaviour
		• **Individual level**
		  • Skill level
		  • Hierarchical position
		  • Service orientation

Fig. 3.9 Selected criteria of market segmentation in the BtB market. Author's own figure

To make this easier not only for your employees but also for integrated agencies, etc., you can use the so-called **persona concept**. **Personas** are fictitious archetypes that represent the target group and give it "a face". They are described as real people. Personas have a life story, hobbies and a philosophy of life, as well as a name and picture. Here are some examples of questions that you should answer for each persona:

- Would Sabine (47) use the product?
- What are the most useful features for Sabine?
- Where would Sabine buy the product?
- Which media would Sabine use to find out about the offer?
- How much would Sabine be willing to pay for it?
- What alternatives would Sabine look at in her decision-making process?
- Etc.

When **creating a persona**, you can follow these steps (see Pruitt and Adlin 2006, pp. 48–52):

- **Family planning**
    First, you define a team that collects data inside and outside your company to identify problems and needs of the defined target segments. The result of this phase is raw data for further persona development.
- **Pregnancy**
    After the first planning phase, you decide how many personas to develop and to what degree of detail. You also define the time horizon and how to implement them in your company. The core of this phase is the development of the persona with all relevant descriptions, which should be summarised in a foundation document (cf. Fig. 3.10).
- **Birth and development**
    To ensure that the personas are used in the planning processes, you develop accompanying communication measures for your team, so that the meaning and seriousness of the persona assignment are understood.
- **Adulthood**
    Adulthood is the time when the persona is used by the company. When developing products and services, as well as advertising measures, you must always ask the following questions, "Would Sabine use this feature?" or "Where would Michael click to now?". It is also important to conduct walk-throughs, develop user scenarios and create style boards with personas so that everyone becomes increasingly familiar with their "life".
- **Retirement**
    You must also ensure that personas stay relevant in these dynamic times. If the established persona no longer adequately represents the target groups, they are to be retired. In this phase you should answer the following questions to improve your use of personas: Was the persona effective? What lessons were learned for the next persona project? Which personas should be used for the next product or for the development of service strategies?

When working on personas, you can use the **document** shown in Fig. 3.10 **as a foundation**.

You should document the results obtained with this foundation and select a photo. You should keep these personas in mind as target persons for all acquisition-related segmentation measures (cf. Kreutzer et al. 2018, pp. 124–127).

In addition to defining these target groups, which are primarily necessary for product/service development and acquisition, a **transaction-oriented segmentation** must be carried out for the already acquired leads and customers of a company. The difference to acquisition-oriented segmentation (in terms of the "prey" definition) is that you often already have transaction data regarding the relationship between your company and your prospects or customers. This means you have the exciting possibility to use this transaction data to segment the already acquired and the prospective customers.

This **concept** is based on the **customer relationship life cycle** (see Fig. 3.11). This involves distinguishing the following three phases:

3.2 Concept of Customer-Oriented Strategies

Feature	Development
Specific details	
Name	Typical name for the age cohort (based on an online search for example)
Age	Typical age
Tagline	Slogan, motto or a frequently used expression
Quote (about the product/service)	Statement regarding the product/service for which this persona was created, e.g. about quality, use or special features of the offer
Family	Persona's family: parents, siblings, possibly also other people belonging to the "clan" who have a strong influence
Marital status	Family situation, e.g. partnership, married, divorced, single
Place of residence	Current geographical place of residence (city/country, big city/small town etc.)
Roles and responsibilities	
Company	Name of employer or self-employed activity
Position	Role at the workplace, e.g. hierarchical classification, area of responsibility
Typical activities	Regular activities and work of the persona that could be relevant to the product or service
Important atypical activities	Activities and work that one would not initially associate the persona with, e.g. particularly rare hobbies, extreme sports, social or political interests
Challenges and pains	Challenges that the persona must face in their job or daily life
Responsibilities	Responsibilities at work and in everyday life
Interaction with other personas, systems and products/services	Contact with other personas in a professional setting or in everyday life, which have a special meaning for the product or the service offer; description of systems and products/services, which are important for the role of the persona.
Goals	
Life goals in the short, medium and long term	Material or spiritual goals, possibly arranged chronologically
Goals in relation to the product or service	Goals that are (should be) achieved with the product or service
Work-related goals	Professional goals
Basic life goals, desires	Fundamental goals, wishes, hopes, expectations
Skills and knowledge	
General computer skills and online presence	Know-how and intensity of hard- and software use
Areas of expertise	Expertise in one or more specialist areas
Frequently used products/services	Products used and services demanded for professional and everyday use
Specialised expertise	Special knowledge, e.g. in a professional or private setting
Knowledge about competitors	Knowledge of alternative products or services offered
Context	
Equipment	Equipment, e.g. professionally or privately relevant technology, materials, aids
„A day in the life"- description	Representation of a typical persona day; this "typical day" does not have to correspond to reality in its entirety, but comprises the relevant, frequently recurring and thus typical activities and contacts
Specific places of use	Places where the product is used, or the service that is to be developed is used
Household and leisure activities	Typical leisure activities and holidays
Relationships with other personas	Defining the personas that are not part of the professional but everyday life
Psychographic and personal details	
Personality traits	Description of personality based on human qualities (honesty, loyalty, curiosity, adventurousness, etc.)
Values and attitude	Political and religious beliefs
Fears, obstacles, peeves	Emotional states that shape how the persona thinks and feels
Personal artifacts (cars, gimmicks)	Description of objects that are particularly important for the persona in relation to the product or service that is to be developed

Fig. 3.10 Persona foundation document. Source: Adapted from Pruitt and Adlin (2006, pp. 230–234)

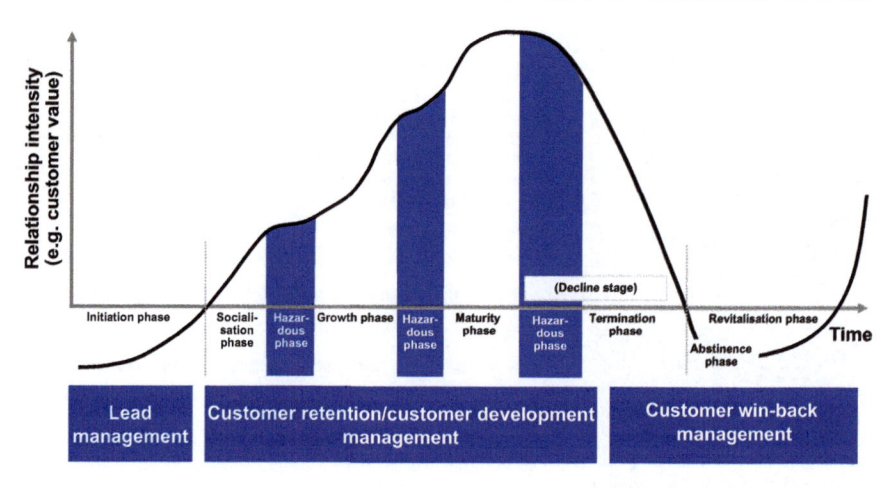

Fig. 3.11 Concept of the customer relationship life cycle. Source: Adapted from Stauss (2000, p. 16)

- Lead management
- Customer retention/customer development management
- Customer win-back management

The concept shown in Fig. 3.11 is relevant because the **interests**, and thus also the **information that people require**, differ considerably in the various phases for both consumers and company representatives. Additionally, your company also has other goals regarding the phase achieved with these people.

The **lead management** phase is mainly about making people or companies interested in your own services (focused acquisition). To communicate with the targeted people, you should **gather contact data** from the start (e.g. mailing address, e-mail address, telephone number or a WhatsApp contact). Using a **lead communication programme**, you can then gradually convert these prospects into customers (cf. Kreutzer 2016, pp. 81–155; Wirtz 2016).

When **managing leads and customers**, you should try to answer the following questions:

- Which people or companies were acquired as leads and customers?
- What characteristics do these groups have?
- Did you reach or motivate people who were described as "prey"?

During the **customer retention/customer development management phase**, for example, after a purchase has been made, it is important for you to thoroughly familiarise the customer with the offer and the company so that you can encourage a follow-up purchase if possible. You should be able to answer to the following key questions to ensure continued customer support and to acquire new customers:

3.2 Concept of Customer-Oriented Strategies

Fig. 3.12 Triad of customer service. Author's own figure

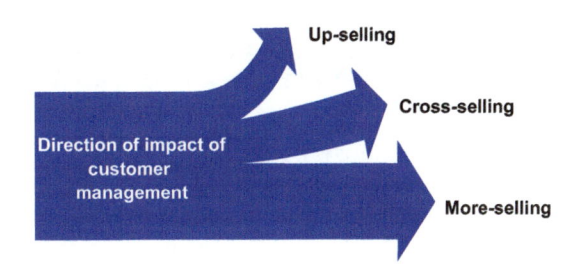

- Which of the target people, groups or companies have become active as buyers?
- What were the initial and follow-up purchases?
- What goods or services did they buy and what were the contribution margins?
- Which purchase patterns can be identified?
- Where do the customers come from (which area)?
- Which parts of the product range are demanded by customers from which area?
- Which winning methods lead to which customer value (e.g. regarding the turn-over and loyalty to a seller; cf. Chap. 6)?
- Which acquisition rates can be achieved with personalised communication (e.g. via mailings) in comparison to non-personalised communication (e.g. via coupons distributed via newspapers; cf. Kreutzer 2016)?
- How to describe the "typical" customer journey?

To increase the value of customers (including customer equity) for your company, you should introduce the **triad of customer service** (see Fig. 3.12). When implementing the technique of **more-selling**, you try to build up customer loyalty so that the customer remains loyal to the product, service or the provider, meaning of the supporting company, and buys "more of the same". A wide variety of customer loyalty systems can be used (see Kreutzer 2016, pp. 159–208).

When **cross-selling** you try to motivate the buyer of a product or the user of a service to purchase further offers from your company. This can be done by various means, such as phone calls, mailings, e-mail, push messages, social media communication or, in both the BtC and BtB markets, through personal sales. Lastly, **up-selling** is an attempt to motivate a customer to acquire higher-quality and thus usually also more profit-generating products or services.

Cross- and up-selling methods can only be used if your company provides relevant offers. Therefore, based on the **Ansoff Matrix** (see Fig. 3.2), one-product companies should determine which forms of product development can be used for their own company to be able to continue supporting customers who "threaten to outgrow" their own product range.

For this approach, you need a lot of information that is gained throughout the process of **customer relationship management**. Only then can you conduct **transaction-oriented segmentation**. To provide support for customers based on their customer value, you should obtain as much of the following information as possible

Address and profile data	Promotional data	Response data

- Address, incl. first name, title if applicable
 	
- Telephone/fax numbers/ e-mail address/social media contact details (ideally with permission to contact them)
 	
- Date of birth/age
 	
- Marital status/household size
 	
- Areas of interest
 	
- Household income
 	
- Household amenities
	- Communication methods, including
	  - Mail about offers
	  - Membership offer
	  - Invitation to events
	  - Provision of coupons
	  - Offers via e-mail
	  - (e-)newsletter
	  - Calls
	
	- Time for communication
		- Date of creation
		- Winning method (i.e. mailing, coupon, online banner, referral)
		- Sales (incl. product range focus)
		- Buying behaviour (incl. bargain hunters, coupon users)
		- Exchange behaviour
		- Purchase channel (preferred branch, online/offline)
		- Payment method (cash, credit card, other forms of financing)
		- Creditworthiness (compliance with payment obligations)
		- Fan on a social network, follower on *Twitter*, *WhatsApp* contact etc.

Fig. 3.13 Selected features to describe your prospects and customers in the BtC market. Author's own figure

during the customer acquisition phase or through customer service (see Fig. 3.13; continued Kreutzer 2016).

These criteria can be used to determine in which segments your company was particularly successful with its products and services. You should look for more customers exactly in these segments, if no drastic strategic changes were made. Acquiring new customers in completely different segments is often a much more expensive alternative. After all, the people from these segments have not felt addressed by the offer so far for very specific reasons. Therefore, a lot would have to happen to win their interest.

> **Remember Box**
> If the conditions have not changed, when acquiring new customers, your focus should be on those that are like the ones you had in the past.
> The guiding principle here is strengthen your own strengths!

To prevent an uncritical, overly comprehensive **collection of information** about customers and prospects, you can use the following key questions to check which characteristics are most important to gather information in a focused manner:

- Does this characteristic help to assess a customer's current or future potential (keyword "customer value", see Chap. 6)?
- Are there plans to align any marketing actions with this characteristic?
- Is it possible to regularly check whether this characteristic is up to date to ensure proper communication with the customer?

By aligning information procurement with these questions, you avoid high costs for collecting and managing data that is not relevant to the company, or for which no suitable maintenance mechanisms exist. Based on experience, five to seven characteristics from the action and reaction data to construct the profile are often sufficient to ensure a properly differentiated service for prospects and customers over several years.

When **gathering and using information**, it is important that you consider the relevant **aspects of data protection**. This applies both to obtaining the necessary permissions as well as using of the data itself. When getting these permissions, the target person must be informed about why the information is being stored and any intended use and/or transmission (cf. Blind and Stumpfrock 2018).

The focus of the final phase of the customer relationship life cycle is **customer win-back management** (see Fig. 3.11). Ideally, as part of **termination** or **churn prevention**, you aim to detect any hints that the customer may want to terminate the contract or switch by analysing his/her behaviour. "Churn" is a made-up word composed of the terms "change" and "turn". To be able to implement countermeasures, you must have customer contact details readily available, as well as further information concerning sales or reactions to different types of communication including mailings, e-mail or push messages.

> **Remember Box**
> You should only focus on winning back those customers who generate a relevant customer value for your company (see Chap. 6).

▶ **Implementation Tips**

- Acquisition-oriented segmentation is essential to acquire new customers in a targeted way and is a mandatory component of every agency briefing.
- Personas should be systematically implemented and used as a basis for all relevant actions to ensure that you are providing appropriate offers for the target groups.
- If you have data on your prospects and customers, you should use this to carry out transaction-oriented segmentation. This enables you to identify particularly interesting subsegments within your prospects and customers that need to be processed in a differentiated manner.

- It is important that segmentation is not an end, but rather enables the company to achieve profitable growth.
- Therefore, you should regularly verify whether the defined segments still contribute to the profitable development of your business.

3.2.4 Market Area Strategy

In addition to the decisions regarding the market field, market stimulation and market segmentation, with the **market area strategy**, you define which geographical area you want to cover. To define your geographic expansion decisions, you can use the starting points found in Fig. 3.14.

The decision about the market area that you want to serve is largely influenced by your company goals and the resources available to you. The competitive situation and economic development in the current key markets also have an impact on this decision. You can use a variety of the analytical tools defined in Chap. 4 to support this decision.

There are various strategies for **international expansion**, as shown in Fig. 3.15. It is possible to differentiate these expansion strategies according to the amount of capital and management that is allocated to implementing the strategy in both the country of origin and host country, respectively (cf. in-depth information about the different strategies Keegan and Green 2017; Hollensen 2017). When using the export strategy the production itself remains in the domestic market and other markets are supplied with or without the involvement of partners. **Licencing**, for instance, grants another company the right to produce and market certain products in a foreign market for a fee.

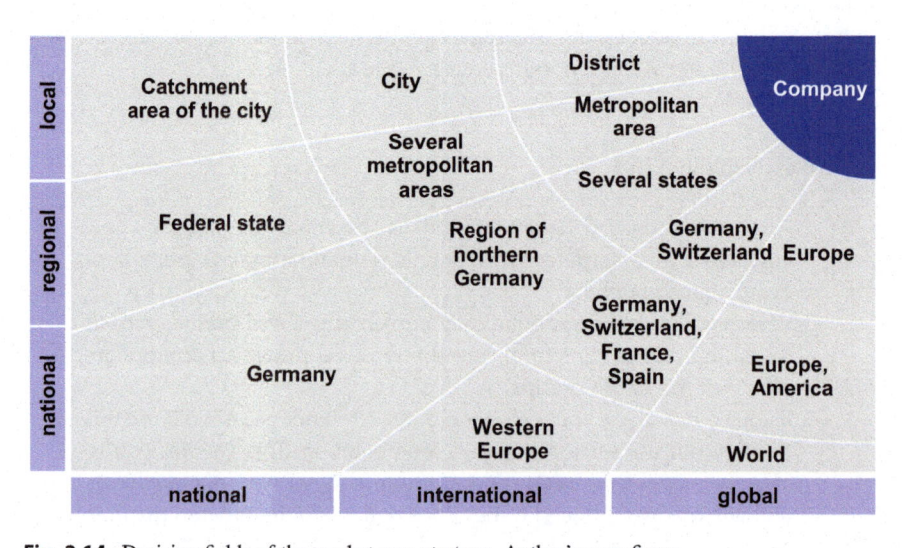

Fig. 3.14 Decision fields of the market area strategy. Author's own figure

3.2 Concept of Customer-Oriented Strategies

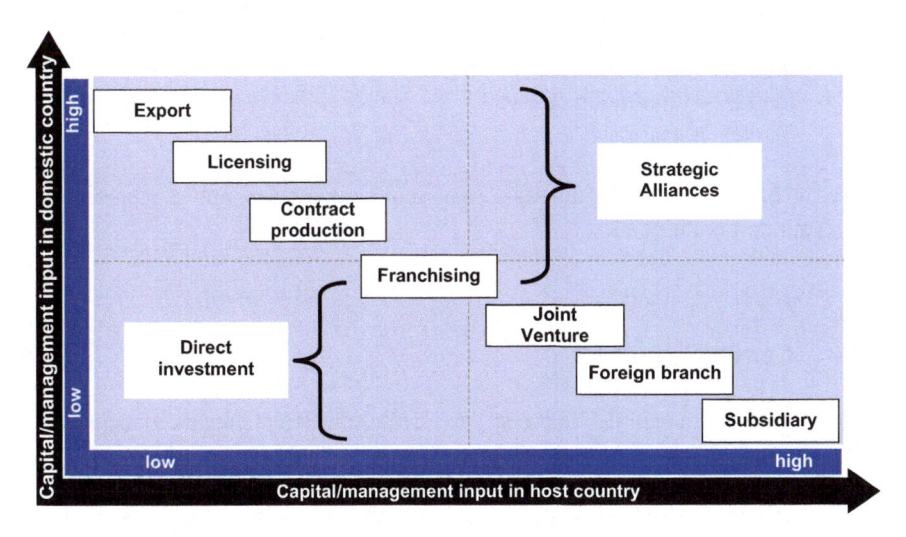

Fig. 3.15 Strategies for international expansion. Author's own figure

In the case of **contract production**, the foreign partner is provided with the technical production know-how which is partly combined with a purchase guarantee. This enables you as an international company to control the quality standard and quantities without having to build production capacities abroad yourself. A popular strategy for international expansion is **franchising**. These procedures are examples of **strategic alliances** because partners work together in the long term on a contractual basis without any interdependence of capital between them.

The implementation of the following strategic concepts is accompanied by significantly higher investments in the host country. These are referred to as **direct investments** (also known as **foreign direct investments**). This can already be the case when implementing a franchising strategy if you set up your own franchise centre in the host country to control the franchise partners. In a **joint venture**, two or more companies set up a new company together without giving up their independence.

Setting up your own **production site** and the establishment of a **subsidiary** are further forms of long-term commitment in a target country. To accelerate the expansion process, it is possible to acquire production units already operating in the host country or entire companies, which would allow you to gain better access to the markets. This is known as an **acquisition** or in the case of a combination of two or more companies as a **merger**. Several of the strategies described are often used over time to better serve developing markets.

▶ **Implementation Tips**
If you use **customer-oriented marketing strategies** in your company, you must make coordinated specifications in these four areas:

- Market field strategy
- Market stimulation strategy
- Market segmentation strategy
- Market area strategy

This ensures that you have a consistent strategic concept to achieve your corporate goals.

3.3 Canvas Concepts

To support your strategy development, you can use different canvas concepts. The term "canvas" or "working area" underlines an important aspect of these tools: the visualisation. The decisive factor in the following concepts is that these approaches enable you to visualise strategically relevant questions more easily, thus making them easier to discuss.

In this context, the **business model canvas** is of utmost importance (cf. Osterwalder and Pigneur 2010). You can use this model as a conceptual template for the documentation and further develop of existing business models and positionings. To do so you develop a visual map that includes the various strategic elements of your business model which can also contribute to the design of customer-oriented strategies (see Sect. 3.2). Figure 3.16 shows nine elements ("building blocks") that must be filled when developing a strategy.

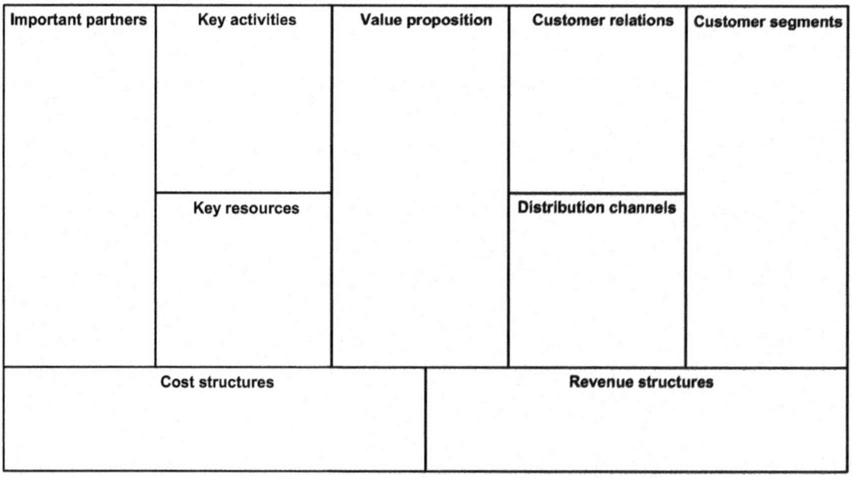

Important partners	Key activities	Value proposition	Customer relations	Customer segments
	Key resources		Distribution channels	
Cost structures				Revenue structures	

Fig. 3.16 Concept of the business model canvas. Source: Adapted from Osterwalder and Pigneur (2010, p. 44)

3.3 Canvas Concepts

The individual building blocks of the canvas model are to be understood as follows:

- **Important partners**
  Companies create buyer-supplier relationships to optimise their own processes and/or to reduce risks of their business model. This also includes entering strategic alliances and establishing joint ventures, even with strategic competitors. You must ask yourself with which (strategic) partners you would like to work together (in the future).
- **Key activities**
  This block involves you and your team determining what you consider to be the most important activities in your corporate value chain that enable you to achieve competitive advantages. A value chain analysis is a good place to start (see Sect. 4.7).
- **Key resources**
  Key entrepreneurial resources include everything that is essential to creating "value for the customer". The resources may include employees, financial resources, patents, production facilities, etc. In this step you examine the most important resources to enrich and further develop your business model.
- **Value proposition**
  The value proposition refers to the products and services that make up your company's product portfolio. It is important that your value proposition ideally differs significantly from that of your competitors in terms of degree of novelty, performance, customer orientation, price-quality ratio and convenience. This raises the central question of what (additional) expectations customers have of your company, or how additional added value can be created for them. This component is closely linked to the market field and market stimulation strategy (see Sects. 3.2.1 and 3.2.2).
- **Customer segments**
  As a company, you must define exactly which customer segments you want to target. Clean market and customer segmentation is an important prerequisite for success. You can also use the persona concepts already presented (see Sect. 3.2.3 on the market segmentation strategy).
- **Customer relations**
  The survival and success of your business largely depends on your ability to build long-lasting and profitable customer relationships. Determining customer value is of great importance (cf. Chap. 6).
- **Distribution channels**
  You can communicate a value proposition and your services to your customers via various channels. You must determine the most successful way to do this (e.g. online and/or offline) and ideally combine it with supplementary added value for the customer.
- **Cost structure**
  All the factors described above are reflected in your company's cost structure. The cost structure also has a clear influence on what kind of market stimulation

strategy can be used. If you want to implement an economy strategy, you must also strive for cost leadership. On the other hand, those who choose a premium strategy do not have to focus so much on cost optimization, but rather differentiate their own offerings through top service, top design and an outstanding quality of material (see Sect. 3.2.2 for more details).

- **Revenue structures**

    The success or failure of your company is reflected by its income. This block involves continuously checking which profits and losses can be achieved with which customer segments and offers. The customer value models are also relevant here (see Chap. 6).

The goal of working with a business model canvas is to first get a deep understanding of the existing business model by analysing the various building blocks. Simultaneously, you can develop new ideas to redesign them. To do so, it is helpful if different teams work on the different building blocks in at the same time. The (new) elements of the business model can then be discussed. Therefore, it is also an important **tool for developing business model innovations**.

▶ **Implementation Tips**

- The business model canvas is a simple and highly effective tool with which you can analyse the existing business model.
- Using the business model canvas, you can also systematically gain new ideas for the strategy process.
- You provide the worksheet for internal workshops. After a short briefing, different teams can complete it.
- It is important that the teams consist of employees from different divisions and hierarchy levels. The motto is "Diversity is key!"
- This requires the hierarchically higher managers to hold back a bit, so that their work neither disturbs the creative process nor (unintentionally) steers it in a certain direction.
- The results developed in the team are then presented and discussed in a larger group.
- This allows you to identify new strategic approaches or gain confirmation for a concept that has already been implemented.

In the digital age, **platform concepts** such as *Uber, Airbnb*, but also *Amazon, Check24, Flixbus* and others are becoming increasingly important (see Kreutzer and Land 2015, 2017a; Müller 2017, pp. 186–190). Therefore, a special **platform canvas** is shown below (see Fig. 3.17).

The first step of using this platform canvas is to work out the possible goals of a platform strategy. One difference to the previously mentioned business model

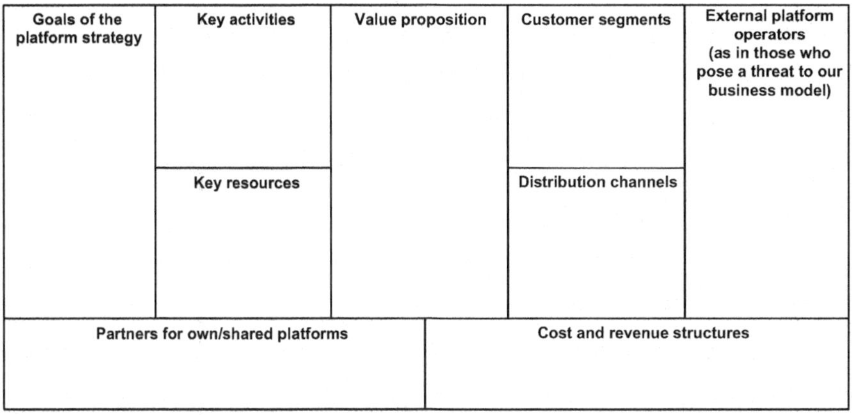

3.3 Canvas Concepts

Goals of the platform strategy	Key activities	Value proposition	Customer segments	External platform operators (as in those who pose a threat to our business model)
	Key resources		Distribution channels	
Partners for own/shared platforms			Cost and revenue structures	

Fig. 3.17 Concept of the platform canvas. Author's own figure

canvas is that you can use this canvas to identify existing external platform operators that could pose a threat to your business model. Additionally, it is necessary to determine which partners could be considered for the development of your own or a shared platform.

▶ **Implementation Tips**

- With the platform canvas, you can analyse the potential threats from established or emerging platforms.
- At the same time, you start a creative process to determine possible goals of your own platform or a platform developed with partners.
- Finally, you also examined which potential partners would be of interest to develop a solution.
- This enables you to stay in control of such threats.

You can also use a canvas concept in another field: **digital transformation**. Sooner or later, every company faces the question of how to go about the transformation into the digital age to a greater or lesser extent (see Kreutzer and Land 2015; Kreutzer et al. 2018; Kreutzer 2018b). An important tool for this is the **lean change canvas** seen in Fig. 3.18. This tool allows you to address the key fields of action of a change process and identify important aspects that are keeping you from and enabling you to progress (see Chap. 11).

▶ **Implementation Tips**

- You should use the lean change canvas soon to determine the challenges the digital age poses for you and your company.

Urgency (three reasons why change is necessary)	Starting point (strategy, key resources)	Vision (key statement defining the company's objectives)	Communication (inwards and outwards)	Parties involved in the change process
				Parties affected
Ability of the organisation to implement the change	Action areas (methods of change management)	Key behaviours	Success factors (change is achieved if ...)	Participants/actors
Necessary investments (personnel, budget; commitment of top/middle management)			Achievable results (profit, growth, pride, morality, growth potential)	

Fig. 3.18 Concept of the lean change canvas. Source: Adapted from Canvanizer (2018)

- Even if you have already started a change process, or are currently in one, this canvas can lead to new and additional insights.
- The target groups for this canvas are the top and middle management, because they discuss the strategic orientation of the entire company in detail.

3.4 Kano Concept

The **Kano model** can be very helpful when shaping the market stimulation strategy (see Sect. 3.2.2). This concept allows you to determine how important different services offered by your company are in achieving customer satisfaction. To determine this, *Kano* investigated the relationship between meeting different customer requirements and achieving customer satisfaction (cf. Berger et al. 1993). It became clear that some of the customer requirements have little or no influence on customer satisfaction (see the lower curve in Fig. 3.19).

Not fulfilling the requirements that are considered **basic requirements** leads to dissatisfaction, but fulfilling them does not bring about satisfaction or enthusiasm. Customers expect these basic requirements to be met. Not fulfilling them leads to dissatisfaction, and it is assumed that these requirements will be met and they do not have an impact on satisfaction. When travelling by plane, these basic requirements include a safe aircraft and arriving at the selected destination. Books, for instance, are expected not to come apart at the binding, even after having worked with it several times. However, even if this is the case, customer satisfaction does not increase.

The customer evaluates **performance requirements** according to the principle "the more, the better". Fulfilling more of the performance requirements increases customer satisfaction (see the middle line in Fig. 3.19). When travelling by plane,

3.4 Kano Concept

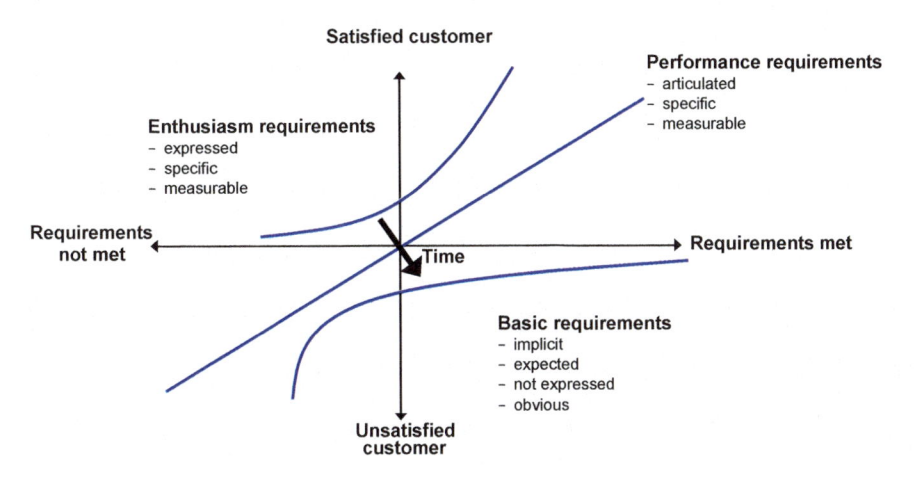

Fig. 3.19 Kano model of customer satisfaction. Source: Adapted from Berger et al. (1993, p. 26)

this includes higher-quality food in economy class, or the free newspapers and magazines. In the case of a textbook, this can be an online platform on which further important learning materials are made available.

Only the third category referred to as **enthusiasm requirements** can trigger enthusiasm in the customer, because unexpected services are provided. However, if such services are frequently provided, there is a risk that they may become performance requirements and thereby also expected (see the upper curve in Fig. 3.19). Taking the example of a textbook, the daily provision of relevant articles, videos, case studies, etc. could lead to enthusiasm, until this is also taken for granted and has thus become a performance requirement.

▶ **Implementation Tips**

- You will achieve the best results if you conduct workshops using the Kano concept. You should invite either the particularly important customers, a cross section of your customers or desired customers to these workshops.
- You can then ask customers themselves about their basic, performance and enthusiasm requirements, although it is better if an external moderator asks them.
- Using a metaplan technique, the results are to be clearly recorded and documented for everyone. In this way you also promote a creative exchange.
- It is beneficial to have employees (e.g. from marketing and sales) participate in these workshops. Ideally, they should have more of a listening role.
- It is often surprising to discover which (new) services would already lead to enthusiasm among customers.
- In many cases, customers have simply brilliant ideas.

- It allows often highlights existing services of which customers have no knowledge. This means that companies often already provide important services, but customers have not yet noticed them.
- Such customer insights and suggestions often provide material for many months of creative work.

3.5 3 Horizons Framework

To determine the strategic need for action in your company, you should use the **3 horizons framework** (see Fig. 3.20; Baghai et al. 2000, pp. 5–17; Blank 2015; oriented to Kreutzer et al. 2018, pp. 73–75). It must be clear that a comprehensive creative renewal of products, services and business models requires not only strategic anchoring in top management and (digital) knowledge in the entire organisation but also additional framework conditions to achieve success. The 3 horizons framework allows you to check how thoroughly your business model should be questioned and, if necessary, revised or even replaced (see Schallmo et al. 2017). You can gain important insights for this concept through the digital maturity analysis (see Sect. 4.10).

Below you will find relevant information about the business models on the different horizons (see Fig. 3.21):

- **Horizon 1 business models**

  Horizon 1 business models describe the status of a company. The existing business model is mapped out and executed. The focus of the analysis are the resulting earnings and cash flows. Finally, they are also a prerequisite for

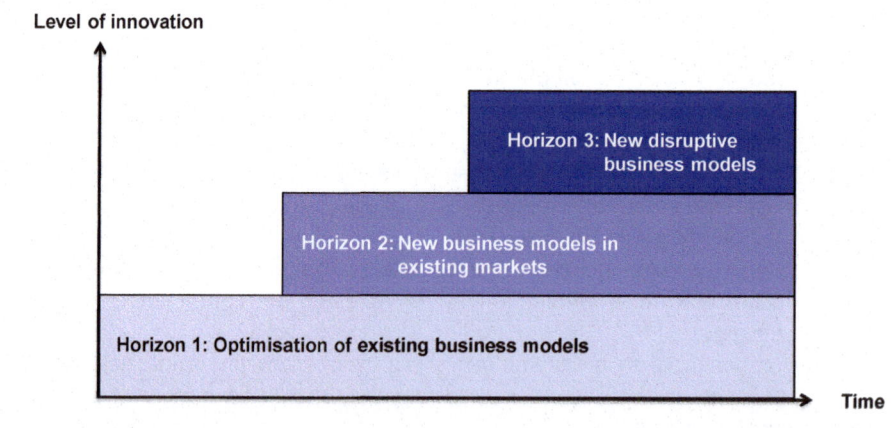

Fig. 3.20 Basic concept of the 3 horizons framework. Source: Adapted from Baghai et al. (2000, p. 5) and Blank (2015)

3.5 3 Horizons Framework

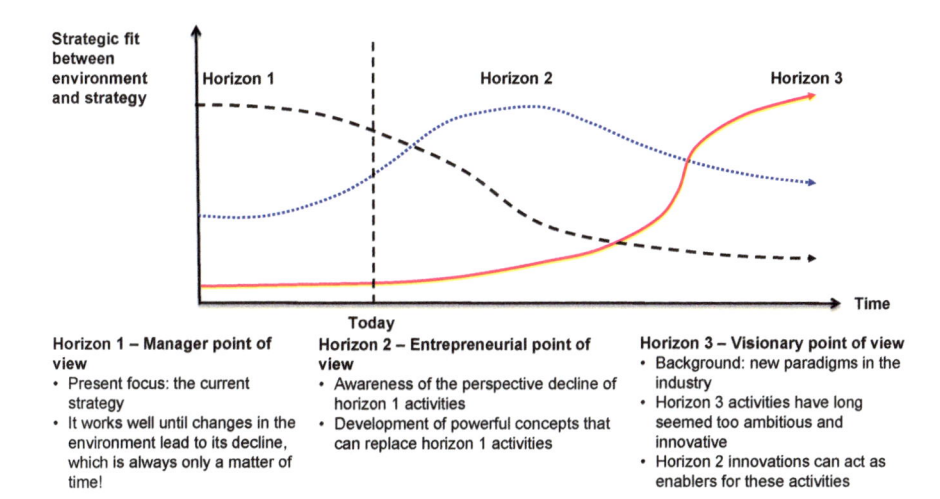

Horizon 1 – Manager point of view
- Present focus: the current strategy
- It works well until changes in the environment lead to its decline, which is always only a matter of time!

Horizon 2 – Entrepreneurial point of view
- Awareness of the perspective decline of horizon 1 activities
- Development of powerful concepts that can replace horizon 1 activities

Horizon 3 – Visionary point of view
- Background: new paradigms in the industry
- Horizon 3 activities have long seemed too ambitious and innovative
- Horizon 2 innovations can act as enablers for these activities

Fig. 3.21 3 horizons framework for strategic analysis. Author's own figure

financing innovation activities. This core business may need to be expanded and/or defended. In these mature business models, it is important to maintain growth and secure profitability through incremental improvements in processes, products and/or services.

- **Horizon 2 business models**

  Horizon 2 business models develop options for business model innovations in relation to relevant markets of the existing horizon 1 business models. New business model initiatives resulting from this are often built up through substantial investments. These business models can already generate initial revenues, although their business peak will often not be reached for another 4–5 years.

- **Horizon 3 business models**

  Horizon 3 business models are highly innovative (often also disruptive) and represent approaches for completely new business logic. To develop such business models, an in-depth analysis of individual company capabilities or customer groups can be carried out that goes beyond the previous day-to-day business. Additionally, you should examine which completely new activities could be profitable for the company (see Sect. 3.2.1 on this market field strategy). This involves exploring strategic options for disruptive change and translating ideas into concrete models.

The 3 horizons framework shows the different ranges of the **business model innovations**. Horizon 1 business models represent existing business logic which focus on the existing organisation, and for which **incremental (digital) optimisation** is particularly relevant. This could be improving customer service by strengthening the service team. Or it could be introducing a customer relationship management system to improve the customer service of an e-commerce company. The level of innovation is relatively low. On this horizon, you only improve the core of the existing business model in certain areas. In this way you can secure and/or expand existing competitive advantages.

Additionally, you need to determine whether your company is also simultaneously working on horizon 2 and horizon 3 business models. The emphasis is on simultaneity! As a first step, you can digitalise non-digital horizon 1 business models.

> **Remember Box**
> The 3 horizons framework draws your attention to a specific strategic challenge. While the day-to-day business is worked on at horizon 1 level, your company must be active at horizon levels 2 and 3 at the same time to shape the future successfully.
> Therefore, the term "ambidexterity" has become prevalent in management rhetoric. You have to master both: the day-to-day business today and shaping the future on horizons 2 and 3, because business models are emerging and declining faster and faster in the digital age.

Therefore, you should use the 3 horizons framework to analyse whether new business models are already in use or being developed in your company on horizons 2 and 3. While the success of business logic on the first horizon can still be measured by classical business-relevant metrics (such as sales development, customer satisfaction indices or the number of newly acquired customers), these indicators cannot be used alone or not immediately for frameworks on horizon 2 or 3. On these levels general learning effects often must be created from iterative testing and gradually developing new service offerings.

> **Remember Box**
> If you use the 3 horizons framework, you should know that during a digital transformation, there is no uniform organisational structure that allows you to perfectly handle the core business while generating (radical) digital innovations.

Ensuring radical and creative renewal of products, services and business models not only requires a strategic commitment by the top management and digital knowledge in the entire organisation (cf. the Digital Maturity Analysis in Sect. 4.10). It is also important to check whether your company fulfils the general conditions to enable new business models, products, services, etc. to be created. You can use the following concept developed by Govindarajan and Trimble (2010, pp. 10–14) as a basis for your analysis:

- Nowadays, the majority of (established) companies are rather unprepared for the development of ground-breaking innovations that may even call their own business model, products and services completely or partially into question. The core of these companies is a so-called **performance engine**. This is referring to an engine whose purpose is more or less to reliably and efficiently produce defined products and services with a desired quality at predetermined costs and often in large quantities. This includes the assembly lines at *Volkswagen* and *Audi* but also the production lines at *BASF*, *Henkel* and *Unilever*. In the performance engine, stability, predictability, routine and zero-defect tolerance are the dominant success factors.

  The **performance engine** usually dominates the entire company. Therefore, all activities that conflict with the known pattern, thus causing uncertainty and inefficiency, are blocked, undersupplied in terms of time and/or resources or even completely shut down. From the point of view of the performance engine, these behavioural patterns are not about avoiding unintentional mistakes but protecting one's own success model.

- This performance engine is contrasted with a network-like concept, which can and may react much faster to changes of the environment. The term **innovation engine** can be used for this. In this area, innovative digital projects with a radical and/or disruptive character can be developed independently of the company's core business. The central guiding principles are an open-mindedness, fault tolerance and the search for future strategically valuable business opportunities that are independent from and uninfluenced by the company's own performance engine.

  An **innovation engine** does not necessarily need to be integrated within your organisation, and often it may not be. The proximity to the operational business can prove to be counterproductive for digital transformation activities. Instead, it has often proven successful to establish a separate **innovation centre** for these transformative activities. The establishment and/or participation in **independent digital companies** can also create the necessary creative freedom. An innovation engine designed in this way would initially only be loosely connected to the current organisation. Linking the corresponding investments would primarily be done at the corporate level.

  Different **tasks** can be defined within the innovation engine. It allows for the development of a digital platform to implement a new business model for a new target group, without having to constantly check whether the purpose of the current activities is being destroyed. Moreover, smart and networked products with deep roots in digital applications can be developed. These "digital versions" can replace current products and services in the analogue sector.

This requires the **resolution of an organisational dilemma**. During this analysis, your task is to determine whether the desired **dualism** already exists. On the one hand, you may find that there is a "hierarchically-mechanistically structured management system of today's operational activities" (namely, the performance engine). On the other hand, "more evolutionary and network-like structures may exist to

Performance Engine	Innovation Engine
(hierarchically structured part of the organisation)	(network-based part of the organisation)
 - Well-defined and proven process and organisational structure - Operational business management based on reliability, efficiency and zero errors - Small steps are needed for change	 - Work in the organisation is done with agility (innovation and speed) - Management of projects with a radical, disruptive, possibly cannibalizing character - Openness, fault tolerance, flexibility and speed are key requirements
Important: this is where you earn money <u>today!</u>	**Important:** this is where you earn money <u>tomorrow!</u>

Fig. 3.22 Creation of dualism in the transformation process. Author's own figure

support successful innovation" (i.e. the innovation engine). Again, the relevance of the term ambidexterity becomes apparent.

Using the areas described in Fig. 3.22 (cf. Kotter 2014, pp. 20–24), your task is to determine to what extent the existing organisation should be further developed towards becoming a **dual or hybrid organisation** in the long term.

It is important to ensure that there is not only an occasional **link between the performance and innovation engine** but that both areas **cooperatively work together as partners**. A prerequisite for success in this collaboration is that all employees of both engines recognise and value the relevance of the other. Only then can the **division of tasks between the performance and innovation engines** be understood in their significance for the long-term survival of your company. In this way, new business ideas emerge in the innovation engine that are indispensable for the sustainable development of the company. However, a prerequisite for this is the provision of the funds generated by the performance engine.

Below you can see how other companies have organised their **innovation engine** to consciously detach themselves from the company's core DNA:

- *Axel Springer Verlag*: Plug & Play Accelerator GmbH, Berlin and Silicon Valley
- *BASF*: BASF New Business GmbH, BASF Venture Capital GmbH, Ludwigshafen
- *Boehringer Ingelheim*: Laboratory BI X
- *Deutsche Telekom*: Hubraum, Berlin
- *IKEA*: Space 10, Copenhagen
- *Merck*: Innovation Center, Darmstadt
- *Microsoft*: Microsoft Accelerator, San Francisco—Berlin
- *Procter & Gamble*: Clay Street Project, Cincinnati

All these innovation engines have one thing in common; they are usually separated from the corporate headquarters, sometimes even located in a different region, and can (largely) lead a creative and cultural life of their own and develop their own DNA. This allows new ideas to be generated, even if they threaten or disrupt existing business activities (in the long term; see also Poguntke 2016).

> **Remember Box**
> If we don't create the thing that kills us, somebody else will!

▶ **Implementation Tips**

- Before you apply the 3 horizons framework, you should first introduce it to your company. For many of your partners, it could still be interpreted as "new territory".
- Demonstrate why it is recommended that every company works on all horizons at the same time (keyword: ambidexterity).
- Check whether the digital transformation process in your company has already begun and, if so, at what level it is.
- Most of the time you will notice that the transformation activities are concentrated on horizon 1 and only partially take place on horizon 2.
- It is most important to ensure that the company's strategy aligns with horizon 3.
- To do this, you should establish a performance and innovation engines in your company.
- You should try to start an innovation engine for your company, so that you can be successful in the future.

3.6 Brand Management Concepts

The starting point of brand management is **defining the brand identity**. This is the core task for internal stakeholders (see Fig. 3.23; based on Kreutzer and Land 2017b, pp. 48–52). Therefore, the brand identity is the "self-perception of internal stakeholders". In part brand management requires the employees of a company who are responsible for brand development to define how the brand should look to the outside world. This process can be based on the following criteria and questions:

- Where do we come from?—our **history**
- What can we do?—our **competences**
- What we believe in?—our corporate **values**
- How do we act?—our corporate **personality**
- What do we do?—our **services**
- Where do we want to go?—our **vision**

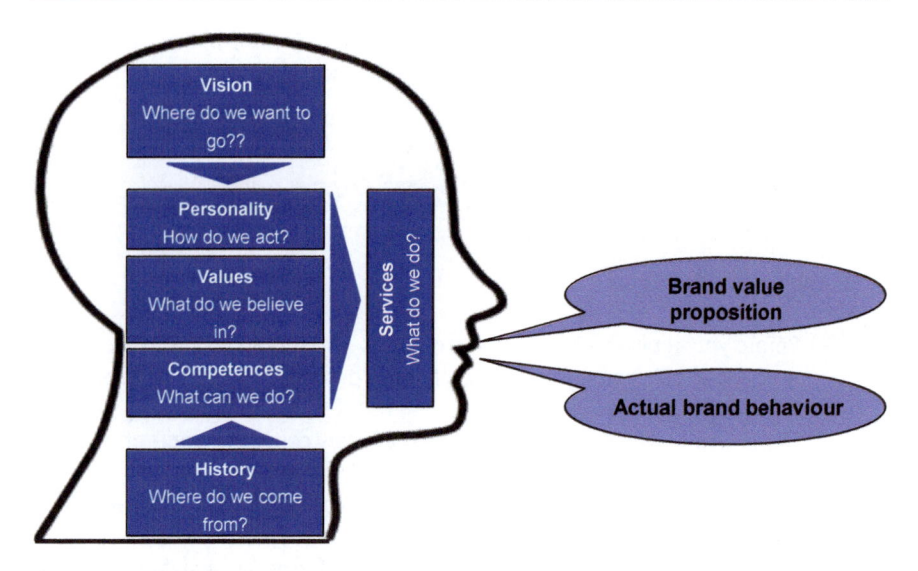

```
                Vision
          Where do we want to
                 go??

            Personality
          How do we act?
                              Services
             Values           What do we do?     Brand value
         What do we believe                      proposition
                in?
            Competences
          What can we do?                      Actual brand behaviour

              History
          Where do we come
               from?
```

Fig. 3.23 Definition of the brand identity by internal stakeholders. Source: Adapted from Burmann et al. (2015, p. 43)

The brand-specific services defined in this way are then translated by you into a **brand value proposition** and **brand behaviour**.

You can also use the **brand identity approach** presented in Fig. 3.24 to build up the brand identity. Using one's own brand competence (Who am I?), it raises various questions which make it possible to define a concrete brand identity regarding four areas (cf. Burmann and Meffert (2005, pp. 51–66):

- What do I offer?—**brand benefits**
- How do I offer?—**brand tonality**
- How do I appear?—**brand image**
- What are my characteristics?—**brand attributes**

The **brand identity approach** shown in Fig. 3.24 can also be used as a checklist to build up or expand the identity of a brand.

When creating a **customer-brand relationship**, various aspects influence the **brand image** among external target groups (especially customers, but also other stakeholders). This represents the "perceived image of external stakeholders". **Brand awareness** is initially built up through brand activities (e.g. advertising, PR, sales promotion). The **brand attributes** that are communicated in this way become known as **functional** and **symbolic benefit associations** of the brand. All these elements are reflected in the **brand expectations** of external stakeholders (see Fig. 3.25).

To implement the brand image, companies can use the five instruments of the marketing mix referred to as **marketing diamond**, namely, product, price,

3.6 Brand Management Concepts

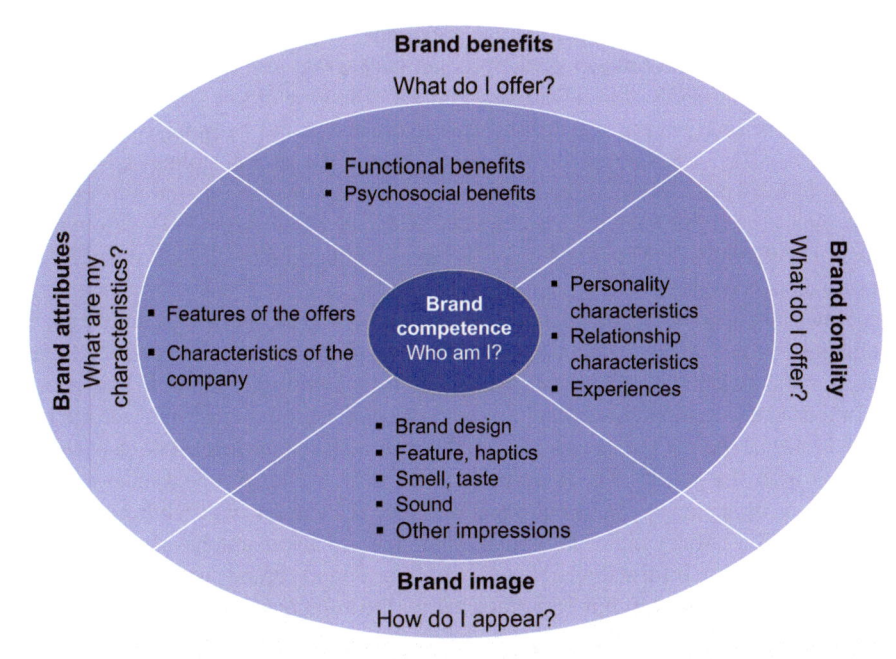

Fig. 3.24 Brand identity approach. Source: Adapted from Esch et al. (2005, p. 211)

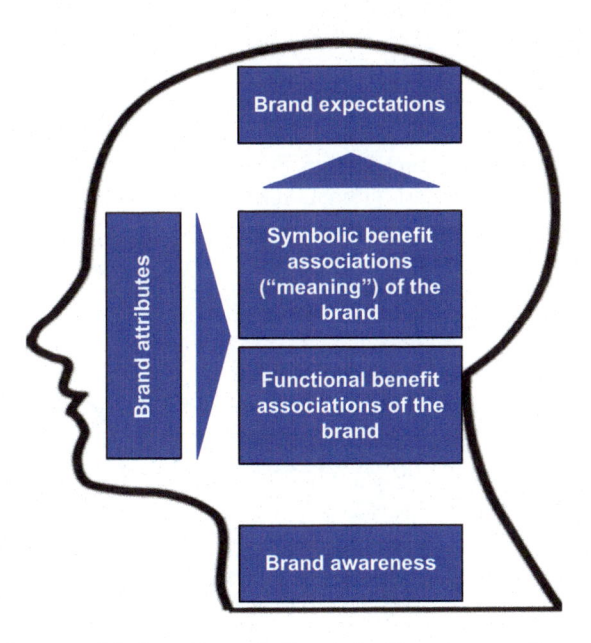

Fig. 3.25 Development of the brand image in the minds of target groups. Source: Adapted from Burmann et al. (2015, p. 57)

promotion, place and people. It is important to ensure that the messages communicated by the product or the product packaging correspond to the content transmitted at the POS or in advertising and PR. The type of sales presence (online and/or offline) and pricing also influence the brand image. Furthermore, colour codes and the logo have a lasting effect on the brand image. Personal customer care plays a key role (keyword "service"), because there is often a direct and therefore also very emotional contact between the brand and the user (see Meffert et al. 2015; Homburg 2017; Kreutzer 2017). The brand image is largely influenced by all the content these instruments convey.

However, operational brand management in the digital age also requires other influential brand image areas that impact the **overall brand user experience** to be taken into consideration. First, this includes to **user-generated content**. This refers to brand-related content that users have developed on their own (e.g. fan website for brands on *Facebook*). On the other hand, this also includes the **interactions of third parties with the brand**. The importance of these two areas in brand management has grown dramatically in recent years, because the rate at which information is communicated online, and even more so shared via social media, has never been so fast or penetrating. Information about "brand failure" and "brand success" spreads in real time and can largely not be influenced by the companies to whom the brands belong.

Based on this knowledge, you must ensure that your brand management includes influencing the areas of **user-generated content** and **interactions of third parties with your brand** through your own brand communication. This is necessary to guarantee that the brand user experience corresponds with the defined brand identity as much as possible. However, it should be noted that companies cannot exercise direct control over these fields. Consequently, they must now consider many more **brand user experience impact factors** than ever before. Figure 3.26 shows the significantly more complex task of brand management in the digital age.

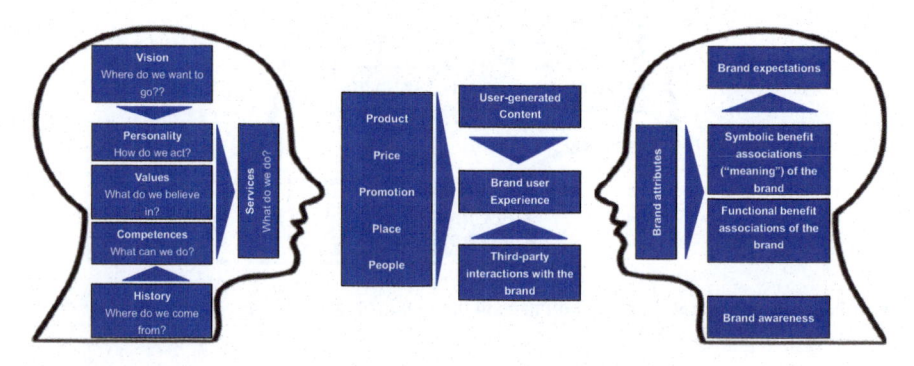

Fig. 3.26 Holistic brand management in the digital age. Author's own figure

3.6 Brand Management Concepts

> **Remember Box**
> The term brand user experience clearly indicates that digital brand management is no longer just about creating a brand image in the customer's mind. Instead, it is more a matter of ensuring that the most convincing and coherent holistic experience possible with the brand is achieved. The aim is to motivate customers to buy and to establish a stable customer-brand relationship. This field is the core of customer experience management.

Furthermore, brand management also involves the continuous development of your range of products and brands. To do so, you can use a tool called the **brand-product lines matrix**. You start by defining the "existing brands and product lines". The use of this tool is shown using the *Alphabet Group* (formerly *Google*; see Fig. 3.27).

Through **line extension** (also known as product differentiation), you aim to transfer the established brand name to other products within the existing product line. In this example, this was done by establishing *Google Search* and *Google Universal Search*. With a **brand extension** (also referred to as a brand transfer), you use the established brand name for new product lines. Such products are often also manufactured by third-party companies, which acquire the necessary licences from the trademark owner. Another option is acquiring other companies with their products and key services, or fostering innovative developments within the company, as *Alphabet* did several times. A few of *Google*'s activities can be found in Fig. 3.27 (such as *Google Adwords, Google Pay*).

		Product lines	
		existing	new
Brands	existing	**Line extension** *Google Search, Google Universal Search*	**Brand extension** *Google AdWords, Google My Business, Google Wallet, Google TV, Google Pixel, Google Play*
	new	**Multibranding**	**Brand and product line innovations** *YouTube, Nest, Picasa, Android, Double Click*

Fig. 3.27 *Alphabet* as an example of a brand-product lines matrix. Author's own figure

Multibranding refers to establishing more brands in addition already existing ones to exploit the market potential. **Brand and product line innovations** involve launching completely new product lines with new brands. *Google/Alphabet* did this by acquiring companies such as *YouTube, Nest, Picasa, Android* and *Double Click*. It is often difficult to determine whether a company's product lines fall into the "new" or "existing" category (cf. also the information about the market field strategy in Sect. 3.2.1, because these areas are directly related).

To offer a more complete range of services, you can use different **service strategies** to make them even more attractive for your prospects or already acquired customers. The concept shown in Fig. 3.28 can help you more strongly **differentiate your offer from the competition**. First, you can first differentiate your services by determining whether the service provision takes place before, during or after the purchase. Moreover, it is recommended to differentiate according to whether the services are provided on a more product-related or personal basis. Using Fig. 3.28, you can conclude which (additional) service fields should be used to differentiate yourself from the competition. You can also use this concept to analyse your competitor's approaches.

Other **pre-sales services** allow you to encourage sales by letting the customer physically experience the product. For instance, this includes test drives or product presentations in houses. Today, this is done at *Tupper parties* or through household product demonstrations by *Vorwerk* in private households, for instance. If you can provide convincing examples of how the product is used by other companies, then offering reference visits can help to initiate a sale in the BtB segment (e.g. of IT systems or software solutions). These also include the innovative concepts, which fall under the basic ideas of **interactive value creation** and **customer integration**, and already comprehensively integrate target customers in the development process (see Sect. 8.2).

		Pre-sales services	Sales services	After-sales services
Product-related services		• Free, time-limited product provision (e.g. test drive, trial subscription) • Sampling	• Packing service • Product/service individualization (customising)	• Delivery • Installation/assembly • After-sales service • Maintenance • Hotline • Remote assessment
People-related services	**Related to the product**	• Product demonstration at POS/at home • Detailed advice • Reference visits with users • Expert conference	• Financing services (including instalment payments, 0% financing) • Introduction to product use	• Free/obligatory trainings • Organisational development
	Unrelated to the product	• Event invitations • Information service	• VIP waiting lounges • Gifts and extras	• On-/offline support programme • Customer magazines • Customer Loyalty Programmes

Fig. 3.28 Concept for services development. Author's own figure

Sales services should help support the actual purchase. Payment methods are particularly important in this area. You can offer special support for customers by providing VIP waiting areas or preferential treatment (e.g. by a key account support).

After-sales services include services designed to facilitate the use of the purchased goods, such as training and maintenance. They also include installation services, insurance, pick-up/repair services and on-site services. You can determine the most important services for customers through design thinking, scrum and lean startup processes (see Sect. 7.3 and Chap. 8).

> **Remember Box**
> The process of brand management starts once and never ends, at least if the brand is on the market.

▶ **Implementation Tips**

- The tools mentioned above offer a good starting point for the comprehensive field of brand management.
- For startups and smaller companies, the tools described here are sufficient to take the first steps towards brand management and to proceed in a goal-oriented manner.
- Large companies are well advised to further develop tools for brand management.
- You should regularly use the brand-product lines matrix to generate ideas for product/brand innovations. The matrix allows you to come up with interesting solutions.
- The same applies to the concept for developing services. It encourages creativity in certain areas to enable you to find for profitable innovations.

References

Ansoff, H. I. (1979). *Strategic management*. New York: Wiley.
Baghai, M., Coley, S., & White, D. (2000). *The alchemy of growth*. Cambridge: Perseus.
Becker, J. (2013). *Marketing-Konzeption, Grundlagen des ziel-strategischen und operativen Marketing-Managements* (10th ed.). Munich: Vahlen.
Berger, C., Blauth, R., Boger, D., Bolster, C., Burchill, G., DuMouchel, W., Pouliot, F., Richter, R., Rubinoff, A., Shen, D., Timko, M., & Walden, D. (1993). Kano's methods of understanding customer-defined quality. *Center for Quality of Management Journal, 2*(4), 3–36.
Blank, S. (2015). *Innovation at 50x*. Accessed March 21, 2018, from http://steveblank.com/2015/08/21/innovation-50x-in-companies-and-government-agencies/

Blind, J., & Stumpfrock, R. (2018). Rechtliche Rahmenbedingungen des Online-Marketings. In R. Kreutzer (Ed.), *Praxisorientiertes online-marketing* (3rd ed., pp. 561–584). Wiesbaden: Springer Gabler.

Burmann, C., & Meffert, H. (2005). Theoretisches Grundkonzept der identitätsorientierten Markenführung. In H. Meffert, C. Burmann, & M. Koers (Hrsg.), *Markenmanagement, Identitätsorientierte Markenführung und praktische Umsetzung* (2nd ed., pp. 37–72). Wiesbaden: Springer Gabler.

Burmann, C., Halaszovich, T., Schade, M., & Hemmann, F. (2015). *Identitätsbasierte Marketingführung, Grundlagen – Strategie – Umsetzung – Controlling* (2nd ed.). Wiesbaden: Springer Gabler.

Canvanizer. (2018). *Create a new lean change canvas*. Accessed March 16, 2018, from https://canvanizer.com/new/lean-change-canvas

Esch, F.-R., Langner, T., & Rempel, J. E. (2005). Ansätze zur Erfassung und Entwicklung von Markenidentität. In F.-R. Esch (Hrsg.), *Moderne Markenführung, Grundlagen – Innovative Ansätze – Praktische Umsetzungen* (4th ed., pp. 103–129). Wiesbaden: Springer Gabler.

Govindarajan, V., & Trimble, C. (2010). *The other side of innovation – How to solve the execution challenge*. Bosten: Harvard Business Review Press.

HARIBO. (2018). *Von der Hinterhofküche zum Weltmarktführer*. Accessed March 20, 2018, from https://www.haribo.com/deDE/unternehmen/geschichte.html

Hollensen, S. (2017). *Global marketing* (7th ed.). Harlow: Pearson.

Homburg, C. (2017). *Marketingmanagement, Strategie – Instrumente – Umsetzung – Unternehmensführung* (6th ed.). Wiesbaden: Springer Gabler.

Keegan, W. J., & Green, M. C. (2017). *Global marketing* (9th ed.). Essex: Pearson.

Kotler, P., & Keller, K. L. (2015). *Marketing management* (15th ed.). Harlow: Pearson.

Kotter, J. P. (2014). *Accelerate – Building strategic agility for a faster-moving world*. Boston: Harvard Business Review Press.

Kreutzer, R. (2016). *Kundenbeziehungsmanagement im digitalen Zeitalter, Konzepte – Erfolgsfaktoren – Handlungsideen*. Stuttgart: Verlag W. Kohlhammer.

Kreutzer, R. (2017). *Praxisorientiertes Marketing, Grundlagen – Instrumente – Fallbeispiele* (5th ed.). Wiesbaden: Springer Gabler.

Kreutzer, R. (2018a). *Praxisorientiertes Online-Marketing, Konzepte – Instrumente – Checklisten* (3rd ed.). Wiesbaden: Springer Gabler.

Kreutzer, R. (2018b). *Führung und Organisation im digitalen Zeitalter kompakt*. Wiesbaden: Springer Gabler.

Kreutzer, R., & Land, K.-H. (2015). *Digital darwinism, branding and business models in Jeopardy*. New York: Springer.

Kreutzer, R., & Land, K.-H. (2017a). *Dematerialization – The redistribution of the world in times of digital darwinism*. Cologne: FutureVisionPress.

Kreutzer, R., & Land, K.-H. (2017b). *Digital Branding – Konzeption einer holistischen Markenführung*. Wiesbaden: Springer Gabler.

Kreutzer, R., Neugebauer, T., & Pattloch, A. (2018). *Digital business leadership – Digital transformation – Business model innovation – Agile organization – Change-management*. Wiesbaden: Springer Gabler.

Meffert, H., Burmann, C., & Kirchgeorg, M. (2015). *Grundlagen marktorientierter Unternehmensführung, Konzepte – Instrumente – Praxisbeispiele* (12th ed.). Wiesbaden: Springer Gabler.

Müller, H.-E. (2017). *Unternehmensführung, Strategie – Management – Praxis* (3rd ed.). Munich: De Gruyter.

Osterwalder, A., & Pigneur, Y. (2010). *Business model generation*. Hoboken: Wiley.

Poguntke, S. (2016). *Corporate Think Tanks: Zukunftsforen, Innovation Center, Design Sprints, Kreativsessions & Co.* (2nd ed.). Wiesbaden: Springer Gabler.

Porter, M. E. (1996, November–December). What is strategy? *Harvard Business Review*, 61–78.

References

Porter, M. E. (2004a). *Competitive strategy: Techniques for analyzing industries and competitors.* New York: Free Press.

Porter, M. E. (2004b). *Competitive advantage: Creating and sustaining superior performance.* New York: Free Press.

Pruitt, J., & Adlin, T. (2006). *The persona lifecycle – Keeping people in mind throughout product design.* Amsterdam: Morgan Kaufmann.

Schallmo, D., Rusnjak, A., Anzengruber, J., Werani, T., & Jünger, M. (2017). *Digitale Transformation von Geschäftsmodellen.* Wiesbaden: Springer Gabler.

Stauss, B. (2000). Perspektivwandel: Vom Produkt-Lebenszyklus zum Kundenbeziehungs-Lebenszyklus. *Thexis, 17*(2), 15–18.

Wirtz, B. W. (2016). *Direktmarketing, Grundlagen – Instrumente – Prozesse* (4th ed.). Wiesbaden: Springer Gabler.

Tools for the Strategic Analysis 4

4.1 Preliminary Remark: Planning the Implementation of Analytical Tools

A comprehensive **company and environment analysis** is essential to successfully plan strategies, as well as measures for their implementation. Knowledge about the activities of competitors and customers, in addition to changes in your own industry and the wider environment, provide the relevant background information for your actions. However, at the same time you must also look inward to be able to incorporate the strengths and weaknesses of your company into the planning process. **Various market and marketing research tools** are available to carry out these analyses (cf. fundamentals of Koch et al. 2016; Altobelli 2017).

The **5D concept of marketing research** shown in Fig. 4.1 provides you with an essential orientation for the target-oriented use of a wide variety of analytical tools (this chapter) and forecasting methods (see Chap. 5).

> **Remember Box**
> Whenever you start a research project, you should follow the 5D concept. Too many researchers still start by designing the questionnaire, without having clearly defined in advance which findings are to be gained at all. You can and should avoid this!

The first step of any research project is the **definition phase**, in which you clarify research questions (see Fig. 4.1). You can focus on the following questions:

- What image does your company have?
- What are the characteristics of your target group?

```
┌──────────┐ ┌──────────┐ ┌──────────┐ ┌──────────┐ ┌──────────┐
│Definition│>│  Design  │>│   Data   │>│   Data   │>│ Documen- │
│          │ │          │ │collection│ │ analysis │ │  tation  │
└──────────┘ └──────────┘ └──────────┘ └──────────┘ └──────────┘
```

- Definition of the research question
- Definition of the marketing research goals
- Definition of those responsible for the project
- Definition of the research budget and timeframe

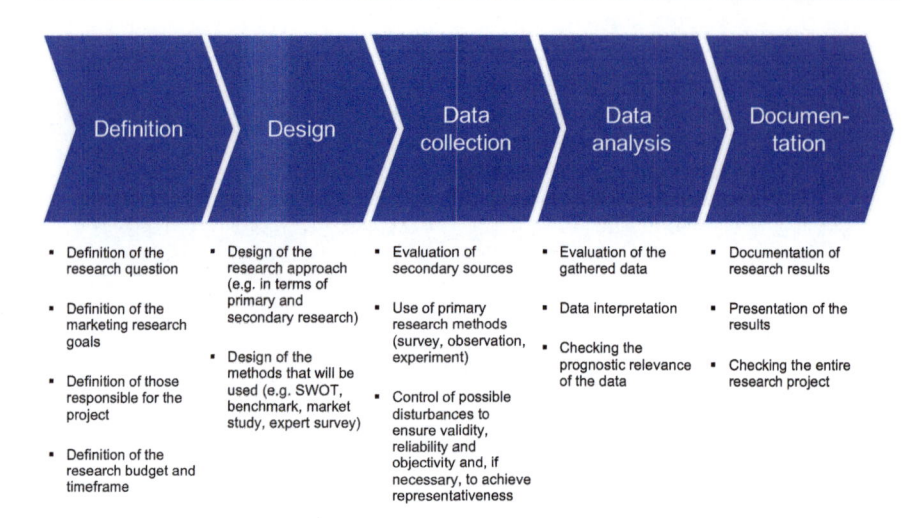

- Design of the research approach (e.g. in terms of primary and secondary research)
- Design of the methods that will be used (e.g. SWOT, benchmark, market study, expert survey)

- Evaluation of secondary sources
- Use of primary research methods (survey, observation, experiment)
- Control of possible disturbances to ensure validity, reliability and objectivity and, if necessary, to achieve representativeness

- Evaluation of the gathered data
- Data interpretation
- Checking the prognostic relevance of the data

- Documentation of research results
- Presentation of the results
- Checking the entire research project

Fig. 4.1 5D concept of marketing research. Author's own figure

- What are the cause-effect relationships between different marketing tools and the company's turnover?
- What are the causes of a decline in sales and profits in your company?
- How does your company compare in the competitive environment?
- What are the reasons for the unexpected success of a new competitor?
- What other challenges can we expect to face in our own industry in the coming years due to digitisation?
- Which disruptions or structural interruptions are emerging in your industry?
- Which platform concepts are particularly successful, and which success factors underlie them?
- In which areas can your company learn from its competitors or other companies to reduce costs or achieve a higher benefit contribution for customers?
- Which communication concepts will enable access to the younger target group in the future?
- How important is social media for my company?
- In which countries should new production capacities be built?
- Which countries should the sales strategy focus on?
- Which companies are interesting candidates for acquisitions?

Only when you have considered these questions and identified possible gaps regarding the current amount of information can you precisely work out your **research goals**, against which the results of the research project can later be measured. This includes the question of whether you want to carry out an explorative, a descriptive or a causal study.

In an **explorative study** a subject area must be researched or explored to gain initial knowledge and insights. Representative results are not expected from these types of studies. An explorative study can deal with the phenomenon of how new

Chinese competitors present themselves in Europe. Observations and interviews with experts could be used to conduct such as study. Furthermore, you can evaluate certain case studies of selected Chinese suppliers, for instance. The focus lies in the "context of discovery", whereby the need for information is rather qualitative than quantitative.

A **descriptive study** involves describing certain phenomena in more detail and recognising possible explanatory patterns. This may take the form of a comprehensive analysis that systematically records the success of platform concepts and attempts to explain their success. Using this information, you can make forecasts on possible developments and plans of action (cf. Sect. 3.3). Thus, the problem is defined much more precisely than in an explorative study. It is important to describe exactly what is currently happening in a certain area. Such a research project is more focused on quantitative information, because a description requires both qualitative and quantitative data.

In a **causal study** the validity of causal hypotheses (i.e. cause-effect relationships) are examined. Hypotheses are assumptions about certain relationships that must be analysed through a study. Causal hypotheses refer to causal relationships between different variables. You can determine how big of an influence the "amount of a fashion brand's online advertising budget" has on the "amount of sales of the brand". Such causal studies often include experiments.

At this point, the important question also arises as to whether a more qualitative or quantitative methodological approach should be used. In **quantitative research**, which is still dominant in many areas, the aim is to be able to express the results exactly numerically. These include the market share, market volume and market potential of the company in the competitive environment, for which larger samples are surveyed. This is not necessary for **qualitative research**. This type of study is more descriptive and nonnumerical in nature. It involves determining the motive structures on which purchasing behaviour is based. Smaller samples are often used (cf. Naderer and Balzer 2011).

Moreover, you should define what the research project is **accountable** for in this phase. Among other things, it must be clarified whether an in-house market research department should take over the task and/or whether an external market research company should be involved for certain parts of the project. Additionally, it is necessary to clarify the **budget** and define the time horizon of the research project to provide timely information support for upcoming decisions.

During the **design phase** you formulate the **design of the research approach** (see Fig. 4.1). Among other things, you determine whether to use only secondary research or alternatively, or rather additionally, primary research. **Secondary research** (also **desk research**) refers to gathering information about interesting facts from existing findings and/or studies. You can conduct online searches and review studies carried out by relevant market research companies. This procedure has the advantages of providing both immediate and easy access, because the extraction and processing can be done at your own desk. Since no new data is collected, it is also much more cost-effective than primary research.

At the same time, information from secondary research is an important basis for refining the research question and for interpreting the data that you collect. However, you should be aware of the limitations of secondary research. This includes the fact that the information gained in this way often does not provide precise answers to your own research questions. Additionally, you often cannot gain competitive advantages from information that is available to the public, since the lack of exclusivity means that this data is also accessible to your competitors. Moreover, secondary data is often outdated and difficult to compare with other data. Lastly, a key disadvantage is that you can often no longer know who collected the data, how the data was collected, when this took place and which collection units (e.g. whether consumers or companies were surveyed) were the focus of the study. This means you cannot say with certainty whether the data is reliable, i.e. whether important corporate decisions should be based on them (cf. remarks on studies in Sect. 1.3).

Therefore, **primary research** (also **field research**) is of particular importance. Primary research involves gathering information about a subject area possibly for the first time. You can conduct surveys, make observations and/or carry out experiments. Seeing as you "go into the field" to collect the desired information, the terms field research is used. Only by doing this you can repeatedly obtain the necessary up-to-date data in the desired form, which is precisely aligned to your research questions, reliable and often also exclusive.

The following **methods of data collection** are available:

- **Primary research**
    - Survey
      Qualitative survey
      Quantitative survey
    - Observation
    - Experiment (often a combination of observation and survey)
- **Secondary research**
    - Internal sources
    - External sources
      Publicly available sources
      Commercial sources

In the design phase you must also determine which **methods** should be used, such as a SWOT analysis, benchmarking or different forecasting procedures. Furthermore, you must also clarify which **variables** are to be collected (e.g. only considering the development of gross national product or also the purchasing power, inflation rate and amount of corruption when assessing a country).

During the <u>**data collection phase**</u>, you often first evaluate **secondary sources** to determine the need for time- and cost-intensive primary research (see Fig. 4.1). Important **internal secondary sources** include data from the finance department (who already has cost, sales and results analyses) and the results of earlier primary surveys (such as competitive analyses, customer surveys and market analyses). Often your own planning and strategy departments also have interesting studies. Additionally, you must check if there is any relevant data in your CRM system.

4.1 Preliminary Remark: Planning the Implementation of Analytical Tools

Good **external secondary sources** include the federal statistics offices, studies by associations and market research institutes, press releases, databases such as *Statista* and *EBSCO* and other sources that are accessible online or offline (see Altobelli 2017).

Three concepts are used for primary research itself. You can often use a combination of them as well:

- Survey
- Observation
- Experiment

A **survey** (including an opinion poll or interview) is a research method in which a conversation is conducted with the aim of systematically obtaining information about attitudes, opinions, behaviour, knowledge, motives and intentions of people. Regarding the **methodology of surveys**, the following forms of **quantitative surveys** can be distinguished:

- **Personal interview** (face-to-face or by phone)
- **Written survey** (using an online or offline questionnaire)

Usually standardised questionnaires are used to obtain a larger number of comparable answers to the same types of questions. These answers can later be extensively evaluated particularly using multivariate methods.

The **methodology of surveys** can also be divided into three **qualitative** forms:

- **Individual interviews** (e.g. as an exploratory interview to explore a subject area or as an in-depth interview to identify the respondent's motive structures and attitudes)
- **Group interviews** (e.g. in the form of group discussions)
- **Workshops** (if necessary with creative tasks to develop new product ideas, focus groups are often used)

These are nonstandardised surveys because question areas may only arise from the answers of the participants.

There are different types of **participants** that you can use in a **survey**:

- **Prospective customer survey** (e.g. to determine through which type of communication or offers a lead could be developed into a customer)
- **Consumer survey** (e.g. to discover the motives when buying cleaning supplies, flour or a smartphone through in-depth interviews)
- **Expert survey** (e.g. specialists in online marketing or digitisation to identify further developments; see Sect. 5.4)
- **Supplier survey** (e.g. to determine how your value chain can be linked with that of suppliers to exploit the possibilities of the Internet of Things)
- **BtB customer survey** (e.g. to analyse how your value chain can be linked with that of the business customers)

When using an **observation** method, the subjects must be perceived in a specific way that is oriented towards the defined research questions. You can observe customers in both brick-and-mortar and online shops; people reading newspapers, magazines and mailings; or people watching TV. Processes can also be the focus of an observation, for instance, if you want to determine the user-friendliness of a website by observing the search and purchase behaviour on the site (cf. Kreutzer 2018a). You can also use technical aids in an observation. Eye tracking is frequently used. Since observations primarily involve recording visible and thus measurable (quantitative) phenomena, you often need an accompanying survey of the people involved to draw the right conclusions from the observable behaviour. Assessment centres often have follow-up surveys in addition to observations. These centres systematically determine the competence of applicants through a wide variety of tasks.

Experiments as a research tool refer to a methodical investigation where you systematically obtain data on cause-effect relationships between variables. The goal may be to test certain hypotheses (e.g. the relationship between price changes and demand behaviour). For example, one or more independent variables (e.g. the price) can be altered according to plan to determine their influence on one or more other dependent variables (e.g. demand or quality perception). All other variables that could otherwise have an influence on the dependent variables must remain unchanged. Experiments are particularly successful in identifying causal or cause-effect relationships between variables. Observations and interviews can only lead us to assume such relationships, but not prove them. Consequently, results of observations and interviews often form the basis for the development of hypotheses, which you then test through experiments.

To ensure that you have in fact gathered reliable, and relevant, knowledge when using these tools, you must take the following **quality criteria** into account when creating a study and particularly when measuring facts and circumstances:

- Validity
- Reliability
- Objectivity
- Representativeness

The **validity** refers to whether what was meant to be measured in a study was indeed measured. This means the extent to which the results of the measurement do allow statements to be made about the facts to be measured. A direct survey of whether customers are tempted by "brands" and are willing to pay more for them will often not lead to valid results. The reason for this is the **phenomenon of social desirability**. Respondents provide answers to certain questions (such as the "influence of advertising", the "frequency of brushing teeth" or the "stimulation by force"), which they assume are socially accepted and thus "socially desirable".

Here are a few examples to illustrate the phenomenon. In a survey one can say, "No, of course I will not be influenced by advertising or brands", although this does not correspond to the actual behaviour. This also applies to questions about how frequently you brush your teeth and, depending on the target group, eat at *McDonald*'s or read the newspaper. These possible validity limitations should be considered when interpreting the results.

Reliability (in the sense of "trustworthiness" or "accuracy") concerns whether the same results would be achieved under the same conditions if data were collected again. To ensure this, random errors should be avoided, e.g. due to how the study was designed. If you conduct a survey about soft drinks in an overheated research studio on one day and in "normal conditions" on another day, you may get different results. Further disturbances may occur in designing the study. If "young men" are asked about their sports and leisure activities by "attractive young women", the results can be distorted by the "interviewers" because the interviewees want to impress them. If the same survey is conducted by "older men/women", this can lead to completely different results. One way to avoid this effect would be to have the interviewers in change systematically to reduce corresponding disturbances, because otherwise the study would not be "reliable".

The **objectivity** of the researcher is necessary to obtain "reliable" information. Objectivity, thus the absence of subjective influences, means that the same results are achieved, regardless of which researcher conducts the study. Objectivity refers to the implementation, evaluation and interpretation of the results.

> **Remember Box**
> You know what they say: do not believe any statistics that you have not falsified yourself. We should be aware of the possible manipulations, so that we can avoid them.
>
> Your (long-term) personal credibility also stands or falls based on whether the results that you produce in your department are objective or not.

Moreover, you should verify which collection units are relevant for your research questions. These can include consumers, employees of companies, proven experts or specialised institutions. In the framework of an **exhaustive survey**, all relevant collection units, which are collectively referred to as the population, are surveyed. If a company employs 400,000 people, a **partial sample survey** may be appropriate instead of an exhaustive survey. It would not make sense to carry out an exhaustive survey because it would be impracticable or economically unfeasible due to the expected costs. To collect meaningful information in a partial sample survey, the selected collection units must be representative. **Representativeness** is achieved if the sample represents the population and if the results obtained from this sample can be applied to the entire population. Therefore, the sample must be a representative subset of the population. To ensure that the sample is representative, all elements of a population must have the same chance of becoming part of the sample. The sample size also affects the representativeness of the results. It is easy to imagine that a sample of one person ($n = 1$) is not sufficient to describe the "purchasing behaviour of the Canadian population". Even a sample of 20 participants ($n = 20$) would not be sufficient for this survey (cf. for determining the sample size Altobelli 2017; Weis and Steinmetz 2012, pp. 97–99).

> **Remember Box**
> We should not use the NOMS method. The acronym stands for national one-man sample. Ironically, it expresses what happens frequently in companies. This method brings about phrases such as "my daughter said..., that's why we have to..." or "I heard about a CEO on the golf course yesterday..., that's why it's now time to...".
>
> We should be guided by reliable data and not follow every trend that we come across. However, this means that we should refrain from only using our own intuition as advice.

In the **data analysis phase**, you will extract the collected data (see Fig. 4.1). You can use uni-, bi- and multivariate data analysis methods. **Univariate data analysis** involves only analysing one variable in a statistical calculation (e.g. the frequency distribution of customers by age or gender). In **bivariate data analysis**, two specific variables are analysed simultaneously (e.g. the distribution of customers by age and gender in a crosstabulation). The **multivariate data analysis** includes the simultaneous evaluation of more than two variables (e.g. age, gender and income). The most well-known methods of multivariate data analysis are the multidimensional scaling as well as cluster and discriminant analysis. This involves forming groups of different customers, or checking the group membership. Other multivariable methods attempt to determine the relationships between several variables. These include regression, variance and causal analysis. Conjoint analysis and multidimensional scaling are used as methods for measuring preferences. Factor analysis is a method that is used to reduce data (see Altobelli 2017; Weis and Steinmetz 2012, pp. 281–293; Backhaus et al. 2015).

When interpreting the data, objectivity is of great importance because it can often be interpreted in many ways (cf. also Sect. 1.3).

In the **documentation phase**, you record the entire study, including the study design, the partners involved (e.g. an external market research company) and the results available for future research (see Fig. 4.1). By doing so, you ensure that your study can be used as a secondary source for follow-up studies. Furthermore, the results are presented to the client in this phase (e.g. the board, a planning department or the marketing department). The documentation should be followed by a review of the entire research project to determine possible optimisations for follow-up studies, if necessary. This is called a meta-analysis, because you are analysing the analysis itself using a broader perspective. It allows possible sources of errors and areas of optimisation to be identified. These must also be documented.

4.2 PEST or PESTEL Analysis

To analyse the macroenvironment of a company, you can use the PEST or PESTEL analysis (cf. also Müller 2017, pp. 130f.). These acronyms represent the areas to be analysed:

- **Political factors**
  This section calls for an analysis of how the following criteria affect a target market or a potential production location: stability and reliability of the government system, changes in the government, strength of right/left radical parties, economic policy orientation of the government (e.g. regulations on co-determination, tariff autonomy, promotion of business startups), economic development (e.g. granting subsidies), etc.
- **Economic factors**
  The following factors, among others, have a substantial impact on the economic attractiveness of a country or region: the level of economic growth, internal price stability (inflation/deflation), external currency stability (exchange rate development), interest rate level, unemployment rate, purchasing power and distribution of purchasing power among the population.
- **Social factors**
  When analysing social developments, you should consider the relevance of the following factors: educational level (including literacy rate), age structure of the population, extent of professional activity, cultural diversity, risk of poverty, average family size, society's expectations of companies, the position of women in society, acceptance of nuclear energy or wind turbines, gene products and new technologies.
- **Technological factors**
  The technical environment is highly influenced by the quality of the "hard" infrastructure (the Internet, roads, railways, airports, ports, energy and water supply), as well as the "soft" infrastructure (education system, justice system).
- **Ecological factors**
  To evaluate the ecological environment, you can determine the extent of environmental damage (water, air, region), resource consumption and recycling rates.
- **Legal factors**
  Legal factors have a lasting influence on the attractiveness of countries and regions. To evaluate the situation in a country or region, the following criteria must be included in the analysis: protection of private property (including intellectual property, such as patents, brand names), general legal certainty (extent to which legal institutions can enforce their right) and specificity of laws and guidelines (codification of regulations by tax laws, law against unfair competition, price regulation, trademark laws, laws against restriction of competition, environmental protection laws, customs regulations, minimum wages, workplace ordinance, approval procedures for new products/technologies, etc.).

Depending on your analysis goal, you can concentrate on four fields (PEST) or six fields (PESTEL) mentioned above during your study. It is very helpful to memorise this tool in case you are ever asked to spontaneously make a small analysis (e.g. in an assessment centre)!

> **Remember Box**
> The PEST or PESTEL analysis is a very useful tool to systematically analyse the macroenvironment of a company. You can use the previously defined factors to **analyse** a company's **macroenvironment**. Most companies have no direct influence on this part of the environment (apart from a few large multinational companies). However, all companies themselves are largely influenced by developments in this environment. Figure 4.2 is based on the PEST analysis, because in my opinion the "legal factors" are already included in the "political factors" and the "ecological factors" can be integrated in the "social factors". You should "check off" the areas listed in Fig. 4.2 on a company-specific basis, as these factors are particularly important. In this way, you can analyse which factors influence business activities and must therefore be considered when designing corporate activities.

Additionally, you should carry out an analysis of the **microenvironment** before making important decisions. You should also approach this systematically to allow foreseeable developments to be considered in your planning. Besides **customers** (direct and indirect) and **suppliers**, **competitors** and their activities have a large impact in this analysis. Today, virtually no competing company can shape its activities without considering relevant competitors and their reactions to their own actions. For this analysis, you must also involve **investors**, whether they be real shareholders or banks financing through credit.

Fig. 4.2 Macro- and microenvironment of the company. Author's own figure

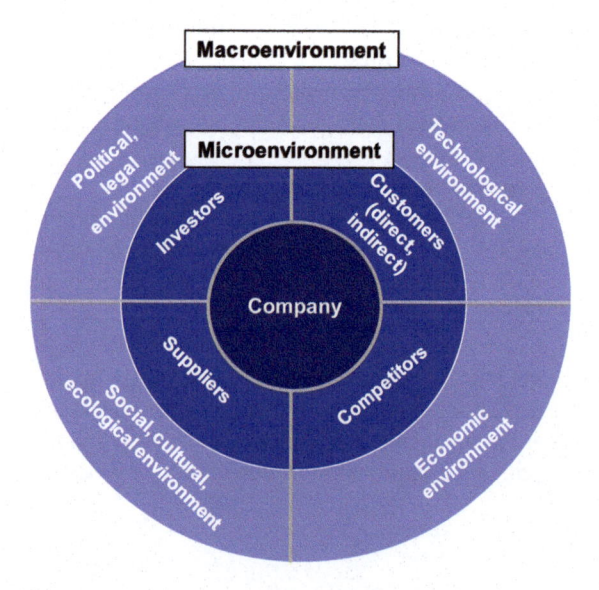

> **Remember Box**
> Analysing the microenvironment enhances your awareness of important developments of direct and indirect market partners and belongs in every toolbox of a manager.

▶ **Implementation Tips**

- The PEST or PESTEL analysis is an easy way to begin a strategic analysis.
- Whether alone or with your team, it allows for the identification of important challenges in a structured manner that will have an influence on the further development of the company.
- To further highlight specific fields of the macro- and microenvironment, you can use additional methods presented in this chapter.
- The various analysis instruments enable you to focus on different aspects of economic activities at the same time.

4.3 SWOT Analysis

The **SWOT analysis** (also TOWS analysis) is a particularly powerful strategic analysis tool that I also like to use. Its aim is to assess one's own performance in the light of relevant competitors while assessing future market conditions.

SW stands for strengths/weaknesses. This includes the comparative advantages or disadvantages a company has when directly compared with its competitors and thus covers the **internal perspective** of the analysis. **OT** stands for opportunities/ threats. It refers to the respective industry and integrates the **external perspective** into the analysis. You can draw strategic conclusions to further develop your company only after a synthesis of external and internal perspectives (see Fig. 4.3). In a one-product company, you can perform this analysis for the entire company. However, if your company is active in different industries and/or with very different offers on the market, you should carry out an analysis for each part of the company separately (e.g. based on strategic business units).

You should pay special attention to one thing when using the SWOT analysis, because this is almost regularly done wrong; company strengths and weaknesses can only ever be identified when they are **compared to relevant competitors**. Only through a direct comparison does it become apparent whether a market share of 12% is a strength or a weakness of the company. If all competitors have market shares between 1% and 3%, this market share is a strength. In this case, the relative market share is between 4 and 12. On the other hand, if the market is dominated by three

	Own strengths	Own weaknesses
Market opportunities	?	?
Market threats	?	?

Identification of company-specific strengths and weaknesses

Identification of market opportunities and threats

Internal perspective / External perspective

Synthesis

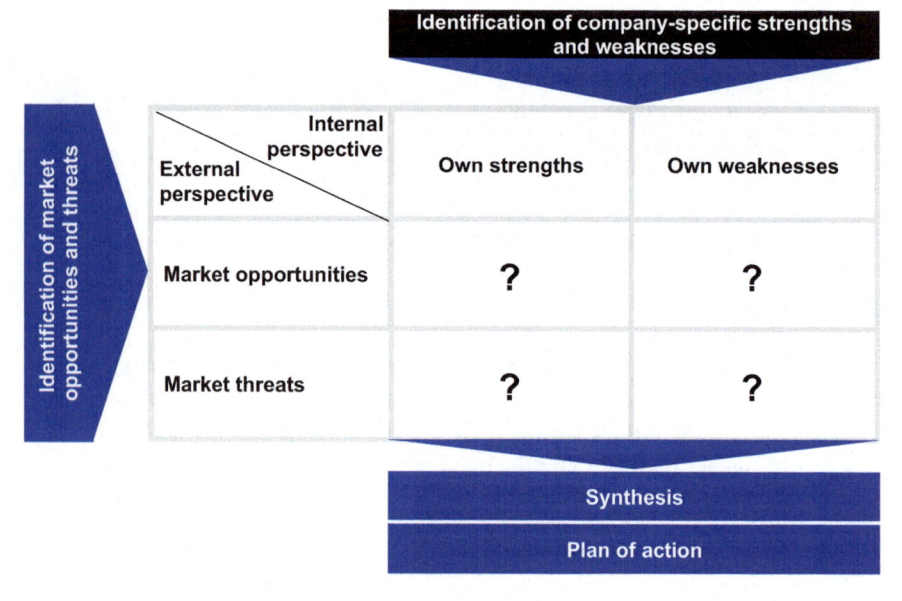

Plan of action

Fig. 4.3 Basic concept of the SWOT analysis. Author's own figure

companies with market shares of around 25% each, the market share is weak (relative market share of 0.48).

> **Remember Box**
> A company's strengths and weaknesses can only be determined in direct comparison with its relevant competitors. That is why saying "strength: we have a large product range" is meaningless and not useful for a SWOT analysis! On the contrary, one relevant analytical result could be: "strength: our product range is 20% larger than that of our main competitor, which is continually proven by high and profitable demand".

Before you can come to precise conclusions, you must first answer another question: how can you **identify the relevant competitors** so that the **relevant market can be defined**? You have two different options:

- Customer-oriented approach of defining the relevant set
- Provider-oriented approach of determining the strategic group

When using a **customer-oriented approach**, you collect the relevant set from the customer perspective. The **relevant set** includes the different offers that the customer considers to be equivalent and takes into consideration when making a purchase decision. This is defined by interviewing customers to find out which other companies or offers directly compete with your own. To determine this relevant set from a customer perspective, you can ask the following questions:

4.3 SWOT Analysis

- Which suppliers does the customer consider to be interchangeable?
- Between which products/services does the customer switch?
- Which products/services does the customer see as similar?

This type of approach can show that a fast-food customer not only switches between *McDonald*'s and *Burger King* but that, from his point of view, a frozen pizza or the kebab stand around the corner is also a relevant alternative. These types of offers would therefore have to be considered in a competitive analysis.

> **Remember Box**
> The customer-oriented approach for determining competitors may require you to consider completely different companies in the analysis than initially planned, because the customer equally considers providers that you "didn't have on your radar".

On the other hand, using a **provider-oriented approach**, you determine the **strategic group** to which your company belongs. This involves grouping companies in an industry that use a comparable strategic concept (cf. Porter 2004a). It is possible that different strategic groups exist simultaneously in an industry. The following questions can be used to identify the strategic group:

- Which companies pursue a comparable strategy?
- Which companies have a similar promise to their end customers?

An example should clarify what is meant by this. In the pharmaceutical market there is a strategic group of **generic suppliers** (such as *Hexal, Ratiopharm* and *Stada*) that distinguishes itself from **companies who conduct their own research** (examples of these include *Bayer, Merck, Novartis* and *Sanofi-Aventis*). When it comes to airlines, **low-cost airlines** such as *easyJet, Eurowings* and *Ryanair* constitute such a strategic group by implementing the same business model. This sets them apart from **premium providers** such as *Cathay Pacific, Emirates, Lufthansa, Qantas* and *Singapore Airlines*.

> **Remember Box**
> The strategic group brings together the companies that provide a comparable offer.

Using the **critical success factors** of respective business areas as a basis, you can **analyse the strengths and weaknesses** of your company. To identify these, you should consider which factors have a decisive influence on the success of a company or SBU (strategic business unit) or SBA (strategic business area). Such business units each illustrate a part of the corporate field of activity. When they are formed, an attempt is made to find the most homogeneous product-market combinations possible, which involves an independent, customer-related market task. In this way, the strategic business units determine how the market is seen, especially for an analysis.

By **focusing on strategic success factors**, you can concentrate on gathering and aggregating information about the most important issues. The following critical success factors are often used to **identify corporate strengths and weaknesses**, whose relevance has been confirmed by findings from success factor research:

- Type, image, market position, degree of innovation and quality of products/services
- Overall digitisation level of the company, the process and organisational structure as well as the individual service areas
- Efficiency of production/provision of services
- Sales strength (organisation, size, efficiency, qualification)
- Productivity of the entire organisation and its subareas
- Expenses (overall in R&D, procurement, production, sales, logistics, personnel)
- Financial strength (including dependence on external investors)
- R&D strength (e.g. qualification of the corresponding personnel, available budget)
- Access to key decision-makers in politics and the society
- Qualification, loyalty and motivation of employees
- Market presence (regional, international, global) regarding procurement and sales
- Organisational structure (flexibility, customer orientation, speed)
- Strategic alliances (in terms of connections that the company has, e.g. regarding sales, purchasing, research, production, etc., to establish an ecosystem)

When making essential comparisons with other companies, you should **relativise the sizes** for certain criteria. It is not useful to compare advertising or R&D budgets in absolute figures between a medium-sized chemical company and *BASF*. In this case it makes sense and is necessary to specify the amount of the advertising and R&D budget as a percentage of sales and then to compare it. Another example is when the number of patents filed is used to assess R&D performance. In this case, a division by the total number of employees or, even better, the number of employees in the R&D department must be made to determine a productivity indicator. This is the only way to determine relevant findings for the competitive comparison.

> **Remember Box**
> You should analyse the strengths and weaknesses in teams. By doing so, everyone involved "incidentally" has the same amount of information and can thereby make assessments.

4.3 SWOT Analysis

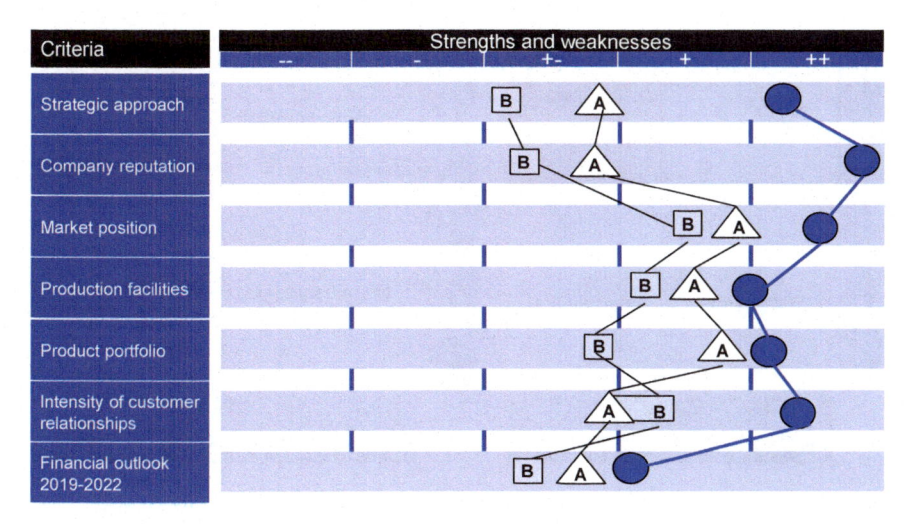

Fig. 4.4 Result of the analysis of strengths and weaknesses in a competitive comparison. Author's own figure

The results of the strength–weakness analysis should be prepared as shown in Fig. 4.4. The own company is shown here in comparison to the two most important competitors A and B.

When analysing your strengths and weaknesses, you should keep in mind a problem area that often also arises in dynamic team processes, namely, the **discrepancy between one's own image and that of others**. The relevance of this discrepancy can be illustrated by the **Johari Window** (named after the authors Joseph Luft and Harry Ingham; Rechtien 1999, pp. 95f.). Four squares are used to distinguish the self-perception and external perception in the personal sphere (cf. left illustration in Fig. 4.5). The first square is defined as the **open area**, because these are the behaviours and motives that are known to me and my environment or perceived by them. The **blind area** in the second square includes the behavioural patterns that others see, but that I do not know myself (e.g. established habits, linguistic quirks). The **hidden area** in the third square refers to aspects which I know myself, but which I do not want to disclose to others. In the fourth square you find the **unknown area**, which includes aspects of which neither I nor others are aware, otherwise known as the unconscious.

In the context of everyday business life, the first square involves the planned, and thus intended, **self-portrayal of the company** to the outside and inside (cf. right presentation in Fig. 4.5). The third square contains the **internal information of the company**, which is known internally and used, for example, for corporate management. This information can and should remain hidden from the outside. Unknown factors in the fourth square include **unused strengths**, such as certain hidden employee talents that do not blossom. However, these also include **unperceived weaknesses**, such as those that may create deficits in R&D that have not yet been noticed either in the company or in the market.

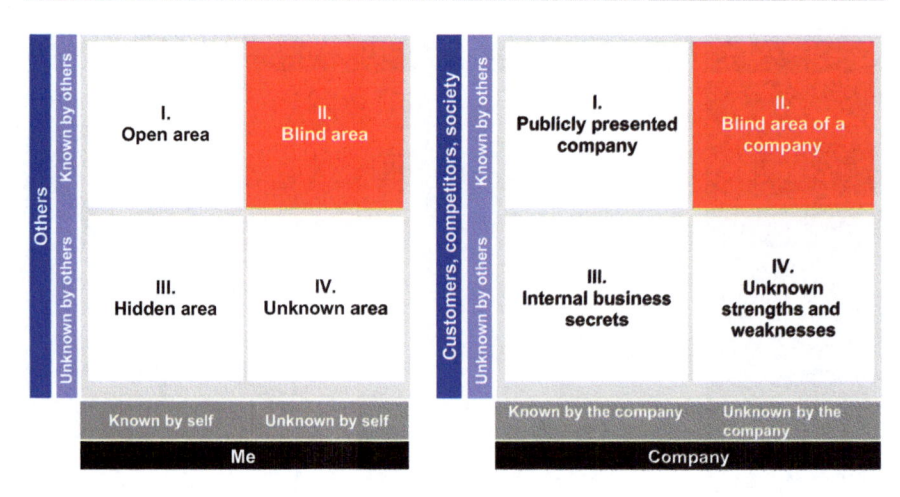

Fig. 4.5 Johari Window for self- and company analysis. Author's own figure

As part of strengths and weaknesses analysis, you should pay special attention to the second square, thus tackling the **blind area of your own company**. What do others know about us as a company that is unknown to us? What do others see that we do not see? This can be a compelling image held by a specific customer group that is not known in the company. These can also be "lousy" quality in the customer service centre or in the online presence as well as a below-average product quality that everyone talks about, but not in the company itself. The analysis is intended to ensure that the second square does not remain a "terra incognita" (an unknown country or an unexplored field of knowledge). Positive aspects found in the first square can be developed, while identified weak points must be eliminated.

> **Remember Box**
> When analysing strengths and weaknesses, you must pay special attention to the "blind spot" of the company. What do others know about us that we ourselves do not know, and therefore cannot turn off?

When conducting a SWOT analysis, you can also use a marketing audit. A marketing audit can allow you to identify possible risks that are caused by the type of marketing management structure at an early stage. The marketing audit can be either strategic or operational in nature. In a **strategic marketing audit**, you systemically compare the changes in the environment and marketing conditions within your own company every 1 or 2 years. Based on the knowledge you obtain, you can revise the systems themselves (e.g. the marketing organisation) or the desired goals and strategies used.

Conducting an **operational marketing audit** involves checking whether the marketing concept of your company is still "on track" once per quarter or year, for instance. A questionnaire is often used to analyse how marketing measures are optimally designed in terms of efficiency and effectiveness. In addition to the

4.3 SWOT Analysis

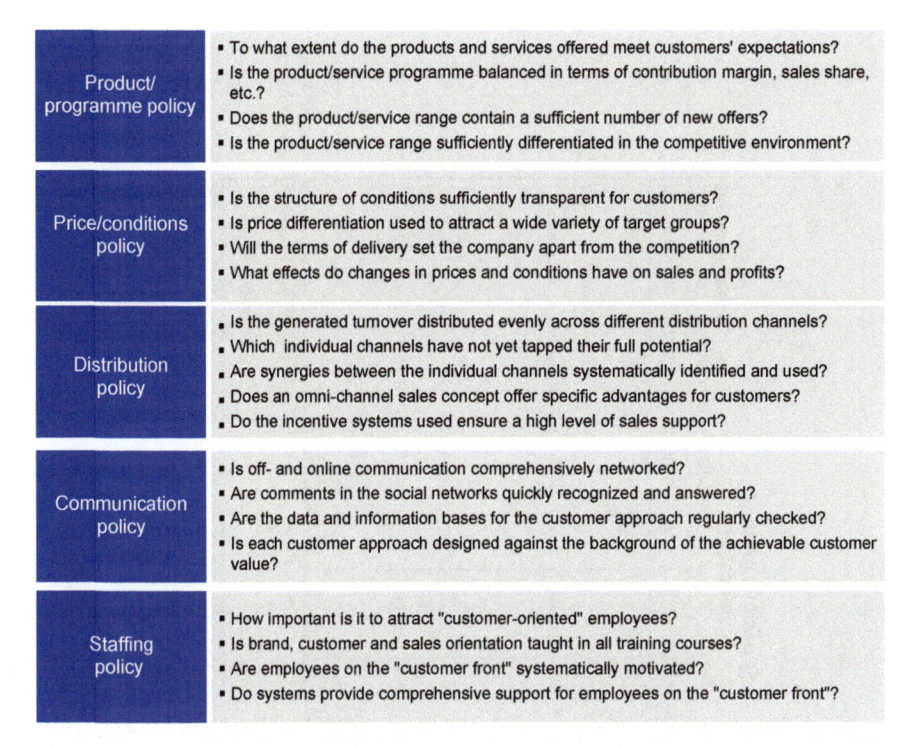

Product/ programme policy	• To what extent do the products and services offered meet customers' expectations? • Is the product/service programme balanced in terms of contribution margin, sales share, etc.? • Does the product/service range contain a sufficient number of new offers? • Is the product/service range sufficiently differentiated in the competitive environment?
Price/conditions policy	• Is the structure of conditions sufficiently transparent for customers? • Is price differentiation used to attract a wide variety of target groups? • Will the terms of delivery set the company apart from the competition? • What effects do changes in prices and conditions have on sales and profits?
Distribution policy	• Is the generated turnover distributed evenly across different distribution channels? • Which individual channels have not yet tapped their full potential? • Are synergies between the individual channels systematically identified and used? • Does an omni-channel sales concept offer specific advantages for customers? • Do the incentive systems used ensure a high level of sales support?
Communication policy	• Is off- and online communication comprehensively networked? • Are comments in the social networks quickly recognized and answered? • Are the data and information bases for the customer approach regularly checked? • Is each customer approach designed against the background of the achievable customer value?
Staffing policy	• How important is it to attract "customer-oriented" employees? • Is brand, customer and sales orientation taught in all training courses? • Are employees on the "customer front" systematically motivated? • Do systems provide comprehensive support for employees on the "customer front"?

Fig. 4.6 Selected questions used in marketing tool audit. Author's own figure

success factors mentioned above, you can also check how well individual tools are working. In this case, a so-called **tool audit** is used. This type of audit is essentially about checking the individual tools of the marketing diamond itself for their target-oriented use. Selected question fields of such an audit are shown in Fig. 4.6.

> **Remember Box**
> A marketing audit involves a critical reflection of individual or all marketing activities of a company. This calls for a comprehensive, systematic and regular examination not bound by instructions. This can be related to the marketing objectives, strategies and tools of a company or a strategic business unit.

Using the product life cycle, you can also carry out an in-depth analysis. This analysis enables you to determine which phase of the life cycle your product is currently in. Strictly speaking, the **product life cycle** is divided into the following market phases (see Fig. 4.7):

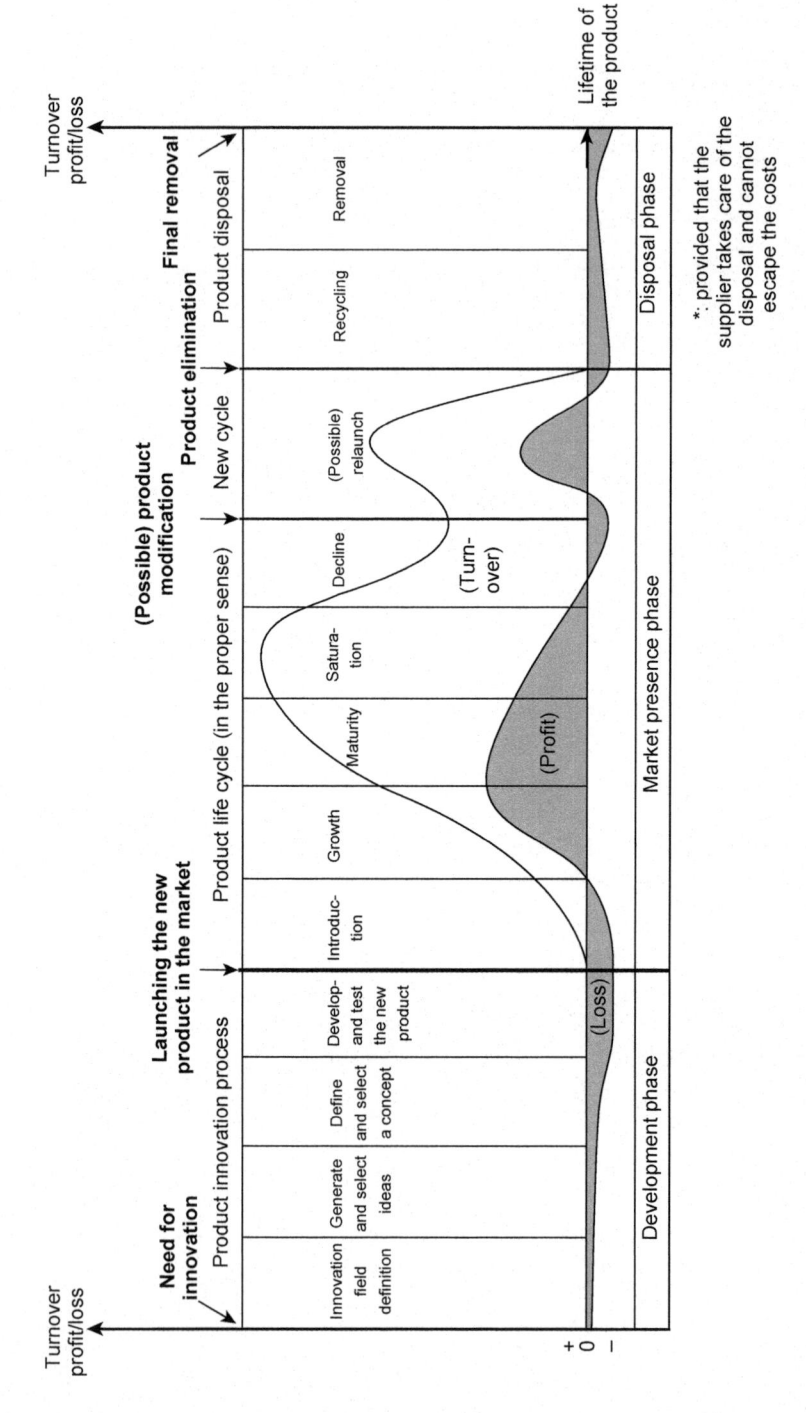

Fig. 4.7 Extended product life cycle as an analysis concept. Source: Adapted from Fritz and Oelsnitz (2006, S. 174)

4.3 SWOT Analysis

- Introductory stage
- Growth stage
- Maturity stage
- Saturation stage
- Decline stage

You can easily determine whether your product is in the introductory or growth phase using internal data, since you actively shape these phases to a large extent. It is much more difficult to tell whether the maturity phase or even the saturation phase has already been reached. This often requires the use of other market research tools. In the extended product life cycle of Fig. 4.7, in addition to the market presence phase, you can also consider the upstream and downstream phases, namely, the creation and disposal phase. The knowledge gained through this analysis increases the awareness for future actions, be it for a relaunch at the start of a new cycle or for withdrawing a product from the market. You can also use this analysis to show which products are currently in the development pipeline (development phase).

Although it is called a "product" life cycle, the phases mentioned are equally relevant for services. You can also use the product life cycle concept flexibly in the following ways:

- **Analysis of the "life" of a specific product** (e.g. the *Volkswagen Beetle*).
- **Analysis of the life cycle of an entire product category** (e.g. SUVs/sport utility vehicles).
- **Analysis of an entire product market** (e.g. passenger vehicles or CDs and DVDs); this is also referred to as a **market life cycle**.
- **Analysis of the life cycle of a company** (e.g. *Amazon* or *Nokia*).
- **Analysis of the life cycle of individual forms of distribution** (e.g. video stores, department stores, online shops, streaming platforms).
- **Analysis of the life cycle of an entire industry** (e.g. of the stationary retail trade in comparison to online trade).

> **Remember Box**
> The life cycle analysis is a very flexible tool that can provide you with exciting insights. The concept cannot only be used as ex post analysis (i.e. a retrospective analysis). It can also be used to forecast the future life cycle of the object under investigation.

The next step of the SWOT analysis is to analyse and evaluate the **opportunities and threats of the industry** in depth, in terms of the expected future developments. Sometimes it is possible to access information gained from the analysis tools already presented and those to come.

In this phase of the SWOT analysis, the opportunities and risks of the entire industry must be identified. This is not about the opportunities and risks of your own company! Unfortunately, this is all too often done wrong. By already addressing the opportunities and threats of our own company at this stage, the logic of the analysis is destroyed.

> **Remember Box**
> In the SWOT analysis, the analysis of opportunities and threats must relate to the entire industry! It requires an industry not a company focus! Otherwise, it is not possible to do a proper synthesis of the internal and external perspective.

The following areas can be analysed to determine the **opportunities and threats for the industry** as a whole:

- Market development (growth/stagnation/shrinkage)
- Access to new/old distribution channels
- Probability of new competitors entering or established competitors leaving the market
- Probability of forward or backward integration of other companies
- Price development for basic raw materials and other materials
- Support or obstacles through legal initiatives
- Availability or expiry of funding programmes
- Probability of market maturity through alternative technologies or products
- Changes in information and purchasing behaviour (e.g. due to changes in values, demographic developments, the Internet)

This includes analysis fields that are also discussed in Porter's **classic 5 Forces analysis** (2004b). It is a good idea to integrate these fields as well. This is an **industry structure analysis** focusing on five drivers of industry competition. As part of the SWOT analysis, which is supported by this concept, you can carry out an in-depth microanalysis to determine the opportunities and threats. The basic idea is that the attractiveness of an industry is significantly influenced by the market forces. These, in turn, have a direct impact on the strategic behaviour of the companies operating within the market.

Porter's analysis concept is based on the idea that the attractiveness of an industry is primarily determined by the five **competitive forces** shown in Fig. 4.8. The stronger the five competitive forces are, the less attractive the corresponding industry is, since it will probably be particularly difficult for you to achieve lasting competitive advantages. A strategic consequence of low sector attractiveness can be that you do not enter a certain sector or end your own involvement there. However, an attempt can also be made to change the rules of the game in the sector or to leave the beaten paths of market development through innovations. The individual drivers of industry competition that influence these decisions are discussed below.

A key driver of industry competition, which you should analyse first, is determined by the **rivalry between companies** that are already active in the industry. Among other things, this is particularly strong if:

4.3 SWOT Analysis

Fig. 4.8 Basic concept of *Porter*'s 5 Forces analysis. Author's own figure

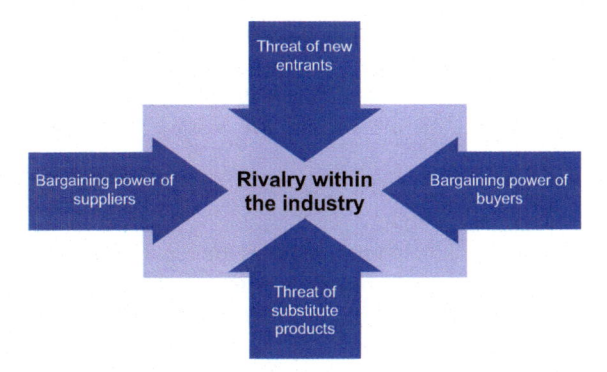

- Threat of new entrants
- Bargaining power of suppliers
- **Rivalry within the industry**
- Bargaining power of buyers
- Threat of substitute products

- Many and large competitors are active in the market, who face fierce competition.
- There is only a low or negative market growth, meaning that own growth is primarily achieved by replacing the competition.
- Companies have a high fixed cost burden and therefore accept orders that are not very attractive in terms of price, which increases the pressure on sales prices.
- There are significant cost differences between suppliers, which intensify price competition.
- The products and services are largely standardised and thus exchangeable for customers (low switching costs in terms of costs incurred by changing providers).
- There are high market exit barriers, so that even marginal providers (who do not make profits or even losses) remain in the market because existing investments, etc. cannot be sold at a profit.

Essentially, this concerns the **competitive position** your company has achieved within your own industry. Does it occupy a dominant market position, is it more in the midfield or does it have a competitive position that is difficult to defend and may even not be viable? At the same time, the strategic directions of the relevant competitors must be identified. Which companies are planning a significant expansion of their market position? Which ones rely on "holding on" or "harvesting"? Which ones are preparing to leave the market? If you pinpoint on the position and the strategic direction of your company in the light of the other driving forces of industry competition, you can make well-informed strategic decisions.

> **Remember Box**
> You can integrate the "rivalry between companies" results into the strengths and weaknesses part of the SWOT analysis. The other analysis steps of the 5 Forces approach provide findings for identifying opportunities and threats.

The **threat of new entrants** section of the 5 Forces analysis refers to new companies with comparable offers entering the market (see Fig. 4.8). The probability of this is particularly high if:

- Only low economies of scale can be achieved, and therefore even small companies are able to work quickly and competitively.
- Experience curve effects can be tapped, so that companies that have been operating on the market for a long time do not have any significant cost advantages.
- Customer loyalty is low due to low switching costs, and the acceptance of new suppliers is high.
- Only weak brand personalities are represented on the market, which facilitate the interchangeability of the products in the eyes of the customers.
- Only a small capital requirement is needed to create a new company (e.g. a publishing house in comparison to an automobile manufacturer).
- There is easy access to the relevant sales channels.
- There is a low degree of regulation (by-laws etc.), so that even newcomers can move into the market without large previous investments.
- The costs of leaving the market are low (low exit costs).

If the **suppliers** of companies occupy the focal point of the 5 Forces analysis with a high **bargaining power**, this reduces the attractiveness of this industry (see Fig. 4.8). The supplier power is high when:

- One supplier or a few suppliers have a heterogeneous customer base (supply monopoly or oligopoly) allowing the suppliers to easily influence the delivery conditions in their favour.
- There is little competition between different suppliers because their delivery programmes differ significantly.
- There is a lack of adequate substitutes.
- The suppliers are relatively independent of their customers because there are a sufficient number of potential buyers.
- Customers incur high switching costs when changing suppliers (e.g. when replacing *SAP*'s ERP software).
- The products supplied are highly individualised for individual customers, making it difficult for customers to change their source.
- Current suppliers can easily become competitors for current customers through forward integration.

Industry attractiveness also suffers when existing companies are exposed to **threats from substitute products** (see Fig. 4.8). Substitute products differentiate themselves from new entrants by offering a different solution for a specific customer problem. The eBook or ePaper, the electronic presentation of book and newspaper content, can pose a major threat to classic book and newspaper publishers. In the hotel industry, new products of the so-called sharing economy, such as Airbnb, are considered a considerable threat (cf. Kreutzer and Land 2017b). Overall, a major threat scenario can be assumed if:

4.3 SWOT Analysis

- Alternative offers are easily available.
- Substitutes have substantial price, performance and/or convenience advantages in comparison to the "original".
- Existing products and services are completely or partially devalued by new technologies.
- The target groups are "willing to change", and it is easy to make such a change (low switching costs).

Buying power is another field of 5 Forces analysis (see Fig. 4.8). A high **buying power** means that the buyers are in the dominant market position and can exert a significant influence on the conditions of the existing suppliers. This situation exists when:

- Few customers make up the demand (e.g. in food trade there are a few large retail chains, or the automotive sector has only a few large car manufacturers). The buying power in a demand monopoly (e.g. the state for certain military equipment) is even more obvious than in a demand oligopoly.
- There is a high price elasticity of demand because substitutes are readily available, and buyers therefore respond to price increases with a significant drop in demand from the corresponding supplier.
- Standardised products can be marketed, which enable the supplier to be easily changed due to low switching costs.
- A poor economic situation prevails, in which customers are under high cost pressure and must therefore put pressure on prices.
- Customers can become competitors of their existing suppliers through backward integration.
- Alternatives are easy to use and available to buyers (this development is massively reinforced by price comparison sites available online).

This **analysis concept from Porter** is very powerful but also requires precise application. This means that you must always define exactly which company is at the centre of the analysis. If this analysis is carried out for the *Volkswagen* Group, you must first analyse the intensive **rivalry of the manufacturers active on the market** (e.g. between *Volkswagen* and *Hyundai, Toyota, Ford, Opel*). Additionally, *Volkswagen* will be challenged by **new entrants** from the Chinese automotive industry. *Volkswagen*'s **suppliers** (including *Bosch, Continental* and *Recaro*) often have only limited bargaining power, as they tend to be highly dependent on *Volkswagen*. **Substitutes** for *Volkswagen*'s classic drive systems are electric and hybrid vehicles and the emerging autonomous cars and buses. Substitutes for the classic sale of vehicles are mobility concepts that provide users with mobility when it is needed through car sharing (e.g. *Car2Go, DriveNow, Flinkster*). In broader sense, local and long-distance public transport can also be regarded as a substitute. *Volkswagen*'s direct **buyers** are initially the authorised dealers and the customers they serve. However, these also include large customers, such as the police, *Deutsche Post* or *Sixt* car rental. The indirect buyers are private customers who purchase their vehicles from the dealer.

On the other hand, if such an analysis is carried out for the company *Bosch*, completely different power constellations exist. In this case, *Volkswagen* (along with *Daimler* and *BMW*) becomes a customer of *Bosch*, while substitutes for *Bosch*'s own products include solar-powered drives, since they are not provided by *Bosch* itself. An analysis for *Sixt* car rental, in turn, makes *Volkswagen* a supplier, while substitutes can be seen in private car-sharing concepts. The customers of the car rental are companies, their employees and private individuals.

The findings of this industry analysis can be incorporated into the **analysis of opportunities and threats**. It is important that you identify these by focussing on the industry, and not on the company itself. Even if people often talk about the opportunities and threats of a company, a SWOT analysis requires these areas to be analysed independently from the company, as has already been emphasised several times. Only by doing so can the **synthesis of internal and external perspectives** be logical and consistent. If company specifics would already be included in the external perspective, the picture would be distorted during synthesis, or this could no longer be consistently represented. Figure 4.9 shows which questions must be answered during the synthesis.

Figure 4.10 depicts an **example of such a synthesis** for the **consumer goods market**. It becomes clear once again that opportunities in the market or industry cannot be exploited by all companies. However, an optimal situation presents itself when you can use your own strengths to tackle opportunities or threats in the industry, which can lead to competitive advantages. Companies face large problems if they cannot overcome threats or take advantage of opportunities in the market due to their own weaknesses. Consequently, a company will lose competitive strength. The results obtained can provide you with (crucially) important insights for the company's strategic orientation but also for the orientation of innovation and acquisition processes.

External perspective \ Internal perspective	Own strengths	Own weaknesses
Market opportunities	With which opportunities in the market can we make the most use of our strengths?	Which opportunities in the market can we not take advantage of due to our weaknesses?
Market threats	What threats in the market can we profit from based on our strengths?	From which threats in the market do we suffer the most due to our weaknesses?

Fig. 4.9 SWOT matrix—synthesis of the external and internal perspectives within the SWOT analysis. Author's own figure

4.3 SWOT Analysis

External perspective \ Internal perspective	Own strengths	Own weaknesses
Market opportunities	High internet-related expertise and access to online distribution channels / Increasing acceptance of online sales platforms	No adequate product offerings / Trend towards organic products and wellness offers
Market threats	Innovative product line for the 50+ generation in stock / Dramatic shifts in the age structure	Pre-existing focus on medium price and quality / Increasingly price-conscious shopping

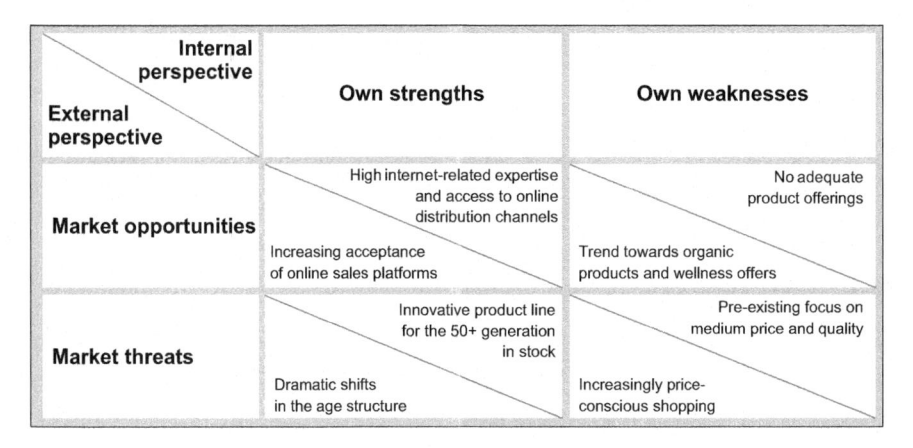

Fig. 4.10 Example of a SWOT synthesis from the consumer goods market. Author's own figure

The company analysed in Fig. 4.10 must introduce organic and wellness products, since they currently have no adequate solutions. Furthermore, the company should also consider whether a second brand should be launched to cater to the trend of increasingly price-conscious shopping. This type of analysis allows to consider customer expectations in the development process of a strategy. In this case these expectations are still very generic and that further marketing research tools must be used to clarify the exact requirements and their revenue potential.

As shown in Fig. 4.3, only the synthesis provides you with the necessary information to derive concrete measures. The concepts discussed in Chap. 3 can help you with this.

> **Remember Box**
> The findings of a SWOT analysis can be visualised using portfolio analyses.

▶ **Implementation Tips**

- You should include the SWOT analysis in your standard repertoire and use it once a year to identify relevant developments and changes at an early stage.
- It is recommended that you carry out this analysis as a team to increase a deep understanding of the industry and the company.
- To determine strengths and weaknesses, you must first analyse the relevant success factors.
- Additionally, you should systematically determine who you and your customers consider as your relevant competitors.

- You must define the opportunities and threats of the entire industry, not merely focusing on your own company.
- The 5 Forces analysis is a very powerful tool for enhancing the content of the SWOT analysis.
- During the synthesis stage, you combine the findings of the internal and external analysis to make strategic conclusions based on them.

4.4 Scoring Model

The **scoring model** is a concept that is both very easy to implement and meaningful. The terms **point rating model** or **cost-benefit analysis** are also used. You can use a scoring model anytime when you want to evaluate different alternatives or objects systemically. This model enables you to more transparently portray these evaluations, thus also making them more comprehensible.

Scoring models can be used flexibly with wide range of questions. Using the same methodology, you assign different weights or emphasis to evaluate various factors. Below you can see in which fields scoring models are already used today:

- **Defining customer value**

    When calculating the customer value, the following criteria are used in scoring models: sales, contribution margin, number of referrals to friends, etc. (see Sect. 6).
- **Determining the creditworthiness of potential customers**

    Before granting a loan or agreeing to deliver with an invoice, companies determine the expected creditworthiness based on several criteria (e.g. previous payment history). This scoring model includes the number of credit cards and current accounts, the previous payment history, current loans or the frequency of housing changes.
- **Selecting of production sites**

    When choosing suitable locations, a scoring model incorporate tax incentives, personnel costs, access to raw materials and the quality of the hard and soft infrastructure.
- **Assessing target markets**

    To position countries in a country portfolio (see Sect. 4.5), a scoring model can assess how interesting target markets are based on their political and economic stability, economic growth, the intensity of competition and the importance of one's own corporate image.
- **Choosing media**

    For instance, to select the best media for one's own company, a model could be based on criteria such as reach, costs, as well as image affinity to one's own offer and to the company.

- **Selecting distribution channels**
  To select distribution channels, a scoring model can consider the control options of sales partners, costs, customer frequency and the image of the potential partners, among other things.
- **Choosing employees**
  Within the company, scoring models are also used to determine the most qualified internal and/or external applicants for an open position.

> **Remember Box**
> The scoring model is a tool that is very easy to use, which allows you to systematically and objectively make decisions. You can adapt it flexibly to a variety of questions.

How should you proceed if you want to use a scoring model for these or similar questions? To develop such a model, you must first define which **characteristics** to use so that you can assign values to different alternatives or objects. When developing the scoring model, you must ensure that the considered criteria are independent from one another to avoid unwanted multiple entries of the same facts. These characteristics are then given a **weighting** to express the different importance of the characteristics. The weighting factors must add up to 1.0. The relevant characteristics, such as the weighting factors, should be determined in an intensive team discussion. This is very exciting, because during these discussions, valuation patterns that are often rather intuitive become transparent and can therefore also be discussed. This alone makes this approach highly valuable.

In the next step, all **criteria** must be **operationalised**, i.e. made measurable, and **given points** (scores) based on their different characteristics. Keep in mind that a higher score describes a "better" situation. Multiplying the points by each weighting and summing up all criteria results in a total point value for each alternative that is to be evaluated. This makes it possible to compare and evaluate ideas.

In Fig. 4.11 you can see how this type of **model is used to evaluate new product ideas**. By using a scoring model, the (often subjective) preferences for different product ideas become visible. If you evaluate all ideas with the same scoring model, it becomes very easy to see which have the greatest chances of success, namely, those with the highest scores. It also helps you realise which ideas you might want to remove. Furthermore, often ideas must have a minimum value (e.g. Sect. 3.3) if they are to be pursued. This prevents mediocre ideas from being more thoroughly explored only because there were no convincing alternatives!

The advantage of such scoring models is that qualitative and quantitative criteria can be incorporated into an evaluation. Additionally, as already mentioned, subjective assessments (the famous "gut feeling") are summed up into an overall assessment by involving several people. Moreover, documenting the evaluation process makes it possible to check how accurate the assessments were 1 year later. This

Assessment criterion	Relative weight (A)	Assessment of new product idea (B)					Result (A x B)
		1	2	3	4	5	
Market potential	0.25		X				0.50
Market growth	0.20			X			0.60
Price willingness	0.10					X	0.50
Intensity of competition	0.15					X	0.75
Development expenses	0.15			X			0.45
Production needs	0.15				X		0.60
Sum	1.00						3.40

1: very unfavorable, 5: very favorable
Minimum value to pursue an idea: 3.3

Fig. 4.11 Scoring model for evaluating a new product. Author's own figure

counts as an important prerequisite for a "learning organisation", because experience with the scoring approach can be used to optimise processes.

▶ **Implementation Tips**

- It is a good idea to use scoring models if you must choose between different alternatives or objects and if you need to include several quantitative and qualitative criteria that are of different importance.
- You should develop and use scoring models in teams.
- If the model is not sufficiently selective and all alternatives or objects achieve similar results after the first run, in the sense of using the model, you can calibrate (i.e. fine-tuned) as needed.
- The model itself and the results must be documented so that the quality can be checked at a later point in time.

4.5 Portfolio Analysis

Even though the portfolio analysis is no longer "in its prime time", even today it still belongs in your strategic analytical tools toolbox. This method remains relevant because this analysis allows you to obtain a very good overall view of the performance of your company. This overview can refer to different perspectives:

- Positioning of the entire company in the competition
- Positioning of your company within the corporate group

4.5 Portfolio Analysis

- Positioning of own SBUs or SBFs in the group
- Positioning of country commitments
- Positioning of products
- Positioning of technologies
- Positioning of customers
- Positioning of employees

Depending on your specific questions, you can develop your own portfolio analyses. Below you will find the general methodology on which the various portfolio approaches are based.

> **Remember Box**
> The portfolio analysis is a powerful analytical tool that you can adapt flexibly to a variety of questions.

The basic structure of the classic **portfolio analysis** of the *Boston Consulting Group* (also known as the **BCG portfolio**, or **market share market growth portfolio**) revolves around **two positioning drivers** (see Fig. 4.12). The first is **market growth**, which as a descriptive element of the product life cycle expresses the general acceptance of the offer by the customer (cf. also Sect. 4.3). Whether there is high or low growth depends on the industries being analysed. The **specific market position** of a company is expressed by its relative market share, which is an indicator of the extent to which experience curve effects have been achieved. To determine this, you must divide your own market share by that of the largest competitor. As already mentioned, this enables you to position individual products, SBUs and SFUs, independent companies or country activities.

The four quadrants formed by the axes "relative market share" and "market growth", each ranging from "low" to "high", are assigned names for the objects positioned there. **Standard strategies** are also included for the individual fields (e.g. disinvestment strategy, harvest strategy). These strategies should be applied when the objects being analysed find themselves in the respective position, or at least provide you with a strategic orientation. However, these standard strategies should not be used blindly but rather systematically critically examined whether they contribute to the achievement of corporate goals before they are implemented.

The units that are sorted into the **stars** category continue to require high investments from the company to maintain or expand their market position in a growing market (cf. Fig. 4.12). Such investments may become necessary in the production area but also in the product range as well as in sales and communication. In total these investments may lead to a negative cash flow. On the other hand, since the **cash cows** will only experience minimal market growth, the need for investment tends to be low (see Fig. 4.12). If necessary, production capacities and investments in R&D, sales and communication can already be reduced at this point. Therefore, these SBUs can generate a positive cash flow.

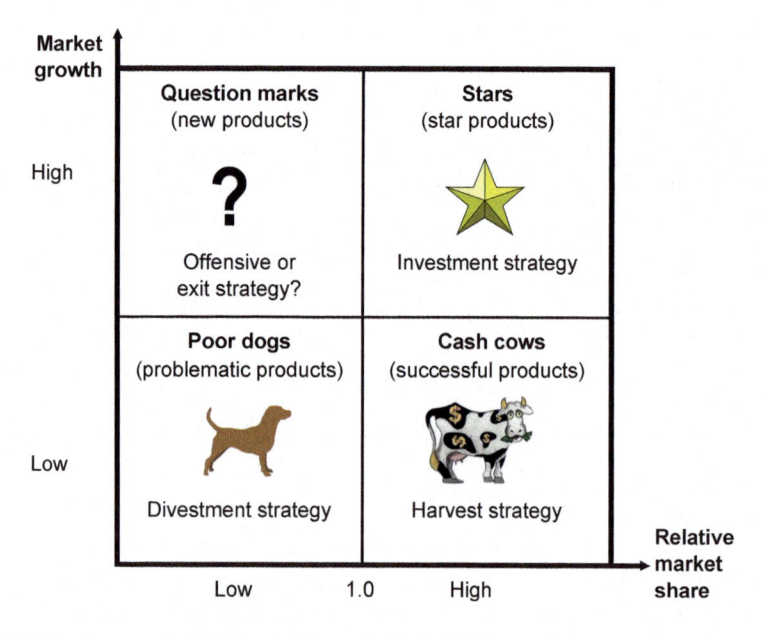

Fig. 4.12 Basic concept of BCG portfolio analysis. Author's own figure

As for the **poor dogs**, in-depth analyses are necessary to obtain concrete indications for the strategic orientation of these products or SBUs (cf. Fig. 4.12). Perhaps the activities positioned here are not profitable but nevertheless indispensable for the company. If this is not the case, these activities can be terminated, sold or incorporated into joint ventures with other companies. It is also possible that increased R&D investments could give these activities new momentum. The activities identified as **question marks** require high investments to expand their current weak market position in a growing market that is growing rapidly (cf. Fig. 4.12). The name indicates that it is unclear whether these activities will be future stars or poor dogs. This must be determined through in-depth analyses.

A portfolio analysis enables you to determine whether a company has a **balanced mix of products, SBUs/SBFs, companies** and/or **country commitments**. This also answers the question whether there are sufficient "new products" or "emerging markets" in the pipeline ensuring that the company will continue to operate successfully in the market in the future. Achieving such a **balance of corporate activities** is the central guiding principle of a portfolio analysis, which was derived from the financial sector (fundamentally Markowitz 1952). The aim is to create a security portfolio that is balanced in terms of various criteria. Two of the main criteria are return and risk. As already explained, this approach was transferred from the financial to the real economy to identify whether there are already offers that are balanced in terms of future opportunities and risks or whether countermeasures must be taken accordingly by analysing one's own portfolio.

4.5 Portfolio Analysis

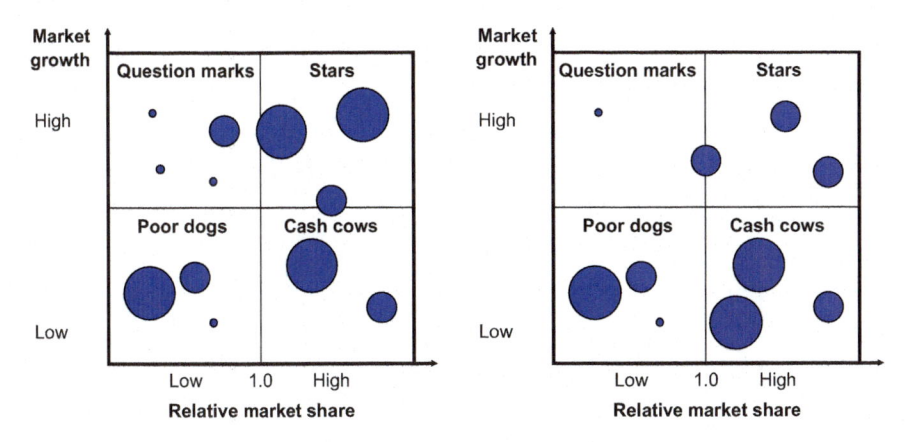

Fig. 4.13 Different product portfolios as triggers of corporate development. Author's own figure

In Fig. 4.13 you will find two different **constellations of portfolios** to illustrate this need for action. While the portfolio on the left has a relatively balanced overall structure, the portfolio on the right clearly shows that there is an in sufficient provision for the future in terms of placing new products on the market early. Firstly, there is a lack of new products in the field called "question marks". Secondly, the company only has a few star products, which also only have a small turnover (recognisable by the size of the circles). Now the company must start innovation processes promptly to overcome the diagnosed deficit. Also, the profits generated by the cash cows must therefore be invested in corresponding future-oriented innovation projects. At the same time, it becomes clear that the current products with high sales are no longer of great importance in the long term (products in the field of "poor dogs").

> **Remember Box**
> The portfolio analysis is a useful tool providing an overview of the company's activities in a highly condensed form and thus supporting the strategic planning of a company.

When using the **BCG portfolio analysis**, you should also consider its limitations. First, you must keep in mind that the underlying two-dimensionality of the analysis does not go far enough. Only depicting an industry and market structure through the criteria of relative market share and market growth does not do its complexity justice. Competitive aspects are only indirectly considered when determining the relative market share. Secondly, there is an overemphasis on growth and experience curve effects, since the criteria were selected based on these. Furthermore, the standard strategies do not have any compelling general validity, so that they need to be put in context with the specific company and market situation.

	Low	Medium	High
High	Invest or divest	Invest	Keep market leadership
Medium	Harvest and divest step by step	Transition	Growth
Low	Divest	Harvest and divest step by step	Harvest

(Vertical axis: Market attractiveness; Horizontal axis: Relative competitive advantage)

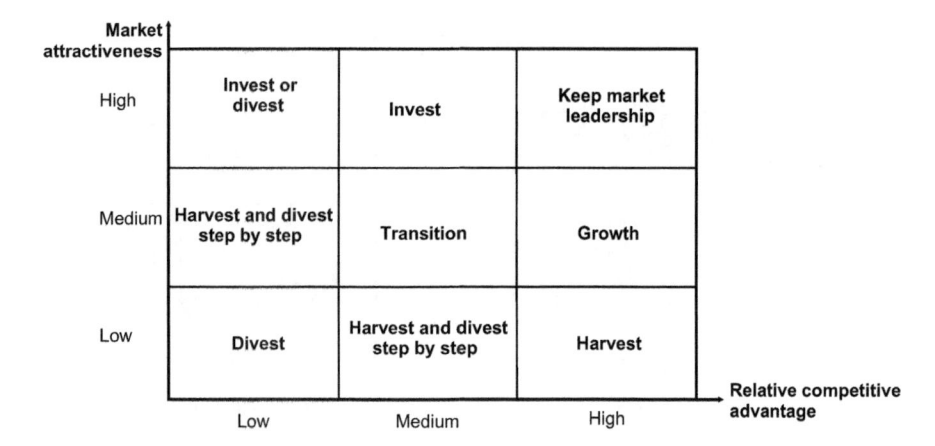

Fig. 4.14 Market attractiveness-competitive advantage portfolio. Author's own figure

The previously mentioned two-dimensionality limitations were overcome by *McKinsey*'s **market attractiveness-competitive advantage portfolio** (cf. Fig. 4.14). This portfolio takes considerably more characteristics into account when describing the market and competitive position of a company. Being able to flexibly choose characteristics allows for tailor-made portfolios. This again demonstrates the flexibility of portfolio analysis.

You can use the following criteria, among others, to determine **relative competitive advantages**:

- **Relative market position** (including market share, growth rate, profitability and size of your own company)
- **Relative production potential** (cost advantages achieved, know-how, licences, location factors, etc.)
- **Relative R&D potential** (e.g. budget, research staff, innovation capability of your own organisation)
- **Relative qualification** of your own managers and employees

You can use several criteria to determine the **market attractiveness**. These include:

- **Market growth and size**
- **Market quality** (including industry profitability, phase in market life cycle, intensity of competition, number and structure of customers, market entry barriers, threat of substitution products; cf. the comments on the 5 Forces analysis in Sect. 4.3)
- **Supply of energy and raw material** (e.g. negotiating power of suppliers, security of resource supply)
- **Environment** (e.g. dependence on the economy, orientation of legislation, public opinion on activities in the sector)

4.5 Portfolio Analysis

Due to the large number of criteria that must be considered, a portfolio analysis is often prepared by strategic consulting companies that have comprehensive relevant databases at their disposal. The scoring method presented in Sect. 4.4 links the information to a value which allows for positioning within the portfolio representation. By using numerous criteria, you can overcome the previously criticised two-dimensionality of the analysis. It also enables you to select the relevant company-specific criteria, so that your company situation is properly examined. Nonetheless, more differentiated standard strategies do not provide significant additional insights.

> **Remember Box**
> The market attractiveness-competitive advantage portfolio is a very powerful analytical tool. You can tailor it to the individual needs of your company or industry.

The **technology portfolio** is an example of a specifically designed portfolio analysis. Technological attractiveness and resource strength are located on the axes (cf. Pepels 2016; Bruhn and Hadwich 2017, pp. 153f.). You should use this version of the portfolio if technology is particularly important for success in your industry. The extent of technological attractiveness is determined by the economic and technical advantages associated with further developing a certain technology in the market. Seeing as most companies are now required to digitally transform themselves, the technology portfolio has great relevance (cf. Kreutzer and Land 2015, 2017a; Kreutzer et al. 2018).

The following are particularly useful when assessing the **technological attractiveness**:

- Development potential of the technology (e.g. already mature, or only in the initial development phase; Gartner Hype-Cycle-of-Innovations provides valuable insights, cf. Gartner 2018)
- Nature and scope of the fields to which the technology is applied
- The way in which the use of the technology will develop (diffusion process of the technology), depending on the acceptance of the technology (e.g. for smart solutions, autonomous driving, virtual reality, use of robots in industries and households)
- Time and budget requirements until the technology is ready for the market (time to market)
- Time and budget required for the technology to generate initial value for users (time to value)

The **technological resource strength** is determined by assessing the situation of the company regarding the technical and economic mastery of the technology in comparison to the strongest competitor. This is assessed based on the following criteria:

- Overall financial strength of the company
- Amount of funds allocated to R&D in the company (absolute and as a percentage of turnover or profit)
- Consistency of funds for R&D in the company (trend of key figures in the past and forecast for the future)
- Status and development of the company's innovation potential (e.g. number of employees in total and as a percentage of total workforce; qualification level of employees, e.g. platform strategies and solutions within the framework of the Internet of Things)
- Results of previous innovation commitment (number of patents applied for per year, share of new technologies in annual sales in absolute numbers and percentage terms)
- Efficiency of innovation commitment (number of newly filed patents per year and R&D employees or assessed in relation to R&D budget used)
- Legal competence in innovation management

You then use a scoring model to combine the assessments made using the previously mentioned criteria. The product and process technologies that you consider as relevant can be depicted in a **technology portfolio** (cf. Fig. 4.15). Possibly contrary to the previous assessment that the technological resource strength of the company should be the same for all technologies, each technology occupies a different position in the portfolio. This results from the different positions taken by the competitors of the technologies. Putting the technologies into perspective in this way is a particularly important factor of the technology portfolio. Based on the findings, you can choose to further develop technologies that will enable you to achieve a dominant market position.

Based on the positions in Fig. 4.15, a company can easily see that technologies 1 and 5 are the most important and should be selected for further development, if they are fully compatible with the company objectives. On the other hand, the position of technologies 4 and 6 raises the question whether disinvestment would be the wiser choice, if the company itself is active in this area. To determine which strategy is to be applied, technologies 2 and 3 must be further analysed. If these technologies play a key role in successfully shaping the digital transformation, the efforts must be increased.

> **Remember Box**
> You should use the technology portfolio if technologies are of great importance for your company, e.g. to successfully manage the digital transformation.

4.6 Benchmarking

```
Technology
attractiveness
                ┌─────────────────┬─────────────────┐
                │  Technology 2   │                 │
                │                 │   Technology 5  │
       High     │                 │                 │
                │                 │   Technology 1  │
                ├─────────────────┼─────────────────┤
                │                 │   Technology 3  │
                │   Technology 4  │                 │
       Low      │   Technology 6  │                 │
                └─────────────────┴─────────────────┘
                                                       Relative resource
                      Low              High            strength
```

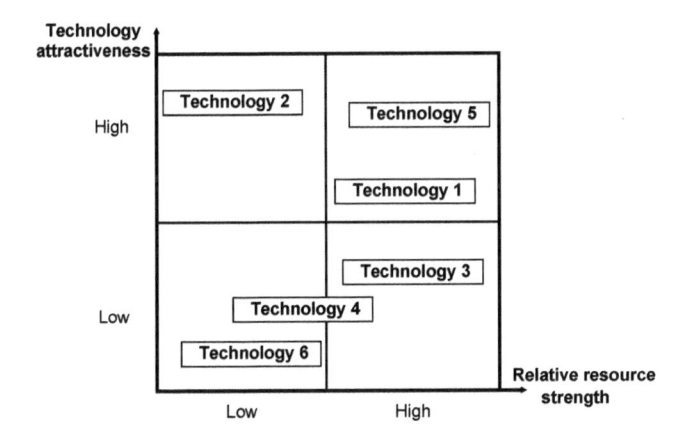

Fig. 4.15 Technology portfolio. Author's own figure

▶ **Implementation Tips**

- A portfolio analysis is a tool which you can use to have a fact-based overview of your own activities.
- The portfolio analysis can be flexibly structured according to the relevant questions.
- It is also recommended to carry out this analysis in teams, possibly supported by consulting partners with a high level of information expertise.
- Relevant analyses should be carried out once a year.
- The results must be documented and included in the annual review.

4.6 Benchmarking

In day-to-day management, you regularly hear the term **benchmarks**. In general, this refers to other companies or offers against which one's own company and its performance should or must be measured, because others define the standard or the frame of reference, i.e. a benchmark. In this sense, benchmarks are standards of comparison for one's own actions. If you want to make such comparisons systematically, and not based on a gut feeling, the concept of **benchmarking** comes into play.

> **Remember Box**
> A benchmark is a standard of comparison for one's own actions. Benchmarking refers to analysing your products, services or processes in comparison with one or more other companies. This allows you to come up with ideas to optimise your own activities.

Benchmarking is a one-time or continuous comparison of your own products, services or processes with one or more other companies. It aims to **identify your performance gap** in comparison to the **best-in-class company** (also known as best-of-breed). Best-in-class companies are those that perform significantly better and can therefore serve as a role model for you.

> **Remember Box**
> Important: Benchmarking is not about implementing a successful model of the past in 2–3 years. That would not cut it!
> Your goal should be to stimulate your own actions by comparing yourself with other companies. It is important to work out your own solution ideas based on the activities of the other companies and, if necessary, even to exceed their approach!

After determining this "benchmark", it is necessary to **develop ideas to close the identified performance gaps**. Thus, benchmarking aims to identify the optimisation potential in the areas of products, services and processes based on concepts already implemented and proven by other companies. Benchmarking can be addressed using the following questions:

- What can my company learn from others?
- What can other companies do that my own company has not yet achieved?
- Which areas can contribute to building up additional customer advantages to further differentiate the performance of my company from the competition?
- In which fields can the approaches of other companies provide orientation to achieve a cost advantage?

Depending on your specific questions, you can use **product/service benchmarking** or **process benchmarking**. If you want to make comparisons with other areas of your own company (corporate divisions, departments, profit centres), you can use **internal benchmarking**. When making a comparison outside of your own company, it is referred to as **external benchmarking**. External benchmarks can also be carried out between companies on a reciprocal basis. The participating companies provide each other with information to carry out the benchmark analyses. However, external benchmarks are generally carried out in such a way that the company defined as the benchmark is not informed of its role. In this case expert

4.6 Benchmarking

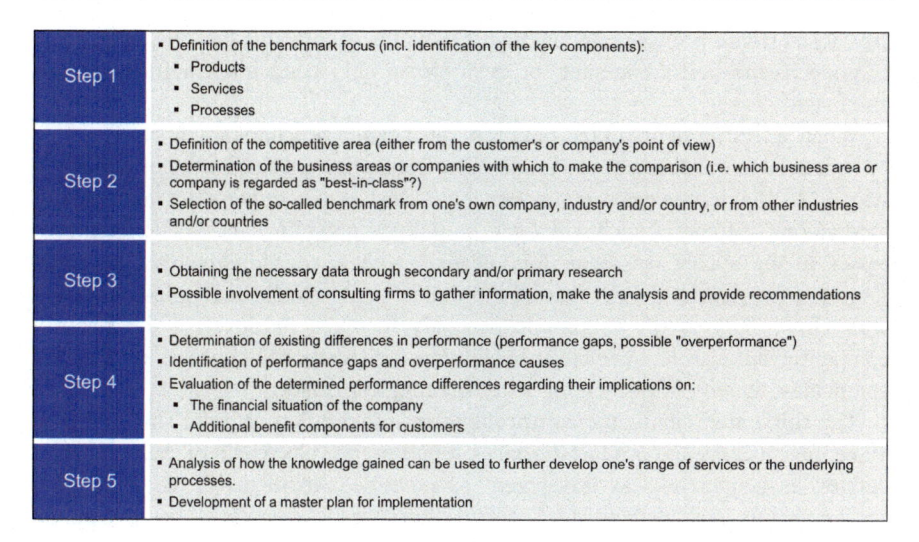

Step 1	• Definition of the benchmark focus (incl. identification of the key components):
	  • Products
	  • Services
	  • Processes

Step 2	• Definition of the competitive area (either from the customer's or company's point of view) • Determination of the business areas or companies with which to make the comparison (i.e. which business area or company is regarded as "best-in-class"?) • Selection of the so-called benchmark from one's own company, industry and/or country, or from other industries and/or countries
Step 3	• Obtaining the necessary data through secondary and/or primary research • Possible involvement of consulting firms to gather information, make the analysis and provide recommendations

Step 4	• Determination of existing differences in performance (performance gaps, possible "overperformance")
	• Identification of performance gaps and overperformance causes
	• Evaluation of the determined performance differences regarding their implications on:
	  • The financial situation of the company
	  • Additional benefit components for customers

Step 5	• Analysis of how the knowledge gained can be used to further develop one's range of services or the underlying processes. • Development of a master plan for implementation

Fig. 4.16 Step-by-step concept of benchmarking. Author's own figure

discussions are led by "neutral third parties" (such as employees of consulting firms) so that the underlying benchmark process remains unknown.

If you select companies from your own industry for the process, this is referred to as **industry-specific benchmarking**. On the other hand, if companies are selected from areas outside the industry, then this is referred to as **cross-industry benchmarking**. Such a cross-industry approach is particularly advisable when benchmarking does not focus on products but on services and/or processes. Figure 4.16 shows the step-by-step concept of benchmarking, which is used as a basis for the different versions.

In **step 1**, you first determine the **focus of benchmarking**. As shown, this can include products, services or processes. For the rest of the procedure, it is helpful if you break down the analysis objects according to their key components (e.g. marketing, sales, logistics, products, HR, purchasing). This makes it easier for you to select the benchmarks (in terms of the comparison objects to be used), since other companies only need to be superior in one subfunction. These can include logistics, R&D, production, customer service, online presence, etc. It also ensures that benchmarking is not about a company comparison but a comparison of specific performance elements.

Depending on these specifications, **relevant competitive areas** are defined in **step 2**. You can also define the relevant competitive areas within a company if you want to compare different company areas or subsidiaries with each other for internal benchmarking. For external benchmarking, a **customer-oriented** or **supplier-oriented approach** can be chosen to define the relevant competitors in product/service benchmarking (see Sect. 4.3).

When searching for offer innovations or process innovations for benchmarking, it is often beneficial to not only look beyond your own industry but also your own country to find the best-in-class company or companies. If the benchmark partners are chosen from a broader field, a possible risk of benchmarking that only makes you as good as the best competitor, or even worse only comparing inefficiencies, is eliminated.

When **selecting benchmark partners** (also called benchmarks), it can therefore be beneficial to use different companies as role models for the components defined in step 1. If *Walmart* carries out a benchmarking to determine offer and service innovations, different benchmarks can be defined regarding the procurement processes in the apparel segment, for instance, with *Zara*, individualised customer service with *Amazon*, individualised products with *Adidas* and goods logistics with *DHL*. This makes it possible not only to reach the level of the superior competitor but also to overtake it by linking the superiority concepts of different companies, thereby implementing an **outpacing approach**.

The **third step** entails the **comprehensive information search**. The goal is to make the concepts and products/services found in the value chain of the companies defined as benchmarks as transparent as possible. Additionally, the underlying success factors must be recorded. Seeing as this phase is often very time-consuming, it becomes clear why consulting companies specialise in benchmarking. Frequently, only they can ensure comprehensive access to the required information and make the complex comparison processes possible.

The **fourth step** involves **identifying the existing differences in performance**. On one hand, you can identify performance gaps when your own concepts and procedures are inferior to those of the benchmarks. On the other hand, performance gaps can exist because processes or components of products or services are not provided efficiently enough. However, "overperformance" is also a possibility if you find out that services provided by the company do not generate any corresponding customer benefit, for instance. In conclusion, it is a matter of evaluating the differences in performance regarding their implications for the financial situation of the company and for the achieved or achievable customer benefit.

Benchmarking provides you with information about processes and/or specific product or service designs that have enabled other companies, but also competitors, to achieve cost leadership or strong differentiation in their competitive environment. These findings can be used to initiate an outpacing strategy for your own company. This can provide you with further important information to design customer-oriented strategies (see Sect. 3.2).

In the final **fifth step**, it is necessary to identify areas of optimisation by **finding differences between the best practice approaches and your own concepts** and to define appropriate methods to implement these new approaches. To overcome the defined performance gaps and to reduce overperformance, it is recommended to come up with a suitable master plan. Benchmarking aims to initiate an organisational change process in the company. It can create credibility for setting high standards in a special way, because the performance already achieved by other companies or parts of companies is used as a benchmark. This can be used to show management and employees that no "impossible" demands or aspirations are being made.

▶ **Implementation Tips**

- Depending on the dynamics of your industry, benchmarks should be continuously identified to maintain the dynamics of change in your company.
- A comprehensive benchmarking, if necessary separated according to different performance areas, should take place once a year.
- The results of benchmarking should be comprehensively communicated internally so that it is clear why improvements are necessary in various areas.
- If you have defined important fields of action, immediate consequences must be derived.
- If certain activities that you are carrying out are the "benchmark" and serve others as a positive comparison, this should be celebrated appropriately!

4.7 Value Chain Analysis

It is in the interest to every manager to understand in detail how relevant competitors can reduce their costs or achieve superior customer benefits. Both ultimately contribute to the profit margin of the company. The **value chain analysis** was developed to answer these questions. This is based on the **value chain** concept developed by Porter (2004b), which is also called the **value-added chain.**

By using a value chain analysis, you can achieve the following goals:

- **Determining of the causes of competitive advantages** both for your company and for other companies
- **Recognising the potential to achieve competitive advantages for your company** (focus: sources of additional customer benefits and/or starting points for improving your financial situation)

The value chain analysis is essentially about identifying starting points where your company can achieve competitive advantages, thus providing information to support the strategic planning process (see Sect. 3.2). This objective makes it have a partial overlap with benchmarking. However, in contrast to benchmarking, a value chain analysis examines your company's entire process of creating good and/or services and compares it with that of other companies. This is often not the case with benchmarking.

You should focus the value chain analysis on the key corporate activities to ensure that the analysis process remains manageable. These key activities include those with a high customer-specific differentiation potential and/or with a considerable portion of the costs. These activities can be found in the most diverse areas of a company. You first assign each of these activities to one of the following types:

- **Core processes** (also known as **direct activities**)
  The activities assigned to the core processes are directly involved in creating value for the customer.
- **Supporting processes** (also known as **indirect activities**)
  These include activities that contribute only indirectly to the production of goods and/or services. A classic example of this is the corporate infrastructure, which includes human resources, controlling and R&D.
- **Quality assurance**
  This category includes activities that contribute to ensuring high quality in a wide variety of company areas. These include quality tests and continuous production monitoring.

When classifying your activities into one of these categories, you should consider the specific situation your company is in, as well as the industry. For this reason, the classification shown in Fig. 4.17 is only an example of implementation. For consulting companies, human resources count as a core process, since their reputation and success depend on the qualifications of their own employees. In classical market research companies, market research, differentiated in various offerings, is one of the core processes. In research-based pharmaceutical companies, R&D is a mandatory core process, whereas this is not the case with generic drug manufacturers. For an IT service provider, the IT infrastructure represents one of the core processes. To determine supporting and core processes, you must therefore analyse the value chain of your own company.

The **value chain** defined in this way is based on the core idea of Porter (2004b, p. 63). According to this idea, you can describe every company as a **collection of activities** through which products or services can be developed, produced, communicated, distributed, delivered and supported. The company-specific way in which the value chain is designed has a direct impact on its **profit margin**. Every change in the design of the supporting or core processes can therefore also influence the achievable profit margin, since this results from the difference between the achieved turnover and the costs used to create value. The more efficiently or

Fig. 4.17 Basic concept of a value chain. Source: Adapted from Porter (2004b)

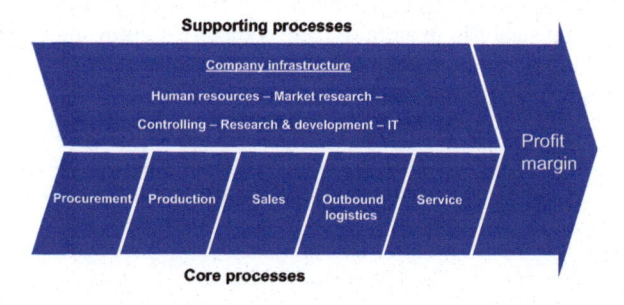

4.7 Value Chain Analysis

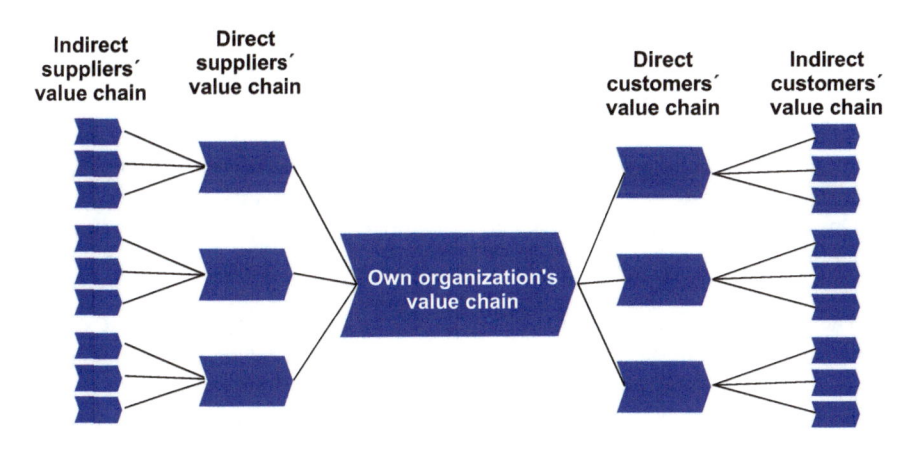

Fig. 4.18 System of value chains. Author's own figure

effectively the funds are used, the greater the value the company can achieve in terms of the profit margin. This makes it clear that any type of activity can be a source of competitive advantage, while the core processes have a particularly large potential.

It is important to note that the value chain of a company is not isolated but rather linked to the upstream and downstream value chains of suppliers and customers in many ways. Together they form a **system of value chains** (or a **value creation network**) which varies from sector to sector (cf. Fig. 4.18; Porter 2004b). Knowledge of the upstream and downstream value chains provides you with interesting starting points for shaping your own value chain to achieve further strategic advantages. This can be achieved by optimally linking one's own value chain with that of upstream and downstream service partners (suppliers and customers). This aspect of linking different value chains is intensively discussed in the context of industry and business 4.0, as well as the Internet of Things or rather Internet of Everything (cf. in more detail Kreutzer and Land 2015).

In larger companies, a **value chain analysis** can concentrate on a service area, a product group or individual strategic business units. This type of focus is required to achieve specific starting points for improving one's own competitive position. In the **first step of the analysis**, the following question areas are answered to determine the **status quo of your company**:

- Which activities are to be differentiated within the scope of value creation?
- Which of these activities represent core, supporting or quality assurance processes?
- Which costs are associated with the different activities?
- To what extent do these activities contribute to the improvement of the competitive position?
  – What customer benefits are generated?
  – What cost advantages result from these?

- Are the activities common in the industry? If not, do they generate a visible customer benefit?
- Are the activities of your own value chain optimally coordinated and linked with each other?
- Are there overlaps, avoidable dependencies and/or synergies that remain unused?
- Is your own value chain aligned with the value chain of your suppliers?
- Does your value chain consider the value chain of your own customers or the purchase criteria of end customers?

The answers to these questions provide indications to **optimise the cost structure** and to **increase the differentiation potential**, which enable your company to achieve competitive advantages. By comparing your own value chain with that of competitors, the value chain analysis can provide further important clues as to how your value chain system should be further developed. In the **second step of the analysis**, answers to the following questions can be used for a direct comparison with relevant competitors:

- What options are there for structuring the value chain within or outside your own industry?
- Which costs of a value chain step are offset by which competitive advantages in your company?
- How does the same value-added process work for competitors?
- Which costs of a value-added stage are offset by which customer advantages in your own company?
- How is the same value-added process structured for competitors?
- Which stages of the value chain must your company perform itself and which can be outsourced (to suppliers, outsourcing partners or buyers)?

Based on the value chain or value-added chain differences identified, you can determine concrete actions to improve your own competitive position in the **third step of the analysis**. On the one hand, it is necessary to identify **areas to reduce costs** by pinpointing product features and/or service areas that generate costs but no relevant customer benefit. Indications of how costs can result from a reduction in the number of variations, from modular production or from a combination of production volumes can also become evident.

On the other hand, you can determine **actions needed to differentiate your own services** from competition. Lastly, it is also possible to identify **ways to optimise the value chain interfaces** both within and outside your company. This highlights activities that should be delegated to suppliers or customers outside your area of responsibility. Additionally, previously outsourced activities that should be reintegrated in a value-adding and/or cost-reducing way may also be identified.

These **actions** illustrate how a value chain analysis is linked to strategy development (cf. Sect. 3.2). Moreover, the insights gained through the SWOT analysis or benchmarking could also contribute in designing the course of action. This information will back up the development of formulating competitive strategies.

4.7 Value Chain Analysis

Based on this type of value chain analysis, it becomes evident why some of the low-cost carriers (such as *easyJet* and *Ryanair*) can generate significant profits despite offering often considerably lower ticket prices than classic airlines such as *Lufthansa* or *Air France KLM*. The following activities explain why the **value chain of low-cost carriers'** costs significantly less, about 50%, than those of classic airlines:

- **Concentration on a few aircraft models or on a single model** (this simplifies service, spare parts supply and flight personnel training)
- **Offer point-to-point connections** (i.e. directly between individual cities, without regional or global network connections), eliminating time-consuming and costly personnel and baggage transfers
- **Significantly lower turnaround times** (the time between landing and restart is often only 25 min)
- **More flying hours per day** (which enables higher revenues and less stand fees at airports)
- **Elimination of many services**, such as a frequent flyer programme, free newspapers and magazines and free food for passengers (on the contrary, food becomes a source of revenue during flights)
- **Higher seat density** (so that more passengers can be transported per flight)
- **Purely online processes** (i.e. no sales offices; if tickets are sold via travel agencies, customers usually must pay a certain amount to them; baggage details and check-in processes for obtaining boarding passes can only be done online; additional costs are incurred at the airport for printing them, e.g. at *Ryanair*)
- **Landing at airports outside the city** (particularly with *Ryanair*, e.g. with "Frankfurt/Hahn", where the Frankfurt airport is 120 km away from the one in Hahn; this strategy is currently being changed by *Ryanair*)

The large number of differences in services within the value chain enables low-cost carriers to often provide the "flight" much more cost-effectively than so-called network carriers and still operate profitably.

> **Remember Box**
> Value chain analysis is a very important tool for determining cost differences and differentiation points between different companies. This allows a deep comparison of your own business model with that of competitors. This can provide important insights to further develop your own value chain.

Nowadays digitalisation makes it possible, and in many cases necessary, to complement the classic value chain with a **digital (information) value chain**. Figure 4.19 illustrates how this can be done. The physical value chain is equally penetrated and enriched by a digital value chain. In this way, various efficiency and effectiveness reserves in the value chain can be put into practice. These reserves must also be examined during the value chain analysis.

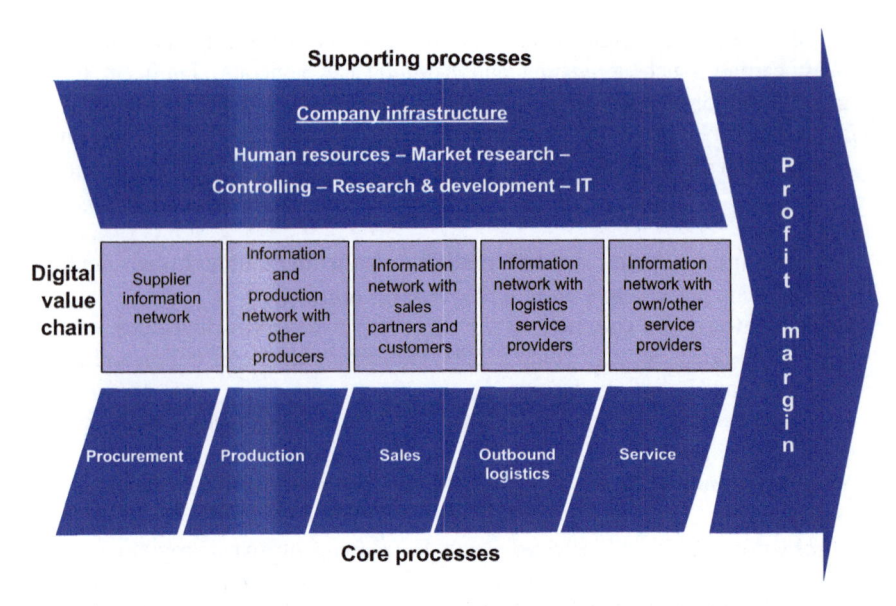

Fig. 4.19 Physical and digital value chain. Author's own figure

> **Remember Box**
> The physical value chain is increasingly penetrated by a digital value chain. Therefore, it must also be integrated into the value chain analysis.

▶ **Implementation Tips**

- The value chain analysis supports you in a complex process of systematically identifying the cost advantages and customer benefits of your competitors.
- The use of this method is always necessary when competitive advantages are lost and/or new competitors (with different value chains) enter the market.
- Step-by-step the various levels are first defined and then examined to gain a deep understanding of the value creation of your relevant competitors.
- Consulting firms that have a deep knowledge of the value creation processes of suppliers in an industry can also often help carry out this analysis.

4.8 Gap Analysis

The **gap analysis** is a simple tool that allows you to both analyse and visualise your goals. In the planning process, this enables you to check to which extent you are achieving your goals based on your existing business. Furthermore, you can see how large the strategic gap is that needs to be filled by new activities. These results can be directly used to develop customer-oriented strategies (see Sect. 3.2).

You carry out the gap analysis in several stages. In the **first step "Definition of the target level"**, you determine which sales or profit targets (or better EBITDA) you seek. In this case, the starting point could be the current turnover or EBITDA. Depending on the expectations of your management and/or your stakeholders, you can then define which sales volume or EBITDA you want to achieve in 5 years (top line in Fig. 4.20).

In **step 2 "Forecasting the further development of the existing business"**, an estimate is made of how sales or EBITDA will develop if no major changes occur. The findings of other analytical methods can be incorporated into this forecast. This line is labelled in Fig. 4.20 with "Turnover/EBITDA from existing business (actual and forecasted)".

In **step 3 "Derivation of the action gap"**, the focus is on the difference between the long-term target figure and the value that will be achieved by simply continuing the activities of the status quo. This gap is visible in Fig. 4.20. This also shows that the existing business is expected to decline as of 2023.

In **step 4 "Defining measures"**, you must develop strategic measures so that the action gap can be closed. Again, these measures can be influenced by the results of other analysis tools to support decisions in customer-oriented strategies (see Sect. 3.2).

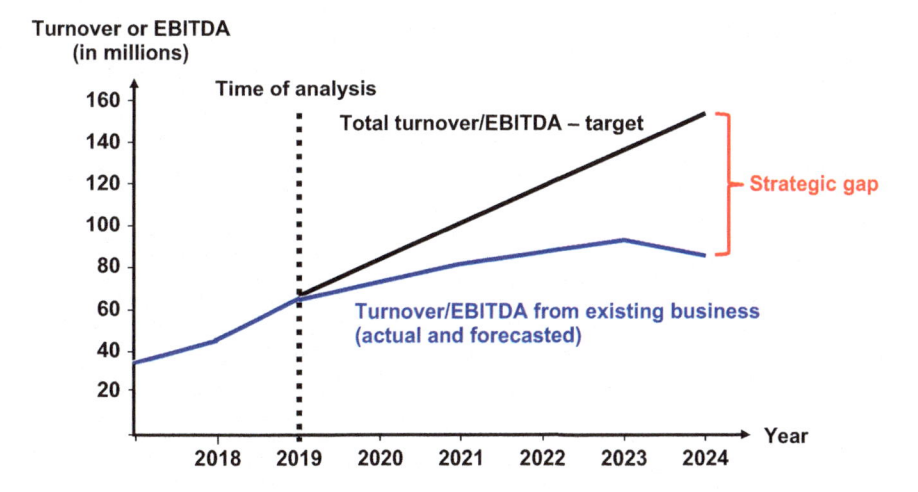

Fig. 4.20 Gap analysis. Author's own figure

> **Remember Box**
> With gap analysis, you can very easily determine to what extent the existing business is sufficient to achieve future financial goals. It enables you to underline the need to start thinking today so that future performance gaps can be closed. This approach can be an important trigger for processing innovations on horizon levels 2 and 3 (see Sect. 3.5.3).

▶ **Implementation Tips**

- The starting point for this analysis is quantifiable company goals, which you can and must actively demand for such an analysis.
- It is important that the target figures of the existing business activities are not simply extrapolated, i.e. updated unchanged, but that a realistic forecast is made.
- Only then can the actual strategic gap be identified and activities initiated to close it.
- Those who lie to themselves about the development of the status quo, and act accordingly less energetically, will be punished even harder later!

4.9 Customer Journey Map

Another important analysis tool is the **customer journey map**. It visualises the process that a person goes through from the first latent need to the act of purchasing and using a product or service. The visualisation helps to recognise the relevant customer needs, as well as possible "pain points".

The starting point for creating a customer journey map is **personas**, which were already defined in Sect. 3.2.3. Next, it is necessary to develop a specific customer journey map for each persona. To do so, you must first define which scenario is to be assumed on a rough timeline from, i.e. with which goals the persona begins the customer journey and which actions are carried out within it. It is also important that the map includes the thoughts and emotions of the users, which are expressed in the different phases.

All these findings will ultimately be incorporated into the **design of the customer journey map**. This links two tools, namely, **storytelling** and **visualisation**. This allows relevant information to be prepared in a "user-friendly" way, because journey mapping creates a **holistic view of the customer experience**. Figure 4.21 illustrates just how complex the customer touch points are that must be considered when creating a journey map nowadays. It becomes clear that the customer often no longer

4.9 Customer Journey Map

Fig. 4.21 Touch points of a customer journey. Author's own figure

differentiates between "online" and "offline" but exists in a "noline" world. We must keep this in mind in our analysis.

To create a **customer journey map**, you should put yourself in the shoes of the customer. Even if the journey maps differ depending on the specific context, they often follow a general model, as shown in Fig. 4.22. In **part 1** of the customer journey map, the "Who?" and "What?" are defined. At this stage you determine which concerns, goals and expectations the persona has at the start of the journey.

In **part 2**, the heart of the journey map, the various phases, actions, thoughts and the overall emotional experiences of the user throughout the entire journey are pinpointed with quotations and/or videos from marketing research. You must check at which customer touch points the persona finds exactly what they are looking for. Where can real customer enthusiasm perhaps even be achieved? At which touch points is the persona rather disappointed by the content provided?

> **Remember Box**
> Creating a customer journey map is a good training in empathy, if it cannot be based on relevant customer surveys! But in any case it is much better to develop a customer journey map based on relevant customer insights.

To find the relevant **content for the customer journey map**, you should answer the following questions:

- How is a need created for the persona with your offer?
- How and where does the persona obtain information in the "Zero Moment of Truth" (e.g. on evaluation platforms, from friends, in forums) before they visit the company's own touch points?

- What importance is attached to the circle of friends and social media?
- Which media does the persona use both online and offline?
- How credible does the persona consider the various information offerings to be?
- What is the significance of the various touch points within the customer journey?
- Which competitive offers are analysed to what extent and via which media?
- What expectations does the persona have of the offers of your company?

In addition to the actions themselves, it is also important to define the possible thoughts and emotional experiences of the persona. These **emotions** can be mentioned in the customer journey map in Fig. 4.22. A short **delineation of the thoughts behind these emotions** completes the picture. Additionally, you can note the **importance of the customer touch points** for the persona in the journey map by assigning values from 1 (low significance) to 5 (high significance). If you find that steps with high significance are rated very negatively on the customer journey, there is a need for action in part 3 (cf. Rainer 2018).

Lastly, in **part 3 insights and responsibilities for the company** can be identified (cf. Fig. 4.22). To improve the customer journey experience, it is first necessary to identify and eliminate possible negative experiences. To do so, it is important to clearly define which expectations customers have when they enter the customer journey. Only then you can satisfy these expectations.

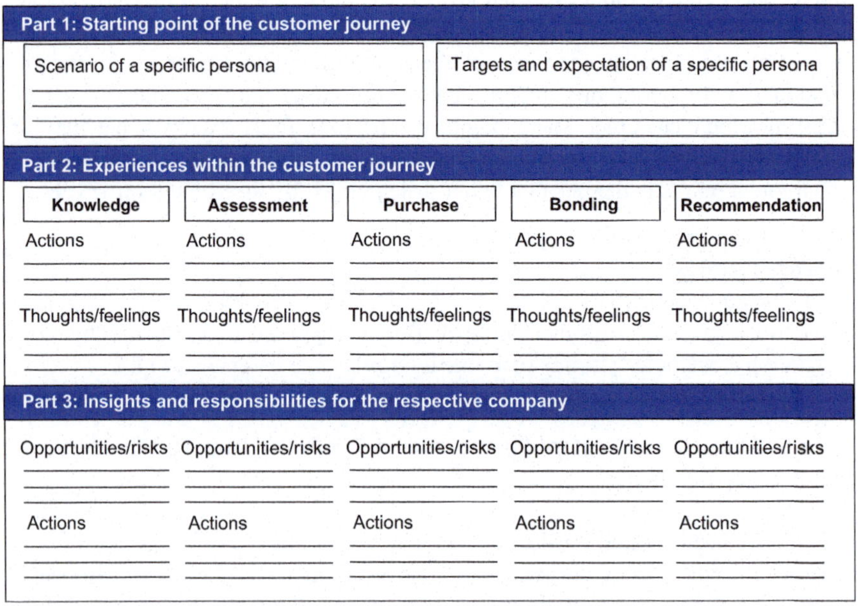

Part 1: Starting point of the customer journey	
Scenario of a specific persona	Targets and expectation of a specific persona

Part 2: Experiences within the customer journey				
Knowledge	Assessment	Purchase	Bonding	Recommendation
Actions	Actions	Actions	Actions	Actions
Thoughts/feelings	Thoughts/feelings	Thoughts/feelings	Thoughts/feelings	Thoughts/feelings

Part 3: Insights and responsibilities for the respective company				
Opportunities/risks	Opportunities/risks	Opportunities/risks	Opportunities/risks	Opportunities/risks
Actions	Actions	Actions	Actions	Actions

Fig. 4.22 Basic concept of a customer journey map. Source: Adapted from Kaplan (2016)

Remember Box
The customer journey map is an essential element if you want to see how your customers find your offers. This not only reveals relevant customer paths but also necessary fields of action.

Based on the insights of the customer journey map, it is important to build up a positive **customer experience** across all or at least many levels (cf. Rusnjak and Schallmo 2018; Kreutzer 2018b). This starts by simply subscribing to a newsletter, making an appointment or downloading interesting information, right through to an online or offline purchase. It is always important to integrate elements of enthusiasm into the customer journey (cf. Sect. 3.4 about the Kano concept).

▶ **Implementation Tips**

- To align marketing concepts with customer expectations, you should develop customer journey maps because they offer an exciting and highly informative framework for action.
- You should involve employees from communication, service, sales and product management areas when developing these maps so that the picture obtained is as holistic as possible.
- Based on the insights gained, you must determine how to manage the customer experience, an approach that is to be developed across different departments.
- You should eliminate possible information and activity silos in your own company, regardless of whether you consider them holistic or not, because all experiences become integrated for the customer, if not before!

4.10 Digital Maturity Analysis

In the digital age, a **digital maturity analysis** is particularly important. This analysis enables you to determine how "fit" or how "mature" your company is for survival when it comes to the challenges of digitisation (cf. Kreutzer and Land 2015, 2017a; Kreutzer et al. 2018). The **digital maturity model** was developed by *Neuland* in cooperation with the *Research Center for Digital Business* at *Reutlingen University*. The digital maturity of a company can be determined based on 32 individual criteria. By using this method, you can determine fields of action and concrete optimisation potentials in individual areas of your company. The findings of the digital maturity model provide the basis for the development of a digital roadmap.

Figure 4.23 describes the basic concept of the **digital maturity model**. To apply it, you analyse the "digital" design of eight different **dimensions**. Each of these dimensions is assigned one of five different states of development. If a company is "**unaware**", it does not realise the relevance of the corresponding dimension. The

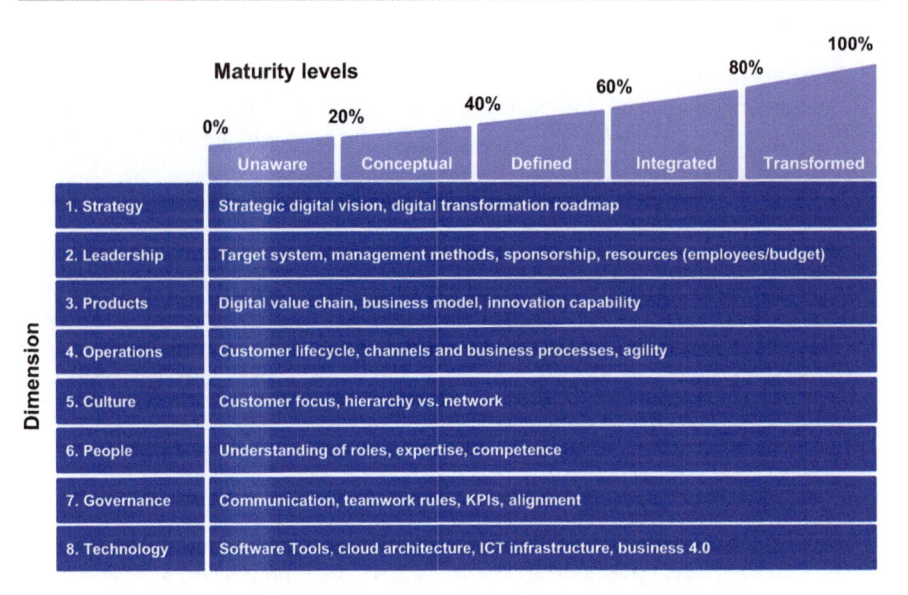

Dimension	Maturity levels					
	0% Unaware	20% Conceptual	40% Defined	60% Integrated	80% Transformed	100%
1. Strategy	Strategic digital vision, digital transformation roadmap					
2. Leadership	Target system, management methods, sponsorship, resources (employees/budget)					
3. Products	Digital value chain, business model, innovation capability					
4. Operations	Customer lifecycle, channels and business processes, agility					
5. Culture	Customer focus, hierarchy vs. network					
6. People	Understanding of roles, expertise, competence					
7. Governance	Communication, teamwork rules, KPIs, alignment					
8. Technology	Software Tools, cloud architecture, ICT infrastructure, business 4.0					

Fig. 4.23 Digital maturity model. Source: Adapted from Peyman et al. (2014, p. 38)

"**conceptual**" state shows that conceptual considerations have already been made in the company for the corresponding dimension. "**Defined**" means the company is already one step further and has created goals, measures and schedules. In the "**integrated**" state, relevant "digital" solutions that have already been integrated are documented. "**Transformed**" is the highest level, for which the necessary changes are already integrated into the company's workflow and organisational structure.

The **first component of the model "Strategy"** measures the maturity level of the corporate digital strategy. It is a core task of corporate management to develop a digital strategy that takes disruptive technological developments and changes in customer behaviour into account. To implement it, you must not only document this digital strategy within the company but also communicate it across all company hierarchies by using a **transformation roadmap**. This strategy can only unfold its transformational effect if it is understood in its entirety by all service providers. Therefore, the digital strategy must also be integrated into the corporate strategy. Awareness of digital transformation throughout the entire organisation is also evaluated in this process.

The **second component of the model "Leadership"** focuses on the role that a company's management team plays in implementing the strategy. The core task of top and middle management is to recognise the relevance of new technologies and to create awareness throughout the company of the necessity of (digital) change. The **management's commitment** to this change, the extent of the functional areas involved and the prevailing leadership culture are important indicators of whether the change management process will be successful.

The third **component of the model "Products"** analyses the extent to which the digital transformation has already taken place in the range of products and services. Among other things, you determine to what extent the degree of innovation of the business model, relative customer advantages and cost superiority over competitors can be attributed to the achieved **depth of digitalisation of the value-added processes** and the end products created by them. The entire range of products and services must be reviewed to see where digitisation can lead to customer benefits and/or cost superiority. Additionally, "digital offers" can top off the product and service range. You must also examine whether the **digitisation of the value chain** is falsely interpreted as a pure "efficiency project" and not as an opportunity to develop innovative product and service concepts.

The fourth **component of the model "Operations"** examines how flexibly business processes can be aligned to new challenges. Furthermore, the extent to which digital channels are already being used internally and/or externally to network value chains is analysed (cf. Sect. 4.7). To create **seamless customer experiences** ("seamless integration"), you must promote the **digitalisation of core processes**. To this end, it is necessary to determine to what extent data and process silos, particularly silos in people's minds, have already been overcome. Moreover, it is essential to examine whether new **technological possibilities** are constantly being investigated regarding their contribution to the company's value creation and, if they contribute positively, whether they are being integrated into company processes. Additionally, you must verify the extent to which the resources required for implementation (especially budgets and personnel) are available.

Every employee of a company must make a multitude of decisions during a working day. Not all these decision-making processes can be regulated using clear guidelines. An example of this is deciding which customer or project should be given a higher priority. When making these decisions employees often refer to the fifth **component of the model "Culture"**, which is based on specific values of the company. In this way, the corporate culture has a direct impact on the daily workflow. It is therefore important that this culture already contains "digital DNA"!

Thus, you should check whether an **innovation culture** already exists in the company to promote digital change. The corporate culture can either brake or accelerate innovation. Concepts, such as the development of "internal incubators" which integrate customers into the innovation process, and other forms of open innovation make it possible to think outside the box. The "Culture" dimension therefore examines how this is structured in terms of transparency, dynamism, communication intensity and willingness to change (cf. Kreutzer et al. 2018).

Remember Box

> Culture eats strategy for breakfast.
> Peter Drucker

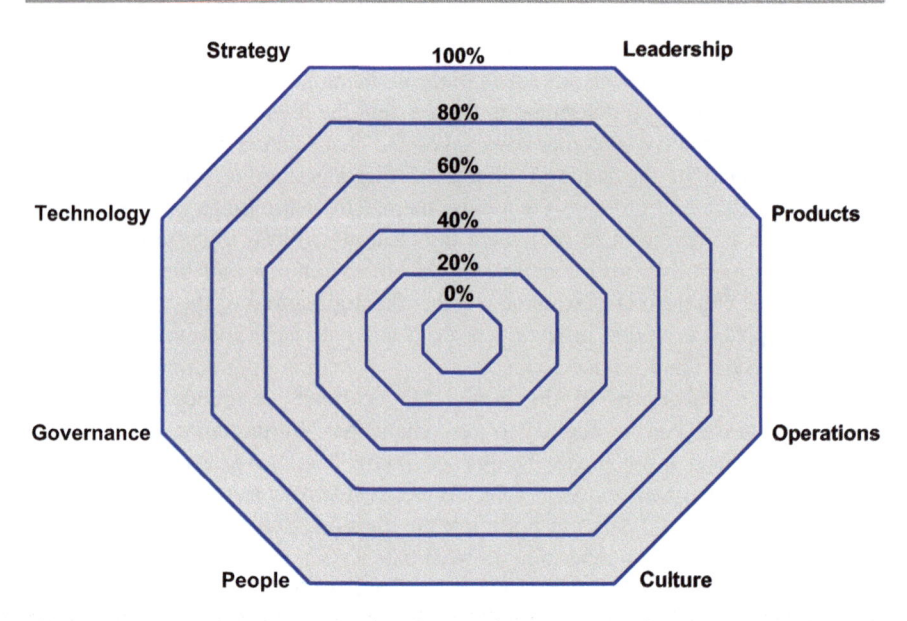

Fig. 4.24 Analysis grid to determine digital maturity. Author's own figure

The sixth **component of the model "People"** analyses how comprehensively it has already been possible to build up digital expertise in the workforce and embrace corresponding learning processes within the company. After all, **new skills** are required in the digital (working) world. For the transformation process, people with "digital know-how" must be placed at central points in the company. You can implement **reverse mentoring** so that young employees can train "older" employees in social media. Furthermore, you must ensure that the resources necessary for the digital transformation are available.

A digital strategy cannot be implemented without an appropriately designed corporate management system. The seventh **component of the model "Governance"** is used to determine the digital strategy is implemented across departments and divisions in both a mandatory and holistic way. Additionally, this step requires you to analyse which control tools are used to measure this. A key prerequisite for implementation is that the **goals of the digital strategy** are measurably defined. Furthermore, all managers must agree that implementing the digital strategy is part of the targets.

Digital technologies can be important "enablers" and thus "supporters" of digital transformation. To succeed, it is therefore crucial to use the necessary technology for data analysis, cross-channel management, process automation and setting up ecosystems, for instance. This is the aim of the eighth **component of the model "Technology"**. At this stage, one of the key questions is to what extent you have already been able to integrate the further development of your IT infrastructure or corresponding cloud solutions as a core area into the digital roadmap. Through their cross-channel interaction (offline-online), customers define new customer management requirements that need to be mapped technologically. The requirements for this further development will therefore largely be driven by the market, customers and thus marketing, and require a flexible design of the supporting systems.

How well your company is positioned overall can be summarised in an **analysis grid to determine digital maturity** shown in Fig. 4.24.

> **Remember Box**
> Even though it is often painful, it is necessary to examine your own "digital maturity". Only this type of analysis can ensure that a crucial digital transformation is based on the "true" status quo rather than speculations.

▶ **Implementation Tips**

- Considering the challenges of the digital age, you should analyse your company based on the dimensions of the digital maturity model soon, the sooner the better!
- It is recommended that every company involve external resources to (critically) analyse its own status quo.
- Based on the findings in the dimensions Strategy, Leadership, Products, Operations, Culture, People, Governance and Technology, you must define concrete actions and create roadmaps to facilitate them.
- To ensure a targeted execution of the defined tasks, you must review the progress on a quarterly basis.
- It is important that the top management is fully committed given the importance of the digital transformation.
- This integration should not be limited to the reporting routines but should also include playing an active role in processing the digital roadmaps.

References

Altobelli, C. F. (2017). *Marktforschung, Methoden – Anwendungen – Praxisbeispiele* (3rd ed.). Munich: UVK.
Backhaus, K., Erichson, B., Plinke, W., & Weiber, R. (2015). *Multivariate Analysemethoden: Eine anwendungsorientierte Einführung* (14th ed.). Heidelberg: Springer.
Bruhn, M., & Hadwich, K. (2017). *Produkt- und Servicemanagement* (2nd ed.). Munich: Vahlen.
Fritz, W., & Oelsnitz, D. (2006). *Marketing, Elemente marktorientierter Unternehmensführung* (4. Aufl.). Stuttgart.
Gartner. (2018). *5 Trends emerge in the Gartner hype cycle for emerging technologies, 2018*. Accessed December 17, 2018, from https://www.gartner.com/smarterwithgartner/5-trends-emerge-in-gartner-hype-cycle-for-emerging-technologies-2018/

Kaplan, K. (2016). *When and how to create customer journey maps.* Accessed March 21, 2018, from https://www.nngroup.com/articles/customer-journey-mapping/

Koch, J., Gebhardt, P., & Riedmüller, F. (2016). *Marktforschung: Grundlagen und praktische Anwendungen* (7th ed.). Berlin: De Gruyter.

Kreutzer, R. (2018a). *Praxisorientiertes online-marketing, Konzepte – Instrumente – Checklisten* (3rd ed.). Wiesbaden: Springer.

Kreutzer, R. (2018b). Customer experience management – wie man Kunden begeistern kann. In A. Rusnjak & D. R. A. Schallmo (Hrsg.), *Customer experience im Zeitalter des Kunden, best practices, lessons learned und Forschungsergebnisse* (pp. 95–119). Wiesbaden: Springer.

Kreutzer, R., & Land, K.-H. (2015). *Digital Darwinism, branding and business models in Jeopardy.* New York: Springer.

Kreutzer, R., & Land, K.-H. (2017a). *Dematerialization – The redistribution of the world in times of digital Darwinism.* Cologne: neuland GmbH & Co. KG. und WirtschaftsWoche.

Kreutzer, R., & Land, K.-H. (2017b). *Digital Branding – Konzeption einer holistischen Markenführung.* Wiesbaden: Springer.

Kreutzer, R., Neugebauer, T., & Pattloch, A. (2018). *Digital business leadership – Digital transformation – Business model innovation – Agile organization – Change-management.* Wiesbaden: Springer.

Markowitz, H. (1952). Portfolio selection. *Journal of Finance, 7*(1), 77–91.

Müller, H.-E. (2017). *Unternehmensführung, Strategie – Management – Praxis* (3rd ed.). Munich: De Gruyter.

Naderer, G., & Balzer, E. (2011). *Qualitative Marktforschung in Theorie und Praxis: Grundlagen, Methoden und Anwendungen* (2nd ed.). Wiesbaden: Springer.

Pepels, W. (2016). *Produktmanagement: A. Neue Produkte am Markt einführen – B. Marken erfolgreich managen – C. Produktprogramme planen und kontrollieren – D. Strukturen und Prozesse implementieren* (7th ed.). Berlin: Duncker & Humblot.

Peyman, A. K., Faraby, N., Rossmann, A., Steimel, B., & Wichmann, K. S. (2014). *Digital transformation report 2014.* Cologne: neuland GmbH & Co. KG. und WirtschaftsWoche.

Porter, M. E. (2004a). *Competitive strategy: Techniques for analyzing industries and competitors.* New York: Free Press.

Porter, M. E. (2004b). *Competitive advantage: Creating and sustaining superior performance.* New York: Free Press.

Rainer, K. (2018). *6 einfache Schritte, um eine Customer Journey Map zu erstellen.* Accessed March 21, 2018, from https://www.chimpify.de/marketing/customer-journey-map-erstellen/

Rechtien, W. (1999). *Angewandte Gruppendynamik* (3rd ed.). Weinheim: Beltz.

Rusnjak, A., & Schallmo, D. R. A. (Hrsg.). (2018). *Customer experience im Zeitalter des Kunden, best practices, lessons learned und Forschungsergebnisse.* Wiesbaden: Springer.

Weis, H. C., & Steinmetz, P. (2012). *Marktforschung* (8th ed.). Ludwigshafen.

Forecasting Methods 5

One of the great challenges in planning is to be able to "predict" the future. After all, you develop strategies and measures, which will be implemented in the future and whose effects will only occur then. Therefore, it is essential that you face possible developments. Various proven measures are available to you to do so.

5.1 Trend Extrapolation

Trend extrapolation is a frequently intuitively applied measure, which does not change current developments and projects them in the future, according to the **motto** "more of the same". The following example demonstrates the "foolishness" of such a rigid approach. With a sailing ship, "more of the same" would lead to a situation in which one would advance too much faster with ten sails than with one or two sails, which, however, is not true!

More precisely, trend extrapolation is the extrapolation of a time series, based on the assumption that the trend underlying a development in the past will continue unchanged in the future. In this time series analysis, empirically observed series from the past are projected into the future with their past regularities, thus "extrapolated". This extrapolation can be done manually by extending a trend line determined in the past, as is the case in Fig. 5.1. This trend line can also be determined using statistical methods if the past development is not as easy to extrapolate as in Fig. 5.1.

> **Remember Box**
> If we are honest with ourselves, we must admit that we often implicitly make such trend extrapolations in our everyday lives. This procedure of simply
>
> (continued)

continuing an existing development is quite simply human nature. However, today, we are in the digital age, the age of disruption with the associated developments and structural breaks.

In this case, "disruption" means the "destruction" of products, services and entire business models by new developments (cf. Kreutzer and Land 2015). The replacement of CDs by streaming services, the threat to traditional retailing from online shops and the (partial) replacement of newspapers and magazines by online offerings could not be predicted by trend extrapolations. This is because trend extrapolation can neither predict a trend reversal nor structural breaks!

Remember Box
Nowadays, you should avoid using trend extrapolation uncritically given the increasing acceleration of changes, especially when we extend trend lines rather intuitively and thus without reflection. This happens more often than we think.

▶ **Implementation Tips**

- You should refrain from using trend extrapolation if it is not very clearly foreseeable that the trends of the past will actually continue unchanged in the future.
- However, in the disruptive age of digitisation, this stability of developments is increasingly unlikely.
- Watch that such unreviewed trend extrapolations made by yourself are not included in your statements. If so, then veto them or question the conclusions based on them.

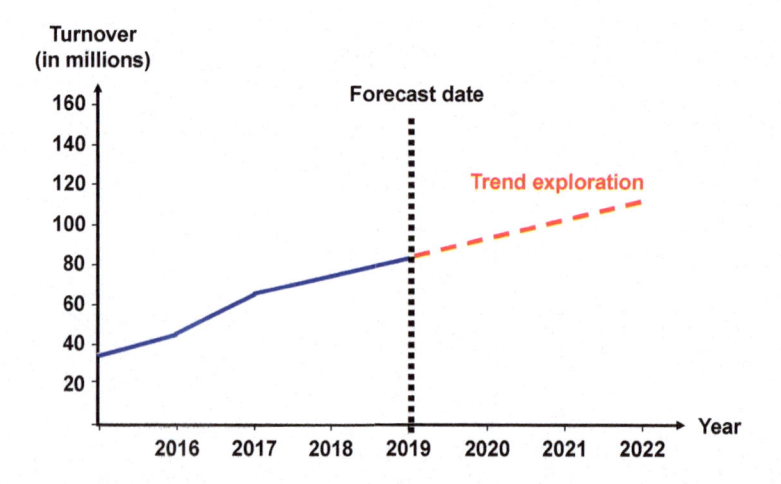

Fig. 5.1 Trend extrapolation. Author's own figure

5.2 Scenario Analysis

A much more meaningful forecasting method is the **scenario analysis**. The core idea behind the scenario technique is that **several possible future scenarios** are developed and described.

> **Remember Box**
> Scenario analysis offers the opportunity to say goodbye to **one** expected future and instead present alternative development opportunities. This enables you to make the uncertainty of the forecaster visible to everyone and thus encourage discussion.

The visualisation of the possible developments takes place in a **scenario funnel**. Relevant future developments based on different assumptions are presented in this funnel, and several trend scenarios are derived. Consequently, the scenario funnel in Fig. 5.2 does not show an exact picture of the future but rather visualises the existing uncertainty by showing various possible developments and results. In scenario development, a distinction is often made between an optimistic scenario (**best case**), a pessimistic scenario (**worst case**) and a realistic or particularly probable scenario (**realistic case**).

It is important that the scenario analysis also shows the development paths, including possible critical events, which lead to the different results. Only then is it possible to understand what can lead to the different scenarios.

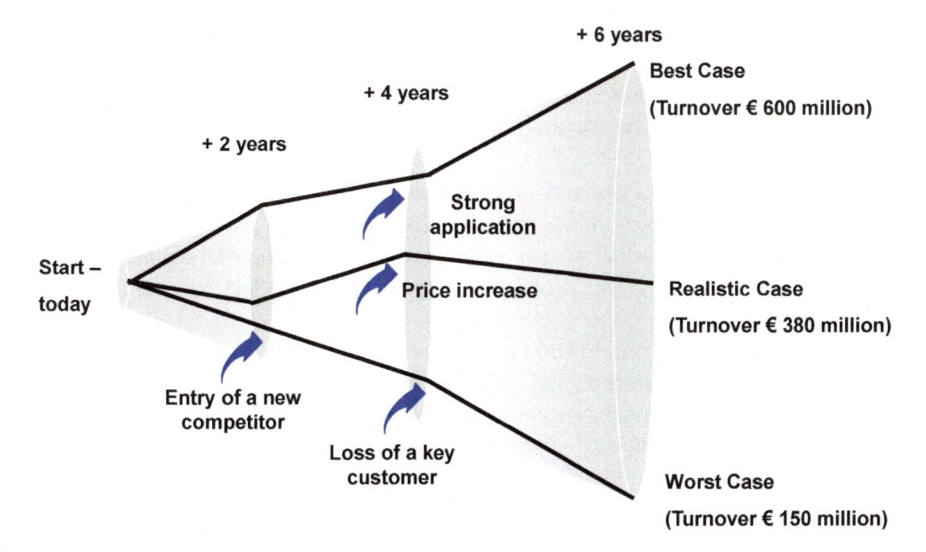

Fig. 5.2 Scenario analysis. Author's own figure

> **Remember Box**
> In most cases, three different scenarios are sufficient to align your company to possible challenges in the future. It also allows for the integration of disruptive developments in the scenarios.

This makes it clear that scenario analysis is not an extrapolation of the past and is not based on historical data. When creating the various scenarios, it is not assumed without examination whether the observations from the past will still be valid in the future. Instead, the scenario analysis tries to identify possible developments and turning points, e.g. the development of an alternative technology (e.g. the breakthrough in autonomous driving), the entry of a new competitor (e.g. from India) or the development of a ground-breaking application case (e.g. for 3D applications in medicine).

Yet, you must remember that the further the view is in the future, the greater the uncertainty. This results in the typical **scenario funnel** (cf. in-depth application in the digital age Kreutzer et al. 2018, pp. 173–175).

> **Remember Box**
> Managers often overestimate the short-term effects of new developments and significantly underestimate their long-term effects.

▶ **Implementation Tips**

- Whereas in the past scenarios were developed for long development periods of 10, 20 and more years, in the current day and age, you must develop the scenarios for a much shorter period.
- Due to the dynamics of globalisation and digitisation, nowadays, the scenarios must be oriented towards the near future of about 2 to 5 years.
- Due to the exponentiality of many developments, you are unable to make forecasts for longer periods in many areas.
- You should develop such scenarios together with top management, marketing, sales and product development, supported by external partners.
- External partners help you to see developments that counteract your own business interests (keyword "disruption") and are therefore often (consciously) ignored by your own company.
- Based on the defined scenarios, different strategic responses must then be developed to ensure that you are prepared should these various scenarios occur.
- The scenarios developed should be combined with the findings of the three-horizon model.

5.3 Analogy Forecast

Analogy is a special form of forecasting. On its own, the term stands for the coincidence of objects or certain characteristics. When using analogies to forecast, you try to learn about the future by making historical comparisons from the past. This assumes that two different phenomena will show a similar development (cf. Keegan and Green 2017, pp. 219f.; Kreutzer 2017, pp. 37f.).

> **Remember Box**
> With a forecast based on analogies, one tries to predict future developments based on behavioural patterns of the same or similar products or services in the past and possibly in other countries.

The basis for **predicting the sale of a new product or service** may be the sale of a similar offer already on the market. The underlying assumption is that the development of sales of these two products will be similar. This is essentially the analogy used. Analogies can also be implemented when it comes to the **expected acceptance of a new technology**. It implies that the acceptance and the expected development of different market segments in Germany (e.g. for the use of music streaming) can be predicted based on the already existing acceptance of this technology in the Scandinavian countries (cf. Fig. 5.3). You should consider the following questions when using this method:

- Based on the market success in the Scandinavian countries, what demand for streaming services can be expected in Germany?

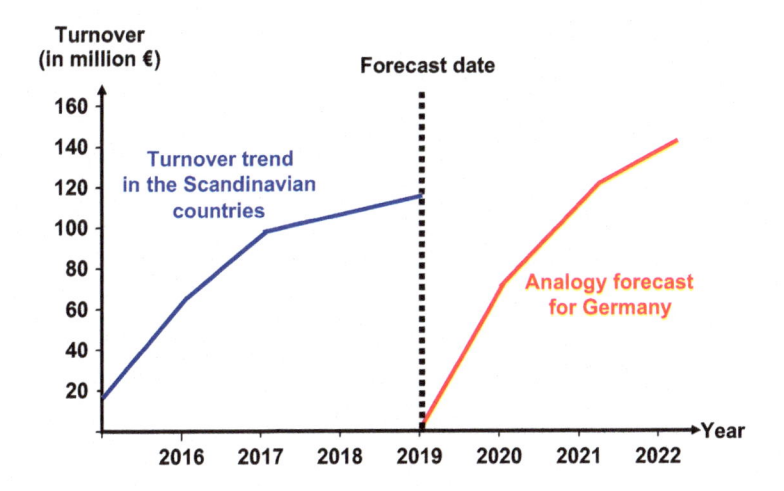

Fig. 5.3 Analogy forecast. Author's own figure

- When can we expect the same level of market penetration in Germany as in the Scandinavian countries?
- Based on the findings in the Scandinavian countries, at which point can initial saturation tendencies be expected for this product in Germany?

When drawing a conclusion using an analogy, you must check whether the necessary prerequisites for the transfer from one product/service to another or from one country to another are met. This includes a comparable openness to technical innovations, as well as a comparable price level for both eBooks and eBook readers.

> **Remember Box**
> When analogies are used, you must ensure that the products/services and/or countries used for the comparison are in fact comparable. Only then can reliable findings be obtained.

▶ **Implementation Tips**

- Analogy forecasting is an effective tool to forecast new developments in your home market, if similar developments can already be observed in other countries.
- It is important that you pay attention to the comparability of the analysed phenomena, so that you don't make any nonsense forecasts.
- Such analogies can be very helpful for a good prognostic approach to new phenomena, because uncertainties about future developments are systematically reduced.

5.4 Delphi Method

The **Delphi method** involves much more effort than the previously described forecasting methods. It is often referred to as a Delphi study or a Delphi survey. The eponym of this approach is the ancient oracle of Delphi, which caused some historical surprises due to its ambiguous predictions! Today, the Delphi method is mostly used to forecast trends, estimate technological developments and predict the future communication, mobility and/or housing behaviour of larger sections of the population or even mankind.

Essentially, the Delphi method is a systematic and multistage survey, usually conducted by experts in the field under investigation. Feedback between the various rounds of the survey is an integral component. The surveyed specialists are provided with the consolidated results of the other experts involved in the Delphi study as input for the next forecast round.

More precisely, the process unfolds as follows (see Fig. 5.4). After determining the research object and formulating research questions, you define relevant experts

5.4 Delphi Method

from the respective research area and recruit them for the survey. Often ten or more experts take part in this type of Delphi study. They are presented with a list of questions and/or assumptions about the object under investigation. In two or more rounds of surveys, the experts are given the opportunity to express their opinion anonymously. This is to avoid coordination between the participants of the study.

> **Remember Box**
> The Delphi method is a multistage survey of experts to address complex questions. Feedback sessions between the survey rounds are used to achieve a resilient result.

After the first round of the survey, you provide all participants with feedback to further stimulate the creative process. Based on the assessments of all the experts, certain assumptions, mean values and other forms of result summaries are presented. There is also the possibility of questioning extreme views and assessments. However, this **pressure to conform** is seen as a point of criticism of the method, because opinions and extreme positions may be "straightened out". Based on the consolidated results, the experts can again make their assessments and statements. This is often followed by a second and possibly a third feedback session. The results are consolidated and documented at the end of the last survey round. Depending on the objective of the study, the results are published publicly or only made available to a smaller audience.

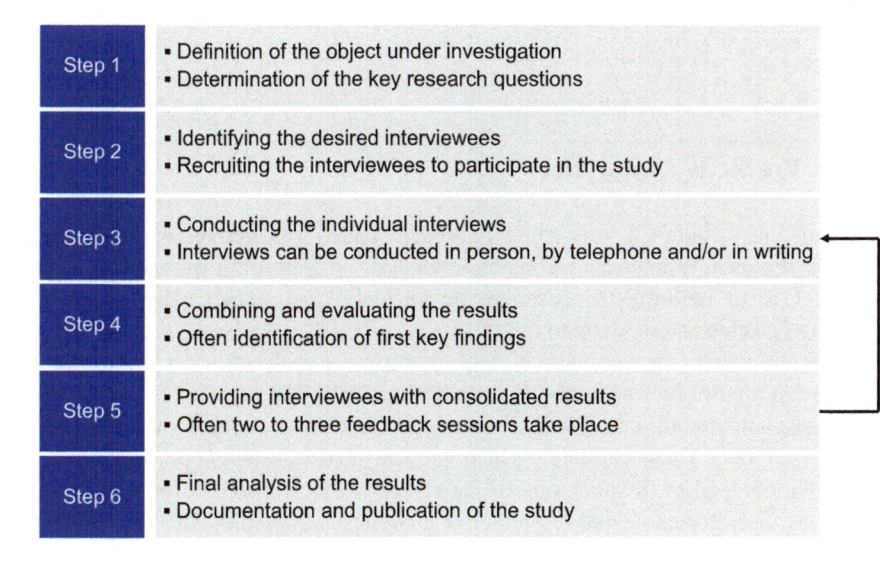

Step	Description
Step 1	• Definition of the object under investigation • Determination of the key research questions
Step 2	• Identifying the desired interviewees • Recruiting the interviewees to participate in the study
Step 3	• Conducting the individual interviews • Interviews can be conducted in person, by telephone and/or in writing
Step 4	• Combining and evaluating the results • Often identification of first key findings
Step 5	• Providing interviewees with consolidated results • Often two to three feedback sessions take place
Step 6	• Final analysis of the results • Documentation and publication of the study

Fig. 5.4 Delphi method. Author's own figure

It is necessary to mention some critical aspects regarding the Delphi method. Firstly, you must question how the "experts" are selected. Since the experts in Delphi studies remain anonymous, they cannot shine in their knowledge community with their statements and will therefore not always choose to take part in such an elaborate study (or only with monetary incentives). Additionally, experts can also represent one-sided opinions when advising companies or associations at the same time. This possible distortion effect is not visible due to the anonymity of the experts. Therefore, while it is difficult to prove, the selection of experts influences the possible result.

It has often been confirmed that particularly experts clearly overestimate the speed of developments, because they themselves deal with them intensively and conclude that they can be implemented quickly. Moreover, despite anonymity, group effects can come into play. Due to the previously mentioned pressure to conform, those who make an extreme assessment must justify this subsequently, even if they are right. This could result in important individual opinions being straightened out and thus invisible during the multistage process.

▶ **Implementation Tips**

- You should critically examine whether it is worthwhile for you and the questions you have determined to design and conduct a Delphi study on the side, which is usually associated with high financial and coordination costs.
- Conducting this type of study for an entire industry or in a larger market in combination with other companies often leads to more productivity and is easier to finance.
- You may also be able to access existing Delphi studies that cover relevant areas.

5.5 Predictive Analytics

In recent years, another forecasting approach, called **predictive analytics**, has become increasingly important. Predictive analytics differs from **descriptive analytics** (classical reporting to describe the "actual") and **prescriptive analytics** (deriving possible action alternatives).

Generally using large amounts of data, prescriptive analytics is an area of **data mining** that focuses on forecasting future developments. The term Big Data refers to these large amounts of data. Predictive analytics focuses on several variables (also called predictors). These variables, which are measured for a single person, a group of people, companies or other objects being analysed, are used to predict future behaviour. Therefore, the goal of predictive analytics is to predict what will happen and why.

5.5 Predictive Analytics

> **Remember Box**
> Predictive analytics are forecasts that are calculated based on, generally large, amounts of data using various mathematical methods.

Thus, to implement predictive analytics, you must have an extensive amount of historical and current data. This can come from your company (including a data warehouse), as well as from other relevant sources. You can use different methods of univariate, bivariate and multivariate data analysis to evaluate this data. These include methods such as neuronal networks, as well as regression and cluster analyses.

In this area, the term **machine learning** has a special meaning. This is a specific form of artificial intelligence, since computer programmes based on machine learning can independently develop solutions for new and unknown problems using algorithms. More specifically, this means that computer programmes develop knowledge and experience "artificially" and thus "independently". It enables a programme to first learn based on historical data and then review the knowledge gained using new data and further develop it independently, without programmers having to intervene again. It is necessary that programmes recognise new patterns and principles from the data, so that they can be used as the basis for future forecasts. This is also referred to as knowledge discovery (see Kreutzer and Sirrenberg 2019).

Predictive analytics can be **applied in a variety of ways**. For example, a bank can use predicators to determine the creditworthiness of a potential debtor before **granting a loan**. The variables age, gender, duration of the current employment, amount of liabilities, number of credit cards, etc. are used as predictors. The default probability of the loan can be determined based on a complex analysis model. Generally, this probability affects whether the loan will be granted, as well as the required collateral (securities) and the interest rate.

It can also be used in the **"Next Best Offer" concept** for a customer. Using the past behaviour of a customer, the next offer with the highest purchase probability for this person is determined on a one-to-one basis. The person then receives exactly this offer via the most successful channel, whether it be through an e-mail, mailing, telephone call, push message or coupon (cf. Kreutzer 2016).

The concept of predictive analytics is also used for the **maintenance of machines**. This is referred to as **predictive maintenance**. This means parts are not replaced when they are broken, but when their wear becomes apparent based on machine data, which is often available in real time. This enables the turbines of airplanes to be continuously monitored during the flight. If required, the necessary spare part is then available to replace the old one at the destination airport after landing (see Kreutzer and Sirrenberg 2019).

> **Remember Box**
> The number of smart objects, i.e. objects that are connected to the Internet, continues to rise dramatically, and they are becoming more and more connected. As a result, an increasing amount of data is generated for predictive analytics.

▶ **Implementation Tips**

- You should examine how relevant predictive analytics are for your company.
- Often there is already a large amount of data available in your company ("small data"), which is only waiting for a qualified evaluation. You should start with these data.
- You can find these data pools of "small data" in your company's CRM solutions, in reports on machine and product failures, etc.
- Once you have successfully implemented forecasting concepts using this "small data" and determined measures to increase success, you should successively integrate further data pools based on their relevance to improve the quality of your forecasts.
- This allows you to open Big Data's treasure chest of knowledge step by step.

5.6 A/B Testing

A/B testing is particularly important in marketing. For instance, you can use it to determine how effectively you are addressing various target groups. Even for specialists, it is impossible today to precisely predict the behaviour of the target audience. In A/B testing, a variant B is used in addition to the original version A (e.g. an e-mail). What makes A/B testing special is that only a single component of variant B can differ from the original version A. Only then can differences in the response behaviour be clearly attributed to this change. This testing procedure can be used for e-communication, mailings, response mediums, advertisements, online banners, keyword advertisements and response mechanisms on the website (e.g. registration for the newsletter or requests to purchase).

> **Remember Box**
> A/B testing is a very effective tool to continuously identify ways to improve one's own communication activities. You should therefore use it regularly.

5.6 A/B Testing

Consider the following example where version B of an e-mail that is being tested is sent to a test group, and the control group receives the original version. Since the original version has frequently proven to be particularly successful in earlier tests, it is sent to more people. The distribution is often as follows:

- Version A, control group: 80% of the recipients
- Version B, test group: 20% of the recipients

If version B turns out to be much worse, the damage (e.g. of lower turnover) is not so high because this version was only used with 20% of the target group. The distribution of recipients between the test and control groups must be random.

With an e-mail, you can test how many **requests are made** with different discounts. You can compare an A version with a 10% direct discount and a B version with a 10 € discount. As already mentioned, you can only change one element at a time to be able to attribute differences in response behaviour to exactly one cause. If several elements are changed at the same time, it is not possible to determine the cause with certainty.

An A/B test can also be used to further develop a corporate website. This is done by randomly directing online visitors to two different versions of the website, which also only have one differing component. The relevant KPIs can then be used to analyse the results. You can determine differences between the conversion rates of the two website versions. This allows you to continually optimise your corporate website to increase the number of visits and pages viewed, as well as the conversion rates. At the end of the special offer, whether it be after a day or a week, you can compare the differences between the results of the two versions. Since only one component of the website's appearance is changed at a time, you can clearly trace the differences in response behaviour back to this change.

Figure 5.5 shows the **design for an A/B website test**. The relevant success factor is RPM (revenue per mille). In this case, the company strives for a particularly high advertising revenue from its own website. Version A generated "5 €" per 1000 visitors to the website, while Version B generated "8 €". Version B was therefore the more responsive version and should be used in the future, if the same circumstances apply.

Before making optimisations based on the test results, you should check whether the result was "random" or "statistically significant" (i.e. "over random"). Differences between indicators or variables in statistics are described as **significant** if the probability that they are random is not above a certain threshold. Therefore, in statistics, "significant" means that an "over random" relationship can be assumed. Consequently, this means that the results were not based on chance! The significance is determined by statistical tests. The selection of the appropriate **testing method** depends on the data material and the parameters to be tested. Only then you can make a mathematically correct estimate of the exceedance of a certain error probability (cf. Altobelli 2017). To determine the **statistical significance**, significance tests must be carried out. Listed below are two appropriate sources:

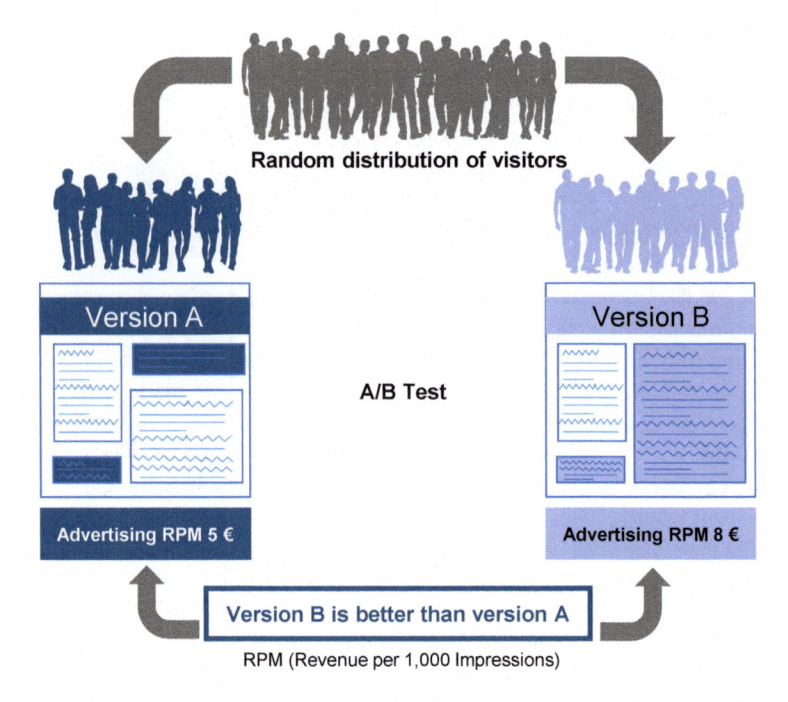

Fig. 5.5 Basic concept of A/B testing—example website optimisation. Author's own figure

- vwo.com/ab-split-test-significance-calculator/
- tools.seobook.com/ppc-tools/calculators/split-test.html

> **Remember Box**
> Before making corresponding adjustments based on the findings of an A/B test, the results must be tested for their significance (i.e. their "over randomness").

You must also ensure that the two versions A and B are assigned to structurally identical groups, so that the results of the A/B test are meaningful. Therefore, an A/A test must be carried out from time to time to **determine the quality of the sample**. As with the already described A/B test, this test is divided into a test group and a control group. However, in the **A/A test**, both groups receive the same information. If there are significant differences in response behaviour at this point, it may be due to an incorrect definition of the test and control groups. This should be avoided (cf. Siroker and Koomen 2013).

> **Remember Box**
> The A/A test is used to check the quality of the sample on which the A/B test is based.

A further development of A/B testing is the so-called **A/B/n testing**. This means not only two, but "n" different versions are used at the same time. The different versions tested can only have one different component from the basis of comparison ("Version A"). This can be the layout of the page, headline, copy text, offer or other picture elements of a website. The achieved results of the individual versions are only evaluated in comparison to the original version, and it is not possible to compare the variants with each other.

> **Remember Box**
> A/B/n testing allows you to test several different versions at the same time in comparison to one original version.

▶ **Implementation Tips**

- A/B testing is a powerful testing and forecasting tool that can ideally be used for all relevant communication measures.
- By using this tool regularly, you will develop your company into a learning organisation, because you are continuously aiming to further optimise the measures that you implement. This gives you a test-driven environment.
- Therefore, you should continuously check the optimisation potential of online and offline communication using A/B tests, as far as it technically possible and economically reasonable.
- A/B tests enable step-by-step learning and should be part of every communication action.
- You should understand testing as a process that begins once and never ends!
- Schedule an A/A test every 6 months to check if your sampling is working correctly—meaning your results are being collected correctly.

References

Altobelli, C. F. (2017). *Marktforschung, Methoden – Anwendungen – Praxisbeispiele* (3rd ed.). Munich: Vahlen.
Keegan, W. J., & Green, M. C. (2017). *Global marketing* (9th ed.). Essex: Pearson.
Kreutzer, R. (2016). *Kundenbeziehungsmanagement im digitalen Zeitalter, Konzepte – Erfolgsfaktoren – Handlungsideen*. Stuttgart: Kohlhammer Verlag.
Kreutzer, R. (2017). *Praxisorientiertes marketing, Grundlagen – Instrumente – Fallbeispiele* (5th ed.). Wiesbaden: Gabler Verlag.
Kreutzer, R., & Land, K.-H. (2015). *Digital darwinism, branding and business models in jeopardy*. New York: Springer.

Kreutzer, R., & Sirrenberg, M. (2019). *Künstliche Intelligenz: Grundlagen – Use cases – KI-journey*. Wiesbaden: Gabler.

Kreutzer, R., Neugebauer, T., & Pattloch, A. (2018). *Digital business leadership – Digital transformation – Business model innovation – Agile organization – Change-management*. Wiesbaden: Springer.

Siroker, D., & Koomen, P. (2013). *A/B testing: The most powerful way to turn clicks into customers*. Hoboken: Wiley.

Customer Value Models 6

6.1 Fundamentals of the Customer Value Concept

In this chapter, I would like to draw your attention to a concept that still receives far too little attention in business practice: the calculation of customer value. Even though **determining the customer value** should be the linchpin of customer relationship management. **Customer relationship management (CRM)** is a conceptual marketing approach that aims to provide target groups with holistic and individual customer-oriented support. The integrated marketing measures implemented to achieve marketing goals are based on the framework of the customer relationship life cycle.

To focus on customer acquisition and support, it is necessary to determine the **value of a customer**. After all, the core of customer relationship management is the goal-oriented development of profitable relationships with customers. Acquiring customer addresses in connection with other profile data provides the basis for a customer approach that is based on profile data and the respective customer value.

The following target groups are initially the focus of **customer value determination**:

- **Desired or target customers** that a company would like to win over ("prospective customer value").
- **Interested individuals**, i.e. people who have already shown a general interest in the company's services and whose communication data are available (e-mail, telephone number, address; "prospective customer value").
- Current and former **customers** who must be supported after making a purchase and won over for additional purchases ("already realised" and "prospective customer value").

Actual and desired customers, as well as interested individuals, can be both consumers and companies or their representatives.

> **Remember Box**
> Customer value is an essential tool to achieve value-oriented customer management.

Recording this type of customer value, e.g. in the form of customer lifetime value (CLV), is still not a high priority for many companies today. Studies repeatedly show that even today less than 40% of companies are concerned with the calculation of customer value.

The following questions will help you to discover the type of action needed to determine the customer value in your company. These questions still continue to remain unanswered in too many companies:

- Who are my best customers and how is their "quality" measured? Is it based on turnover or contribution margin? Is it measured using a past or actual value or as a forecast?
- How loyal are the customers and how is loyalty measured? By the length of the customer relationship, by the number of successful recommendations or by the amount of turnover? In the latter case, a distinction can be made between the absolute and relative level of turnover using the share of wallet. The share of wallet refers to the monetary share of a company in the total turnover a customer generates in a specific product category. If over the course of 1 year a customer spends 410 € at *Zara* and 75 € at *H&M* from his/her annual clothing budget of 750 €, *Zara*'s share of wallet is 55% and *H&M*'s is 10%.
- Which segments are the focus for customer loyalty measures? And why?
- Which acquisition channels and which acquisition measures are used to acquire the best and worst customers? What are the reasons for this?
- Which offers attract the best/worst customers? Why?
- Which support measures are the most efficient for retaining customers? How is this achieved?

If you cannot ask such questions and answer them in an informed manner, you will neither achieve your **effectiveness** nor your **efficiency** goals. It is necessary to achieve these goals so that marketing is not only a strategy leader but also a profit driver. Therefore, to do this function justice, marketing must justify the profitability of its actions and prove the increasingly demanded **ROMI**, the **return on marketing investment**. Determining the customer value is an important basis for this.

> **Remember Box**
> Without determining the customer value, you cannot build a value-oriented customer management.

6.1 Fundamentals of the Customer Value Concept

Fig. 6.1 Task and approaches of value-oriented customer management. Author's own figure

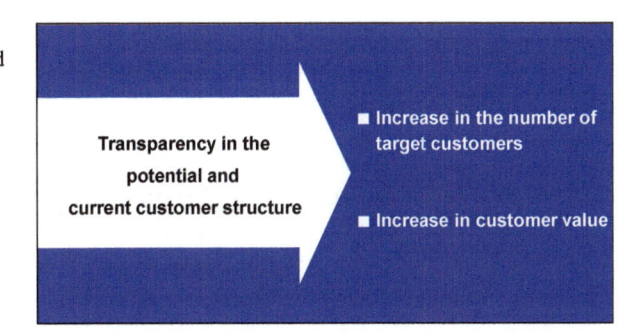

- Transparency in the potential and current customer structure
  - Increase in the number of target customers
  - Increase in customer value

Value-oriented customer management is the development of concepts that contribute selecting and developing profitable customer relationships (see Fig. 6.1). In value-oriented customer management, you have two tasks. On the one hand, this is the selection of the customers that you wish to win over and keep. On the other hand, it is about designing a customer service to increase the customer value. In summary, the tasks of value-oriented customer management can be characterised by selecting, developing, structuring, maintaining and terminating business relationships with individual customers or customer groups based on their value contributions to defined corporate goals (cf. Helm et al. 2017). These value contributions are also referred to as customer value.

This approach of value-oriented customer management is still valid and should encourage you to take appropriate measures within your company. Today, however, it is evident that certain activities need to be more strongly integrated to assess the value of already evaluated potential and current customers. You must keep in mind the **activities of prospective and current customers on social media**, which indicate whether they either have a bond with or reject a company. Therefore, the CLV must be supplemented by a **customer reference value** (CRV).

Furthermore, another target group is gaining in relevance for companies: the **digital opinion leaders**. This refers to people who are not necessarily potential or current customers of a company but who nevertheless have a big influence on its success. This is because by expressing their opinions in blogs, communities, as well as on *YouTube/Instagram* and social networks, these people significantly influence the opinions of many people. Since these digital opinion leaders are not always potential or current customers, this is called only a **reference value** (cf. further information on influencer marketing Kreutzer and Land 2017).

> **Remember Box**
> Due to the importance of (digital) opinion leaders, you should also aim to determine the reference values.

The idea of the **(customer) reference value** will ensure that both target groups are taken into consideration, since they play an important role in leading and forming opinions in the online world. To clarify the required activities when determining this extended (customer) value, the following section will first show you what previous concepts for value determination look like. Based on these concepts, ideas for further development are then presented.

6.2 Methods to Determine Customer Value

To test the **quality of your customer value determining concepts**, you can use the following statements, to see which one applies to your company:

- There are **no concepts** to determine the customer value.
- A general distinction is made between **good and bad customers**, although there is no concrete meaning of the attributes.
- A distinction is made between **large and small customers**. Behind this often lies the generally incorrect assumption that a larger customer is automatically also a more profitable customer.
- When analysing customers, the **length of the customer relationship**, the **recommendation rate** and the **communication intensity** are evaluated.
- A distinction is made between **occasional and regular customers** (e.g. in stationary retail); however, such groups say nothing about turnover levels and impact on contribution margins.
- A distinction is made between **online and offline customers**, but the question of which results these customers generate remains unanswered.
- An **ABC analysis** shows the distribution of customers based on their level of turnover or impact on contribution margins. The concentrated areas that become visible can provide an important orientation for customer loyalty management. However, in the classic ABC analysis, behaviour from the past (i.e. past sales) is rewarded in the present. On the other hand, future high-potential customers who are currently still in the B and C segments do not receive value-oriented support because their potential has not yet been recognised (cf. Fig. 6.2).

With this relatively simple analysis, you can see to what extent your company is dependent on individual customers and therefore how vulnerable it is. As seen in this example, if you generate just under 80% of your turnover with only 20% of your customers, it is very important that you ensure that this turnover with these A customers does not decrease. At the same time, you should ask yourself whether among the B and C customers, who do not have a large share of sales today, there are those with future potential who can replace the existing A customers.

You should not use an ABC analysis statically to shed light on the status quo alone. Dynamic application is required to exploit the full potential of an ABC analysis. By doing so, you are already trying today to identify the A customers of the future within the B and C segments.

Such an ABC analysis can also provide you with important information about other issues. It can help you classify products, distribution channels and sales markets, as well as procurement sources. The dependency on specific products,

6.2 Methods to Determine Customer Value

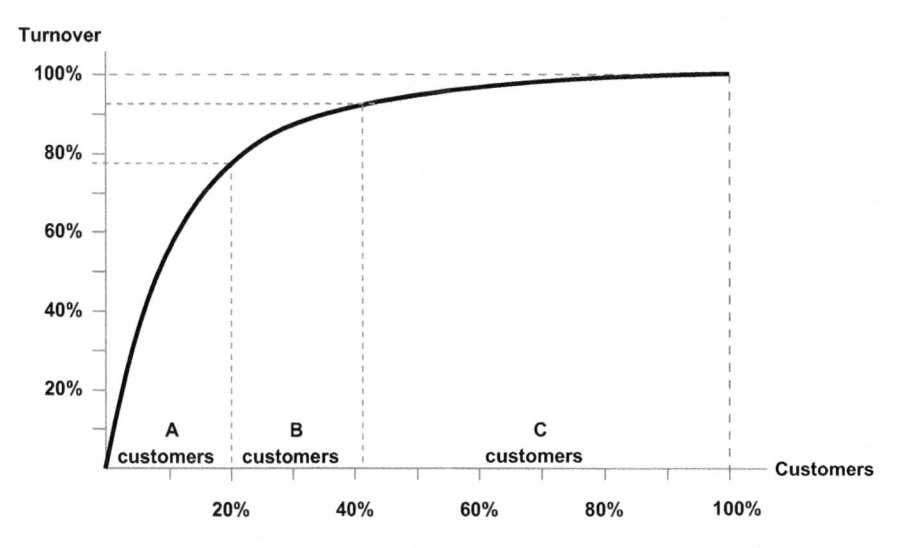

Fig. 6.2 ABC analysis of the customer base. Author's own figure

customers, sales channels, sales markets and procurement sources becomes clear through the determination of **concentration effects**. These results can serve as a reason to take counteraction to reduce excessive dependencies.

> **Remember Box**
> The ABC analysis is an important tool to identify (early) dependencies on products, customers, distribution channels, sales markets and procurement sources.

A study conducted by Verint (2014) involving 78 executives at companies in German-speaking countries shows how "good customers" are defined (see Fig. 6.3). The definitions were not very convincing, because no compelling customer value model was used under any circumstances. To concentrate solely on the **duration of a customer relationship** is not sufficiently value-oriented. Furthermore, it also does not help to focus on the **communication intensity** or **amount of turnover** (without determining the contribution margins achieved). When it comes to referrals, not only this behaviour should be measured alone. Instead, you should determine how many successful referrals have been made and how profitable the recommended customers have become.

> **Remember Box**
> The definition of "good customers" is not yet convincing in many companies.

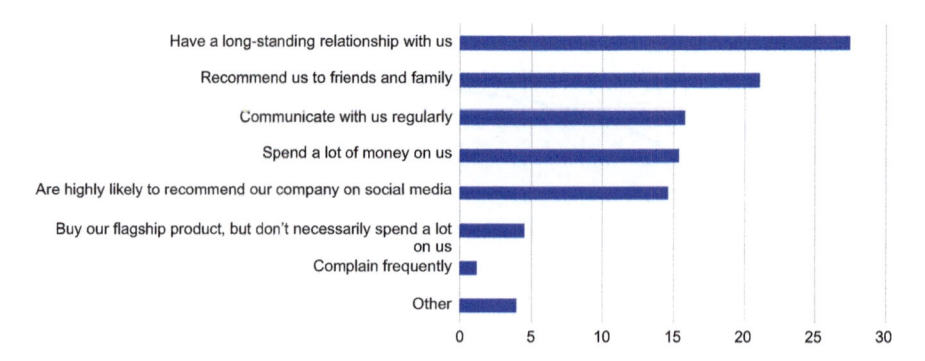

Fig. 6.3 Definition of "good customers" ($n = 78$; multiple answers possible). Source: Verint (2014, p. 1)

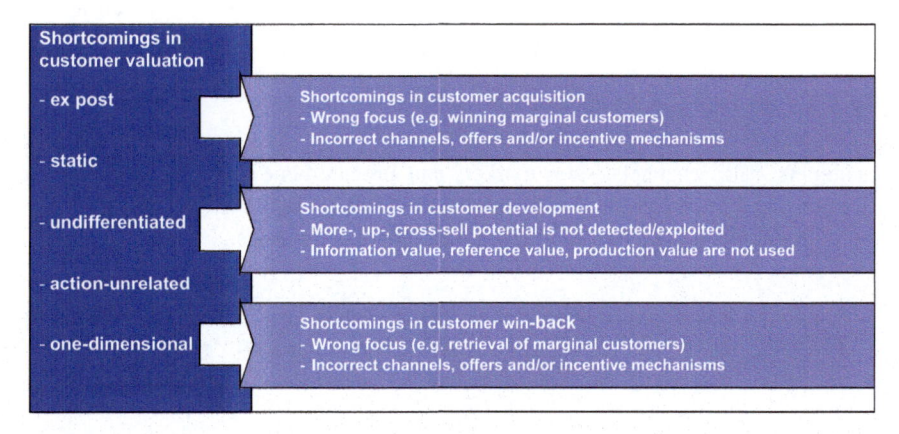

Fig. 6.4 Error sources in the customer management. Source: Adapted from Helm et al. (2017, pp. 20–24)

If similar concepts are used in your company, you should work towards a higher information density to exploit the **knowledge potential for value-oriented management**. The most important error sources that must already be avoided in value-oriented customer management are listed in the first column in Fig. 6.4 and described below:

- Often, a **customer evaluation** takes place **ex post**, without questioning whether the customer behaviour shown in the past can also be expected in the future. Customers with development potential cannot be systematically identified in this way.
- **Static models** are used which are based on a trend extrapolation ("more of the same"), without anticipating possible system breaks or discontinuities in behaviour and not taking them into account when determining customer value (cf. Sect. 5.1).

- An **undifferentiated approach** exists if you don't consider that individual customers or customer groups can develop differently over time.
- The customer rating does not take the way in which a customer was approached, and the offer made into account (**rating is unrelated to action**).
- A **one-dimensional approach** is used if only a single criterion is used to determine the value. This is often the turnover, without considering that this does not correlate positively with the contribution margin for all customer groups.

Below are the consequences of such an approach, which violates the basic rules of value-based customer management:

- **Shortcomings in customer acquisition**

  Insufficient customer value determination may lead to acquiring less relevant (marginal) customers in the future who do not generate any or negative contribution margins for the company. Additionally, communication channels, offers for new customer acquisition and/or specific incentive mechanisms may continue to be used, which do not lead to customers with long-term value, but only attract bargain hunters.
- **Shortcomings in customer development**

  More, up- and cross-selling potential is not recognised or cannot be exploited in a suitable manner. This means mailings are sent to customers who cannot generate additional turnover, while customers with additional turnover potential may not be served. Additionally, it is possible that information, reference and production value of customers is not used, because the evaluation ignores this.
- **Shortcomings in customer recovery**

  A wrong focus is set (e.g. winning back marginal customers), or wrong channels, offers and/or incentive mechanisms are used.

To encourage further developing customer value management, you should first check which **criteria**, if any at all, are currently used in your company to **determine customer value**. Figure 6.5 provides an overview.

Regarding the **time reference**, a distinction can be made between a pure ex post analysis, which only takes past activities into account, and an attempt to forecast future developments (ex ante approach). You must also check whether to use a one-period approach (e.g. by restricting the ordering season to 6 months in online retailing or to a complete fiscal year) or several periods are to be included in the valuation. The decision depends on the seasonal fluctuations of your business area.

You must determine whether **individuals** or individual companies or different **customer groups** are considered. Generally, it is recommended to use powerful analysis and forecasting methods to take a closer look at individual customers, so that the individuality of each customer can be considered. Only evaluating individual customers provides the necessary management information for target-oriented customer support (see Sect. 5.5 for more).

Concept	Characteristics/criterion
Time reference	• Ex post vs. ex ante • One vs. multi-period evaluation
Unit	• Individual customer • Customer groups
Temporal modelling	• Static approach • Dynamic approach
Content modelling	• One- vs. multidimensional concepts • Monetary vs. non-monetary criteria
Value realisation	• Nominal value analysis • Discounting on analysis date
Customer value driver	• Turnover (more-, cross-, up-sell-oriented) • Contribution margin • Reference value (image effect of customers, opinion leaders or multiplier role, value of customer recommendation) • Information value (customer as a source of ideas and creative partner) • Production value (customer as co-producer) • Transaction costs (customer-driven support costs) • Transaction costs (company-driven support costs)

Fig. 6.5 Criteria to determine customer value. Author's own figure

There are static concepts which involve extending the time series of the past into the future (**extrapolation**; see Sect. 5.1). **Dynamic models** attempt to take other influencing factors into account in the forecast. Thus, in principle, the quality of the forecast is higher if relevant behavioural data are included (see Sect. 5.5).

The concepts for determining customer value can also be differentiated according to the number of dimensions included. **One-dimensional approaches** concentrate only on turnover or the contribution margin. With **multidimensional models**, the different facets of a customer value, beyond turnover or contribution margin, can be considered. Furthermore, you must decide whether the approach will consider monetary factors (such as turnover, contribution margin) and nonmonetary factors (such as referrals or positive customer contributions on social media).

The **value realisation** can disregard the time at which the factors determining customer value are deposited or payed out and consider them purely nominally. This differs from concepts that discount future cash in- and outflows to the valuation date ("discount"). In this case, the interest rate used for discounting is particularly important, as it largely impacts the present value of incoming and outgoing payments that are yet to be determined.

The widest range of models for determining customer value relate to **drivers of customer value**. It is necessary to decide which turnover and cost categories are to be considered when determining customer value. The most common criterion is **revenue**, whereby future revenue development is often not differentiated between more-, cross- or up-selling potential. In many cases, only the previous revenue is used as a basis for determining customer value. An important, but still far too rarely used, success variable is the **contribution margin**, which is to be determined customer specifically as the sum of the contribution margins of all purchased products or used services. The challenge for omnichannel companies is to combine revenues or contribution margins from both online and offline purchases into one customer account.

Insofar as contribution margins are determined on the customer side, the offer-related costs for the products supplied or for the provision of services are generally included. It is rare that the **transaction costs** associated with a customer relationship are also considered when determining the contribution margin. These include the customer-driven support costs caused by the customer's specific behaviour pattern (e.g. returning many products, making many calls to the call centre, paying too slowly resulting in interest and handling costs). Additionally, the company-driven support costs must be calculated, e.g. by considering the costs depending on the number and content of advertising efforts (e.g. sending a high-quality catalogue), as well as telephone and e-mail contact or visits to the location. You must also consider these factors for both on- and offline areas.

However, the value of a customer is not limited to monetary values. Both in the BtB and in the BtC market, a customer can also have an important **reference value** for the company. This aspect has great significance in the online age. Nowadays, every single customer has the possibility to have a lasting influence on the profitability and success of companies through his or her ratings. Even people who do not use products or services of a company have this power to express their opinion. Therefore, when further developing value models, opinion leaders or multiplier roles, which can be customers and non-customers, should be given a greater value. Information about a company's own range of services can be communicated to a global target group via social networks such as *Facebook* or *Twitter*.

In the future, you should consider that the **reference value** is particularly important. You can find the reasons for this in Fig. 6.6. A study on trust in advertising forms in Germany shows that online recommendations are ranked as the third most credible form of advertising at 55% (top 2 box), only just below editorial content (57%). Based on this knowledge, you should give some attention to the concept of **(customer) reference value**.

The Internet's diverse interaction possibilities make it increasingly important that you also evaluate the **value of information** coming from customers and non-customers. Today, everyone with an Internet connection can actively generate ideas or be a creative partner of companies by making direct contact with them or getting involved on relevant platforms (e.g. *Submit your idea at Starbucks.com* and *ideas.lego.com*). The relationship becomes even stronger through **production value,** when the customer becomes a co-producer. This can be achieved through a wide variety of concepts and (online) platforms. You should try to find different ways to evaluate the respective engagement of these online-based engagement forms of customers and non-customers.

You can combine the classic criteria for determining customer value into customer value concepts in different ways. One example is the already mentioned **customer lifetime value** (CLV). This is usually the sum of the monetary value contributions (revenue/contribution margin) of a customer, aggregated over the

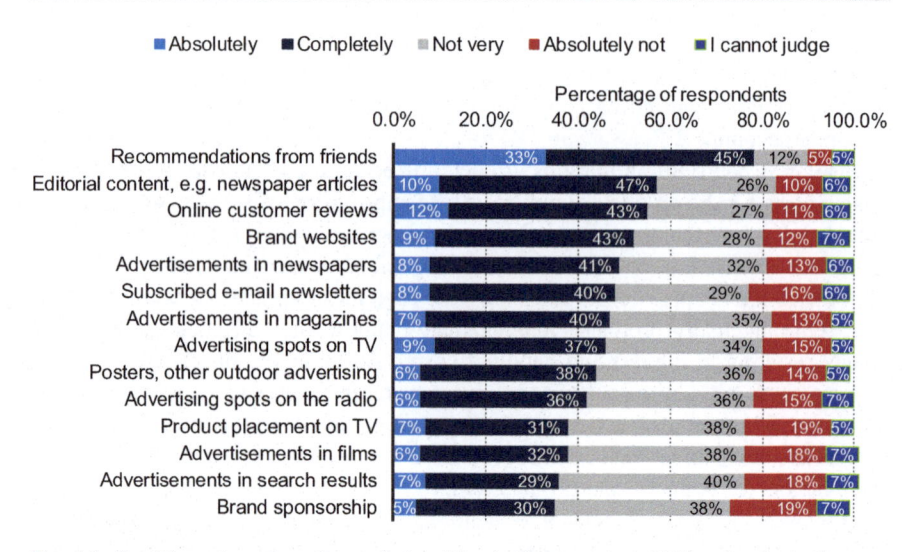

Fig. 6.6 Confidence in various forms of advertising in Germany ($n = 1037$ respondents; German-speaking population ages 18 and over). Source: Statista (2018a)

Criterion	Weighting	Score					Weighting factor x score
		1	2	3	4	5	
Number of trips booked per year	0.3	0 - 1	2	3	4	X >= 5	
Average turnover per travel booking in €	0.5	x < 750	750 <= x < 1500	1500 <= x < 2500	2500 <= x < 3500	x >= 3500	
Referrals (average number of new customers recruited per year)	0.2	0	x < 0.5	0.5 <= x < 1	1 <= x < 2	x >= 2	
Total	1.0						Sum

Fig. 6.7 Scoring model to determine customer values in a travel agency. Author's own figure

possible or desired duration of the relationship with a company. The CLV can be used to decide which investments should be made in the long-term loyalty of a customer.

To determine the customer value based on various criteria, you can use the scoring models presented in Sect. 4.4. Figure 6.7 shows an example of a simple **customer value model** from the point of view of a travel agency.

The **RFMR method** is another scoring model that can be used for many online and offline stores. With this concept, the customer value is determined using the following criteria:

6.2 Methods to Determine Customer Value

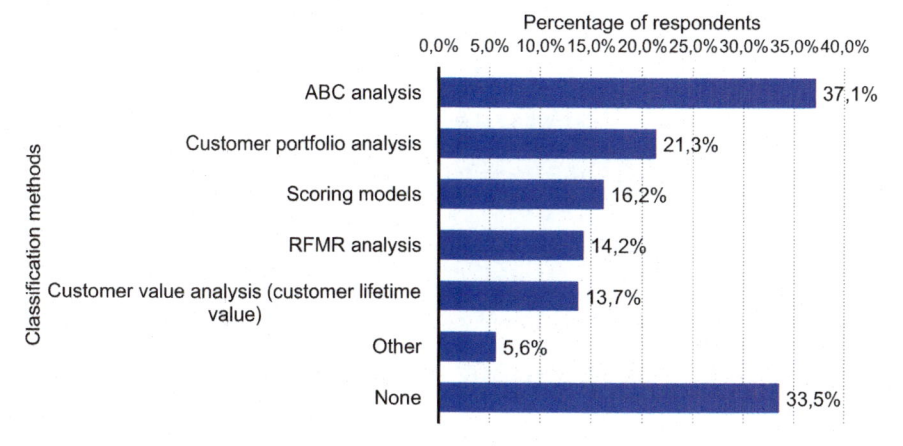

Fig. 6.8 Approaches used to determine customer value ($n = 197$ managers; multiple answers possible). Source: Statista (2018b)

Classification methods (Percentage of respondents):
- ABC analysis: 37.1%
- Customer portfolio analysis: 21.3%
- Scoring models: 16.2%
- RFMR analysis: 14.2%
- Customer value analysis (customer lifetime value): 13.7%
- Other: 5.6%
- None: 33.5%

- **Recency**: How long has it been since the last purchase?
- **Frequency**: How often does the customer make purchases per month or per year?
- **Monetary Ratio**: What amount of turnover does the customer generate when making a purchase?

If the customers of an online shop are evaluated using the RFMR model, the following applies: the more recent the last purchase was, the more frequently the customer makes purchases and the more turnover he/she generates, the higher his/her value for the company. It is assumed that such a customer is highly likely to make further purchases soon. A similar model can be used for a fundraising company. This model can be further developed to include customer- and enterprise-driven support costs when determining the customer value.

It has already been pointed out that only very few companies use qualified **concepts to determine customer value**. Figure 6.8 shows which methods are used by these companies. The **ABC analysis** comes first with 37.1%. Another 21.3% use a **customer portfolio analysis** (see also Sect. 4.5). 37% determine **contribution margins on a customer level**. Furthermore, 16.2% use a **scoring model**. The use of the **RFMR method** at 14.2% and the **customer lifetime value analysis** at 13.7% are also often based on a scoring model. It becomes clear that one-third of the companies do not determine the value of their customers, and more than one-third rely on the ABC analysis, which does not provide very meaningful results regarding the real customer value.

> **Remember Box**
> Even today, most companies still do not use qualified concepts to determine customer value.

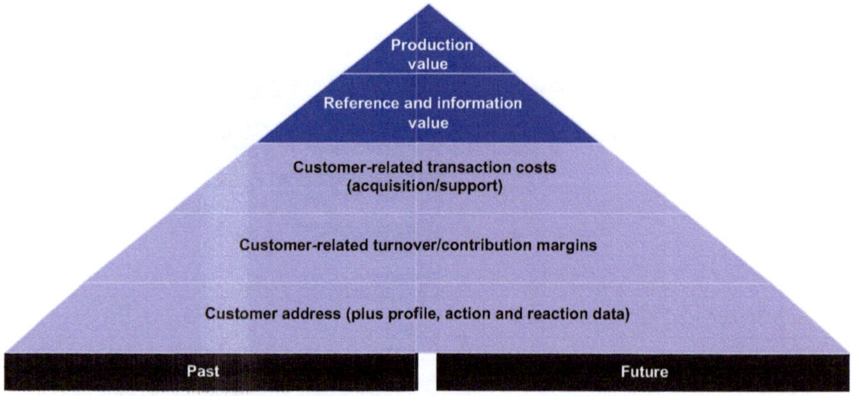
Production value
Reference and information value
Customer-related transaction costs (acquisition/support)
Customer-related turnover/contribution margins
Customer address (plus profile, action and reaction data)
Past
Future

Fig. 6.9 Competence pyramid for determining customer value. Author's own figure

Depending on the specifics of your industry, your goals and the availability of the relevant data, you should develop your own **concept for determining customer value**. You should determine customer value with more accuracy if your company is also able to offer differentiated customer support based on these identified customer values. The differentiation of the customer evaluation must go hand in hand with the differentiation of the customer approach. The conceptual starting points can be found in the **competence pyramid for determining customer value** (cf. Fig. 6.9). Building up a competence pyramid may be a project that lasts for several years. This is particularly important if you intend to evaluate online and offline activities in an integrated manner.

The importance of identifying and supporting digital opinion leaders, be they customers or non-customers, has already been discussed. People who stand out with particularly positive reports and comments about a company are often referred to as **advocates** or **brand lovers**. Which paths can be taken to determine their value (cf. Xevelonakis 2015)?

Figure 6.10 depicts a conceptual approach of a separate model for recording this influencing potential. Firstly, the **size of the network** (reach) that a person can have is important. In the stage, the quality of the network could be evaluated. This is because digital opinion leaders who reach other opinion leaders via their network are more valuable to companies. Furthermore, the **average number of people reached** must be determined. The **number of communicative actions per week** is also an important criterion. However, the most important is the **engagement rate of the recipients**, and therefore, it has the highest weighting. After all, what is the point of a transmitter that reaches many but does not mobilise them? When further developing this model, you can also include the differently weighted type of engagement achieved in the value model.

As seen in the model above, it is possible to score a **(customer) reference value** between 1 and 5. However, not every digital opinion leader communicates in a tone that fits to corporate goals. For those who dominantly refer to a company or its

6.2 Methods to Determine Customer Value

Criterion	Weighting	Score					Weighting factor x score
		1	2	3	4	5	
Reach/size of network	0.2	< 1000	1000 <= x < 5000	5000 <= x < 10,000	10,000 <= x < 50,000	X > = 50,000	
Average number of people reached	0.2	< 1%	1% <= x < 7%	7% <= x < 10%	10% <= x < 13%	x >= 13%	
Number of actions (posts etc.) per week	0.2	<=1	1 < x < 5	5 <= x < 10	10 <= x < 20	x >= 20	
Engagement rate of recipients (likes, shares, comments etc.)	0.4	<=1%	1% < x < 3%	3% <= x < 5%	5% <= x < 7%	x >= 7%	
Total	1.0						Sum

Fig. 6.10 Individual model for determining the (customer-) reference value. Author's own figure

Fig. 6.11 Continuum of social influencers. Author's own figure

brands, products or services negatively, the (customer) reference value is given the sign "−". Those who fluctuate between positive and negative messages are identified with the sign "+−". Only those who continuously give positive references receive the sign "+". It becomes clear that a **sentiment analysis** is necessary to consider the tonality of the statements. This evaluation can be integrated into a continuum of social influencers (cf. Fig. 6.11).

If developing this type of model is too time-consuming for you, you can use concepts from third parties, so-called social scoring services. These also begin by collecting a lot of data from the online sphere. Crawlers are used to search social networks, microblogs (especially *Twitter*), blogs, forums, Q&A portals and other platforms for relevant opinion contributions. Examples of good providers of these **social influencer scores** include Klout (2018) with the *Klout score*, and Brandwatch (2018), which offer *Brandwatch audiences*. Both concepts enable you to determine an individual's online reputation by evaluating their activities on social networks.

> **Remember Box**
> If you do not want to develop reference values independently, you can use the services of social scoring services.

When implementing value-oriented customer management, you should finish by checking whether the "value of the company performance for the customer" is equal to the "value of the customer" and make improvements if needed.

▶ **Implementation Tips**

- When it comes to the important topic of "customer value determination", you should start by critically reviewing your company.
- Check which concepts (if any) are in use.
- Determine how meaningful these concepts are in fact and check where there is room for optimisation.
- Before you tackle them, first analyse the importance that is attached to customer value in your company and which concrete measures are already based on customer values. This will allow you to see how much effort you might need to put into persuading others.
- Develop an appropriate concept together with marketing and sales teams to achieve greater transparency in the value of your own customers.
- Establish concrete acquisition and support measures from the determined customer values.
- In in the next step, you can work on determining a (customer) reference value or use existing concepts such as *Klout* or *Brandwatch*.

6.3 Net Promoter Score

A concept that only takes a few days to put into practice in your company is the **net promoter score (NPS)**. It is a powerful and at the same time easy to use concept to measure the degree of emotional loyalty and trust that customers have in your company. Essentially, the NPS is about the simple question of how many of your own customers would recommend your company (net) to others. The basic concept of the NPS is described in Fig. 6.12.

The only question you must ask to determine the **net promoter score** is "How likely are you to recommend our company, product, service, brand to your friends and colleagues?" The answers can be given on a scale from "0" ("not likely at all") to "10" ("very likely").

Promoters of a company or brand are only those who give a rating of "9" or "10". **Detractors** (critics) are those who only assign values between "0" and "6" when asked whether they would recommend it. **Passives** are those who give a rating of "7" or "8". When calculating the net value of the recommendations, the percentage of detractors is subtracted from the percentage of promoters. The group of passives is disregarded. Consequently, the **formula to calculate the NPS** is as follows:

$$NPS = \text{promoters (in\%)} - \text{detractors (in\%)}$$

6.3 Net Promoter Score

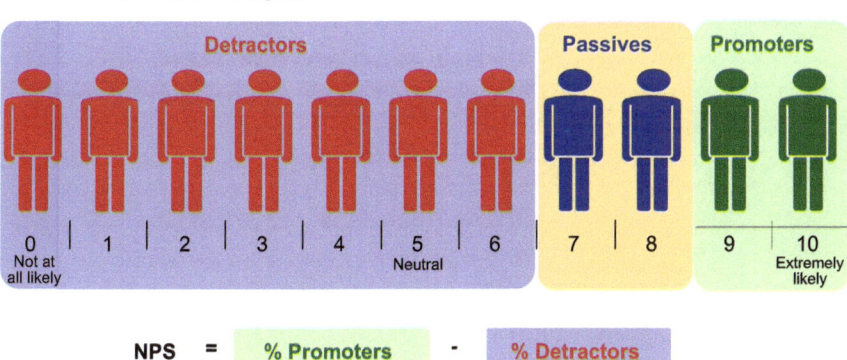

Question: How likely are you to recommend our company/product/service/brand to your friends and colleagues?

Fig. 6.12 Concept of the net promoter score. Author's own figure

In the best case, the **values of the NPS** can be "100%" if all customers have assigned the value "9" or "10". In the worst case, the result is "−100%" if all customers have only assigned values between "0" and "6" (see Reichheld 2003).

> **Remember Box**
> The net promoter score is a simple tool that you can quickly implement. It determines the trust of your customers by measuring the degree of readiness for recommendation.

Figure 6.13 shows how the net promoter score is used in the hotel sector. In this case, the hotel gave out a survey immediately after the visit. It is important that you not only ask for a pure evaluation but also the reasons for it. Only this additional information allows you to trace the evaluations and, if necessary, take corrective action.

It is important that you first determine the initial value of the NPS for your company before changing existing structures and processes. This value, determined at the start, documents the **zero measurement of your company**. Through in-depth analyses, you must discover why this exact value was the outcome and what measures can be taken to improve it, if necessary. This can be done by asking a supplementary "why question" after determining the probability of recommendation. Through this small additional question, you often receive exciting insights into the estimated and criticised performance of your company.

It is also very exciting if you carry out a comparison in the competitive environment. You can work out any advantages or disadvantages of your company position regarding the NPS results. You can find the NPS values for different industries, and sometimes also for individual companies, online on different platforms. You can occasionally use these values as your benchmark (see Sect. 4.6).

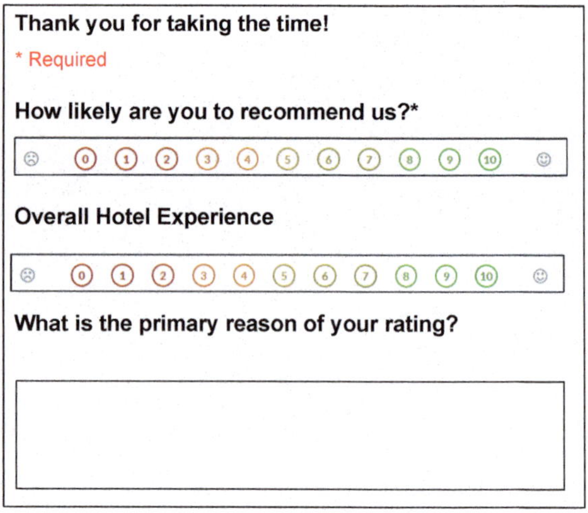

Fig. 6.13 Use of the net promoter score in the hotel sector. Author's own figure

> Thank you for taking the time!
> * Required
>
> **How likely are you to recommend us?***
>
> ☹ (0) (1) (2) (3) (4) (5) (6) (7) (8) (9) (10) ☺
>
> **Overall Hotel Experience**
>
> ☹ (0) (1) (2) (3) (4) (5) (6) (7) (8) (9) (10) ☺
>
> **What is the primary reason of your rating?**
>
> [   ]

▶ **Implementation Tips**

- My recommendation is simply get started immediately and use the NPS.
- Find partners in your company who are as interested in the NPS values as you are.
- Integrate the NPS question into existing processes, be it at the check-out in an online shop or stationary shop.
- You can either ask this question continuously or every quarter for a certain period, if you have a lot of repeat buyers.
- It is important that you discuss the results with all affected departments and establish appropriate measures to improve the analysed status quo.
- This will also help your organisation to "learn" continuously and ideally become better and better!
- Don't forget that optimisation measures are often not realised quickly in practice, and therefore, you must be patient when waiting for NPS values to improve.
- If improvements have been achieved, you should celebrate this appropriately with all responsible employees!
- After all, nothing is more motivating than success!

References

Brandwatch. (2018). *Brandwatch Audiences*. Accessed March 22, 2018, from https://www.brandwatch.com/audiences/

References

Helm, S., Günter, B., & Eggert, A. (2017). Kundenwert – eine Einführung in die theoretischen und praktischen Herausforderungen der Bewertung von Kundenbeziehungen. In S. Helm, B. Günter, & A. Eggert (Hrsg.), *Kundenwert, Grundlagen – Innovative Konzepte – Praktische Umsetzungen* (4th ed., pp. 3–34). Wiesbaden.

Klout. (2018). *Lass andere wissen, was Dir gefällt.* Accessed March 22, 2018, from https://klout.com/home

Kreutzer, R., & Land, K.-H. (2017). *Digital branding – Konzeption einer holistischen Markenführung.* Wiesbaden: Springer Gabler.

Reichheld, F. F. (2003). The number one you need to grow. *Harvard Business Review, 2003*(12), 47–54.

Statista. (2018a). *Welchen der folgenden Werbeformen vertrauen Sie?.* Accessed December 12, 2018, from https://de-statista-com.ezproxy.hwr-berlin.de/statistik/daten/studie/222329/umfrage/umfrage-zum-vertrauen-in-unterschiedliche-werbeformen

Statista. (2018b). *Welche Klassifikationsmethoden setzen Sie zur Klassifizierung Ihrer Kunden ein.* Accessed November 22, 2018, from https://de-statista-com.ezproxy.hwr-berlin.de/statistik/daten/studie/240285/umfrage/anteil-eingesetzter-klassifikationsmethoden-zur-segmentierung-von-kundendatenbanken/

Verint. (2014). *Wertvolle Kunden finden und binden.* Weybridge.

Xevelonakis, E. (2015). *Social influence and customer referral value.* ATINER's Conference Paper Series, MKT2015-1605.

Methods to Create New Products, Services and Business Models 7

Nowadays, it is more and more important to foster a **company's internal innovation potential**. You can use various creativity techniques to do this. These can be used in different areas of the company, such as strategy, marketing, R&D, product management and sales. The goal is to find **new services** for the company or identify **possibilities to further develop existing offers**. Additionally, it poses the important question of how to further develop existing **business models** and find completely new business models. The following methods can help you answer these questions.

7.1 Brainstorming and Brainwriting

The most widespread creative technique is **brainstorming** (for fundamental details cf. Osborn 1963; Vahs and Brem 2015). This is because this method is very easy to use. However, it is necessary to keep some rules in mind. Brainstorming aims to gather as many ideas as possible in a group discussion through "loud thinking". The ideal duration is approx. 30–45 min to ensure all participants are highly concentrated. The number of participants should be limited from five to eight and ideally come from different departments and/or hierarchy levels.

The **moderator** plays a central, and often underestimated, role to ensure that all suggestions are recorded and that the following **brainstorming guidelines** are followed in particular:

- "Every idea is welcomed!"
- "The more impetuous an idea is, the better!" (i.e. quantity before quality)
- "Criticism is forbidden!" (no "idea killing")
- "Free association with proposals!" (i.e. pick up ideas of others and develop them)

The most difficult task of the moderator is to prevent **idea killing**, whether verbal or non-verbal. This is because every change, every innovation, first causes fear that leads to the rejection of these innovations. However, especially when brainstorming, it is important to let ideas and suggestions influence creativity. If the moderator does not consistently reject criticism, all creativity will be killed. This often happens when different hierarchical levels are present and/or introverted people are involved, who are quickly discouraged by criticism.

> **Remember Box**
> During brainstorming, the moderator must ensure that everyone follows the important rules of the game. Otherwise there will be no creative flow.

Brainwriting (also called **method 6-3-5**) is a good way to avoid the disadvantages of brainstorming. This creativity technique involves giving six participants a written problem and asking them to work out three solutions each. These are passed on five times. These sessions last approx. 60 min and enable conflict-free cooperation between different hierarchical levels and personalities, since the suggestions can "only" be answered in writing.

> **Remember Box**
> Brainwriting is a perfect method to involve even the most introverted people in creative processes.

▶ **Implementation Tips**

- Use the brainstorming method whenever you want to quickly develop some new ideas.
- It is important that the role of the moderator is clearly defined and that he or she consistently enforces the brainstorming rules.
- Avoid brainstorming sessions that last for hours because they don't work.
- Use brainwriting if you want to involve more introverted, but often highly qualified, top performers in the creative process. They will thank you for it!

7.2 Attribute Listing

Attribute listing is another simple tool to increase creativity. This is a systematic-analytical method for new product development. The offer in question is first broken down into various characteristics. These are used to describe its current state. Subsequently, you search for different design possibilities in each feature group, so that you can find starting points for creative further development. Through a combination

Characteristic	Current state	Variations
• Form	• Rectangular	• Round, square, trapezoidal, triangular
• Material	• Paper	• With haptic elements (fabric, foil etc.)
• Design	• Hardcover, paperback	• E-book, audiobook, CD, DVD, streaming
• Interactivity	• None	• Online communication with publisher/author • Online tasks with solutions • Online tests • Provision of current background material

Fig. 7.1 Attribute listing for the development of a textbook. Author's own figure

of the newly found characteristics, innovations can emerge which are then to be evaluated based on their realisability. Figure 7.1 shows an example of the development of a textbook.

The same concept can also be used to develop services.

> **Remember Box**
> Attribute listing is a method that enables you to find new solutions for existing product and service concepts.

▶ **Implementation Tips**

- Attribute listing is a less complex method that enables you to quickly generate a few additional ideas.
- It can be used to further develop both products and services.
- Therefore, the method should be part of your toolbox.

7.3 Design Thinking

Design thinking is currently particularly popular among creative methods, and rightly so! That's why this tool belongs in your toolbox. Design thinking is often used to **work on complex tasks**. It is based on the approach used by designers, who present persuasive solutions by completing their tasks in the following phases: observation, understanding, brainstorming, prototype development, refinement and execution. It is possible to jump back and forth several times between phases during this process to ensure the greatest possible learning effects (cf. Stickdorn and Schneider 2010; Lewrick et al. 2018; Schallmo 2017; Uebernickel et al. 2015; Mootee 2013; for an application with media products Quade and Schlüter 2017).

> **Remember Box**
> Don't wait—innovate!

The creative process of design thinking makes use of these considerations through a special methodology and various tools. The focus is on **consistent customer orientation**. This can be used to develop products, services and processes.

You should consider the following **characteristics and principles of design thinking** (cf. Poguntke 2018):

- Building the **team for design thinking**

  Design thinking requires the creation of multidisciplinary teams; the members have different experiences. In this case, diversity means both male and female, young and older, as well as starters and "old hands". Moreover, very different areas of the company should also be included in these teams (from accounting to procurement, production, sales and marketing).

  It requires looking for so-called **T-shape personalities**. These are people with a wide range of interests and a high level of professional expertise. The horizontal part of the letter "T" expresses the necessary wide-ranging and comprehensive knowledge, which the people should contribute. The vertical part of the letter "T" stands for a deep knowledge in a certain field.
- **Procedure of a design thinking process**

  A design thinking process often involves the following steps:
  - **Empathise**: building empathy for the target groups
  - **Define**: describing the task
  - **Ideate**: finding solutions
  - **Prototype**: developing prototypes
  - **Test**: examining the solutions that were found
  - **Decide** (after several iterations, as in test runs): selecting a solution

  A special feature of design thinking is its consistent target group orientation, which is reflected in all steps of the process. During the process, phases of divergence and convergence also alternate. In the **divergence phases**, the focus is on the quantity of solutions. The goal is to develop as many ideas as possible, while respecting the rules of brainstorming (cf. Sect. 7.1). On the other hand, the **phases of convergence** are mainly about condensing and bringing together the gained knowledge and the developed ideas.

  Visualising the developed ideas is very important during all phases. It starts with the defining a **persona** for whom a new service concept, app or product is to be developed (cf. Sect. 3.2.3). This strengthens the desired empathy. Additionally, it is necessary to visualise gained knowledge and the developed solutions with sketches and storyboards. **Storytelling** is used to further foster understanding and empathy. This is done by using concrete application situations, pain points and expectations to tell little stories that further promote understanding (e.g. based on the customer journey map).

An important part of design thinking is **rapid prototyping**. Developing expensive prototypes that are as realistic as possible is deliberately avoided during this process. Instead, it involves using little effort to develop several (simple) prototypes quickly in the early phases and test their functionality with the final users.

This leads to **iterative cycles** (iterations). In other words, several test runs of the same process steps, since new findings lead to new ideas, which mean new prototypes, and thereby new test results. These results represent new insights that drive the creative and evaluation process again. Thus, the process of learning and a step-by-step approach to an ideal solution continues over several rounds.

- **Determining the space and time of a design thinking process**

  The space and time concept must promote the flexibility and dynamic nature of the design thinking process. Therefore, there should flexibility regarding the media that can be used in room. Metaplan boards, flipcharts, high tables and play corners are part of the basic equipment. Furthermore, creative processes can be supported by metaplan cards and post-it notes of different colours and sizes. Different materials, ranging from clay and *Lego* bricks to other building materials, can be used to develop prototypes (see Sect. 7.4).

  It is recommended to use rooms that are separated from the general workplace, so that the participants in a design thinking process are not always distracted by day-to-day business. While these can still be in the same building, they can be optically separated and, if necessary, have large signs indicating "Please do not disturb creative processes". The reason why many agencies offer their clients appropriate locations is so that they can work undisturbed.

  Creativity takes time. Therefore, a design thinking process should not be quickly scheduled in (unlike brainstorming, see Sect. 7.1). Instead, all participants should be able to concentrate fully on the defined task. Therefore, mobile phones, tablets and laptops should simply be turned off (there are buttons on the devices for this, but these are usually rarely used!).

The **process of design thinking** described above is now explained in detail, so that you know exactly what should happen in which phase (see Fig. 7.2).

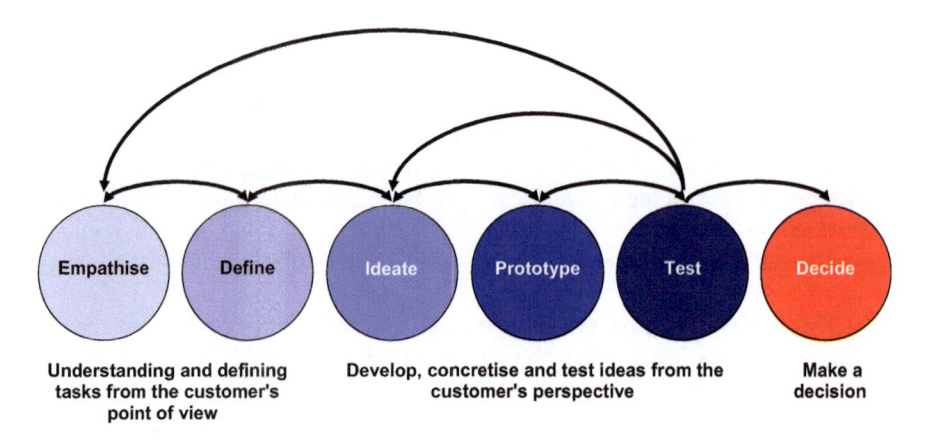

Fig. 7.2 Phases of the design thinking process. Author's own figure

- **Empathise: building empathy for target group**

    The design thinking process starts with the empathise phase (building empathy). It consists of compiling information from various sources and studies that help you to get a good understanding of the initial situation. Insights gained through focus groups and/or in-depth interviews are particularly helpful. These often give particularly comprehensive insights into the disposition of people in the target groups.

    So-called personas are often used to sharpen this perspective. These are fictitious people who each represent very specific target groups (cf. Sect. 3.2.3). They help to achieve a user-centred focus. For these personas, so-called **empathy maps** can be developed that visualise central aspects of the previously researched disposition and express further relevant aspects (cf. Fig. 7.3).

    An empathy map helps you to determine the relevant customer wishes, pain and gain points, as well as the individual needs of the persona. An empathy map allows you to focus on the emotional state of a persona by understanding the individual sensory organs and their perceptions or sensations. That is why the persona is positioned in the centre of the empathy map with the fields "pain" and "gain". Around them, four further areas are defined, which are assigned to the human senses. Each sector is explored with specific questions. These six defined areas must be filled with content that is always consistently from the perspective of a concrete persona! The customer journey map could be used here as well (see Fig. 4.22).

7.3 Design Thinking

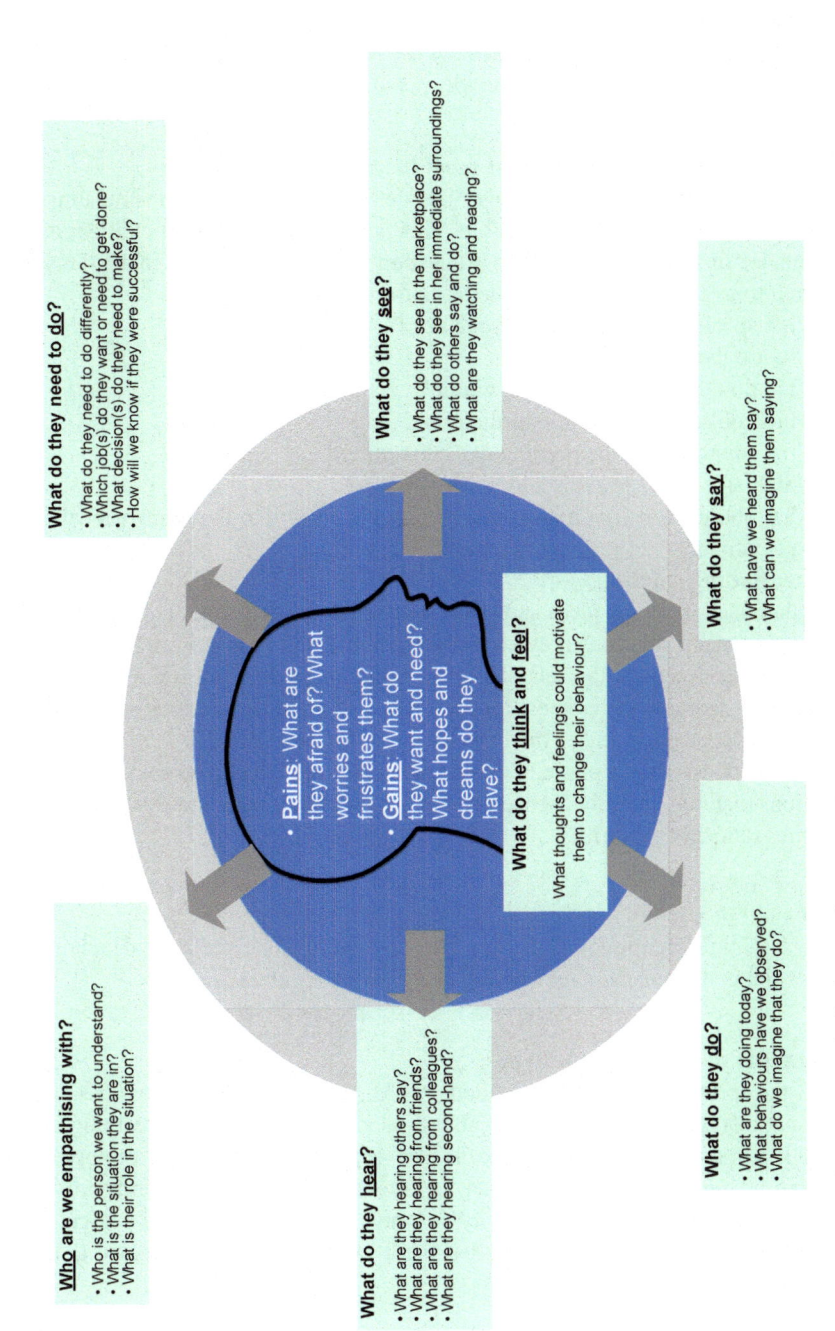

Who are we empathising with?
- Who is the person we want to understand?
- What is the situation they are in?
- What is their role in the situation?

What do they need to do?
- What do they need to do differently?
- Which job(s) do they want or need to get done?
- What decision(s) do they need to make?
- How will we know if they were successful?

What do they see?
- What do they see in the marketplace?
- What do they see in her immediate surroundings?
- What do others say and do?
- What are they watching and reading?

What do they say?
- What have we heard them say?
- What can we imagine them saying?

What do they hear?
- What are they hearing others say?
- What are they hearing from friends?
- What are they hearing from colleagues?
- What are they hearing second-hand?

What do they do?
- What are they doing today?
- What behaviours have we observed?
- What do we imagine that they do?

What do they think and feel?
What thoughts and feelings could motivate them to change their behaviour?

- **Pains**: What are they afraid of? What worries and frustrates them?
- **Gains**: What do they want and need? What hopes and dreams do they have?

Fig. 7.3 Empathy map for a persona. Author's own figure

> **Remember Box**
> Design thinking entirely revolves around the persona, who is the target for the development. You must understand this persona in depth.

- **Define: definition of the task that must be completed**
  Based on the information above, the define phase involves formulating a question that is as precise as possible. This is also called a **design challenge**. It is a matter of formulating the initial question with the persona in mind. This is referred to as the **point-of-view**, the basis for ideation:
  - What specifically does this persona need?
  - Why do they need it?
  - What do they want to achieve with it?
  - Which obstacles might hinder their use?
  - What support does the persona expect from us?
  - Which side could provide additional support?
  - What should a solution, service, or product look like that can meet these expectations?
- **Ideate: finding solutions**
  In the ideation phase, ideas and initial solutions are developed. The first step is to develop many solutions (keyword **divergence**). You choose from the creative methods discussed in this chapter (e.g. mind maps, brainstorming, attribute listing). To promote the creative process, it is also possible to search specifically for the "most absurd idea". This frees the mind for new ideas!

  This is followed by a phase of **convergence**, during which you select possible solutions that will be further processed in the next phase. After the creative phase, a higher rationality returns!

> **Remember Box**
> Design thinking requires alternating between phases of divergence (finding ideas) and convergence (summarising and classifying ideas).

- **Prototype: developing prototypes**
  In the prototype phase, so-called **rapid prototyping** is used (see the explanations about the minimum viable product in Sect. 8.2). For learning and testing purposes, the simplest means are used to create initial prototypes. Depending on the solution, you can use sketches, wireframes, storyboards or 3D models. At this stage, creativity is only limited by time and budget. If processes and service concepts are designed, role plays can also be used to test the functionality of certain processes.

> **Remember Box**
> You should quickly and cost-efficiently check the relevance of developed solutions by using rapid prototyping.

- **Test: examining the solutions that were found**

   The prototypes are shown to users in the test phase. There are various alternatives depending on the knowledge that you have gained. If the prototype fails, you can use the new findings to restart the ideation process. If the users like the prototype but still think it is a bit rough around the edges, their insights can be processed in a new ideation process. If the individuals in the target group accept the prototype (possibly after several iterations), you enter the last phase. This demonstrates the high flexibility of design thinking. Individual phases are simply run through as often as necessary until a compelling solution is found.

> **Remember Box**
> Since developments are ultimately developed for the users, and not for the paying customers, users play an indispensable role in such processes. Users are defined as the persona in the design thinking process.
>
> Nevertheless, often only bosses decide which solutions to use. The actual users, on the other hand, are far too rarely involved in such decision-making processes. You can and should change that! Design thinking systematically "forces" you to do so!

- **Decide: selecting a solution**

   After the target group "accepts" the prototype, the design thinking process is completed. At this point, the solution concepts gained can be transferred to the "classical" organisation, so that they can be developed and introduced to the market.

In summary, design thinking is based on the following **guiding principles** throughout all these phases:

- Fail often and as early as possible (and inexpensively)!
- Failure is an inexhaustible source of learning!
- It is important that the team has a high degree of autonomy!
- Constructive feedback is a must!
- Learn continuously!
- Make solutions tangible!
- Let the customers decide what really is successful!

▶ **Implementation Tips**
- There are (almost) no limits to the use of design thinking. Wherever you need convincing innovative solutions for products, services, processes, you can use the concept.
- It is important that you allow enough time to prepare the creative space so that all the necessary working materials are available.
- You should also create a "cuddly atmosphere" where participants can feel comfortable and be creative.
- When you start the process, you should outline the rules of the game and procedure so that all participants can get emotionally involved.
- If you have no experience moderating such a process and no other trained employees are available in your company, you should use external moderators.
- The moderator plays a decisive role in the success or failure of design thinking, especially when they moderate in a motivating manner and systematically go through the phases discussed above.
- Through professional implementation, you can generate a high level of engagement and commitment from the participants, which benefits the creative process.

7.4 *Lego* Serious Play

Lego **Serious Play** is another tool that you can use to find new approaches to solving problems through a moderated process. The participants, again preferably from different departments, can develop new business strategies, processes and products in workshops. The moderators of these workshops play a key role because they must align the playful components of this approach with concrete tasks of the company.

> **Remember Box**
> Despite its high level of abstraction, *Lego* Serious Play is a concept with which creative solutions can be developed in mixed teams in a playful yet serious way.

The goal is that the participants use various *Lego* building blocks to create highly detailed models as **metaphors for different aspects of the workshop topic**. It encourages an intensive exchange between the participants about these topics that is supported by play. Several interesting effects can be achieved (see Fig. 7.4):

Fig. 7.4 *Lego* Serious Play—material and results. Author's own figure

- Creativity and innovation are encouraged, as cognitive and manual processes are combined by working with *Lego* bricks.
- The basis for this is the so-called hand-brain connection. Since the hands are particularly intensively connected with the brain cells due to their fine motor abilities, thinking in connection with doing leads to a particularly deep and lasting understanding of the topic at hand.
- Problems and tasks, which some of the participants were only vaguely aware of, suddenly become "touchable" and thus "comprehensible", in the truest sense of the words.
- Things can also be very easily modified or "manipulated" by simply exchanging or changing a few pieces.
- Through the ongoing process of constructing, deconstructing and reconstructing, it is possible to both promote creative processes and new develop new solutions.
- Using common "vocabulary", in this case the *Lego* building blocks, breaks down communication barriers between specialist units and across hierarchical levels.
- At the same time, you can address problem areas more openly, because of its playful nature.
- The playful approach simultaneously shifts the attention and redefines roles, which are independent from the classic tasks of the workshop participants. This allows participants to express completely new creative sides.
- The playful approach also inspires participants to perform well and to go beyond classic creative boundaries, be they self-made or externally defined. Ideally, in these situations, a proper flow develops, which encourages the players to rise to their task.
- It has been shown that by constructing real things, it is easier to grasp connections and at the same time develop new solutions.

For which questions can you use *Lego* Serious Play? Firstly, it is possible to support corporate **strategy development** with this approach. The first step is to visualise the internal and external influences on the company. Next, possible strategy scenarios can be played through and evaluated regarding their long-term contribution to the development of the company. However, this approach can also be used to visualise concrete **challenges the company faces** and make them comprehensible, so that solutions can be developed. The *Lego* building blocks then provide the material to promote the analysis of the status quo and to develop solutions.

▶ **Implementation Tips**

- Implementing *Lego* Serious Play requires trained and experienced moderators. Only they can ensure that this approach is used successfully.
- If thematic "laymen" try to moderate such a process, they can only fail.
- Therefore, you should only use this method with external support if you do not have suitably trained staff.
- It is important that the participants of such a workshop understand the relevance of the concept at an early stage.
- However, the approach should not be overcomplicated for the participants by giving them a comprehensive introduction to the theoretical basics, so that they can work with a clear mind.

7.5 Mind Map

A **mind map** is both an important and simple tool. An **analytical-creative search procedure** is a method to systematically promote **creative processes**. You can use this method to develop presentations, lectures and professional articles. You can also plan events or all the things you want to do with your sweetheart in the new year.

We often collect ideas in a structured form one after the other. This is done in a certain order. Ideas that do not fit into a category are rejected and postponed until later, and then they are forgotten. This is exactly where the mind map concept comes in. In the analogue world, you take an A3 or A4 sheet of paper or a whiteboard, if you want to develop the mind map in a team. Various digital mind map versions are also available on the Internet.

When creating a mind map, you place your **main theme** in the middle of the sheet or whiteboard. This can be "Plan with sweetheart 2019" or "Lecture on Digital Darwinism" or "Plan the customer event". Other thoughts and ideas related to the main theme are written on **lines** that connect to the centre **using keywords**.

The lines connected to the main theme are **structured hierarchically**. The lines that originate directly from the main theme represent the main points. This is illustrated using the example of "Plan with sweetheart 2019" (cf. Fig. 7.5). For this topic, the following could be examples of **main points** or main branches:

7.5 Mind Map

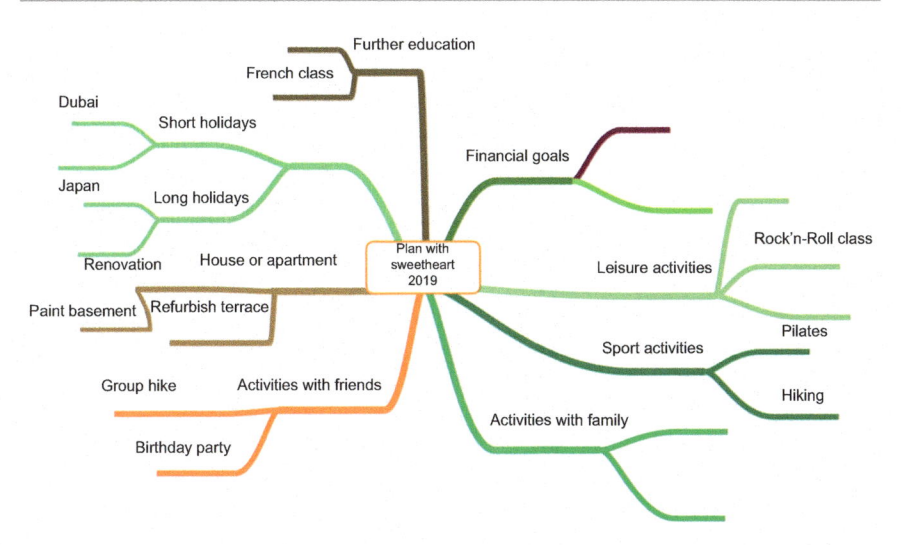

Fig. 7.5 Mind map concept (created with webgreat.de). Author's own figure

- Holidays
- Financial targets
- House or apartment
- Activities with friends
- Activities with family
- Sports activities
- Cultural activities
- Further education

It is not crucial that you recognise and record all these points at once. For example, you may be planning a trip to Dubai before it becomes clear to you that you need a point entitled "holidays". Then insert this theme as the main branch in the mind map. Even before you write "Dubai" on a next branch of the thought tree, perhaps another idea comes to you. You think it makes sense to differentiate between the shorter and longer holidays that you are planning. In this case, you should add these two additional branches first and then add "Dubai" to the short holidays because you only want to spend 5 days there (see Fig. 7.4).

Then you remember that you want to celebrate your birthday in a big way. However, this is not a top point itself, but rather a part of "activities with friends". This means you have already defined the next main branch. In this way, you can be creative, jumping from idea to idea without losing anything. If you have a detail point, first check to which superordinate topic and thus to which main and/or secondary branch it belongs. Then, insert it in the main branch or further sub-points, if necessary. It is important that all branches are connected to each other.

> **Remember Box**
> A mind map allows you to quickly examine and structure more complex processes and projects and to develop further ideas either alone or in a team.

When creating a mind map, usually only key terms or short sentences are used to ensure readability. It is important that you and/or your team have the same idea of what this means. When developing a presentation, it can be useful to develop the planned structure of the presentation as main and secondary branches. Analogous to brainstorming, in this creative process, it is essential that you initially collect as many ideas as possible and participants are not associated with ideas. An evaluative analysis of the result only takes place in a later phase.

You should keep in mind that a mind map does not have to meet any artistic requirements. This very personal tool is about readability and transparency for you and/or your team (cf. Müller 2013).

> **Remember Box**
> You can also use this kind of mind map if you want to plan the next year with your sweetheart or family. What could be nicer than coming together on the first of January and thinking about what you would like to do, achieve, start and/or complete in the next 12 months. This is a small but fine contribution to your own life planning, and an important step towards more joie de vivre (I say this from my own experience).

▶ **Implementation Tips**

- You can easily create a mind map on your own or in a team if you want to quickly bring together a few ideas or gather material for a presentation or an article.
- You simply write your main topic in the middle of an empty sheet, and then you are all set.
- Next, you can collect important keywords that fit to the topic.
- To organise your thoughts, you should always look for suitable headings for these keywords.
- This creates a framework of ideas in which nothing gets lost.
- You can often end this creative process after 30 or 45 min because all relevant factors have been gathered.
- If necessary, look at the result again on the following day and check whether something is missing.
- There is no easier way to support creative processes.

7.6 World Café

Today, the **World Café concept** is of great importance for exploiting the creative and solution potential of larger groups (cf. Brown and Isaacs 2005). This specific workshop method is suitable for groups of about 12–15 participants or more and can be a particularly refreshing way of loosening up larger conferences.

> **Remember Box**
> As a very interactive element, the World Café can be integrated into larger events to encourage participants to communicate, which is often neglected in many plenary lectures. Then, ideally, you no longer hear, "The breaks were the best thing about our conference".

This concept is already being used by many companies when heterogeneous groups must work on joint topics, since it brings together different perspectives. Additionally, it is possible to directly react to ideas, suggestions and evaluations of other participants. Thus, not only are ideas generated in the World Café, but they can be shaped, evaluated and, if necessary, further developed. Ideally, initial ideas can also be developed into an action plan. Moreover, participants who may be working on the same topics for the first time are able to network, especially in large companies.

> **Remember Box**
> The core idea of the World Café is to motivate participants to engage in intensive exchange on predefined issues. This means that many exciting ideas can often be developed in just 1 h. You could call it "analogue crowd sourcing".

You can use a World Café for the following **purposes**:

- Strategy development
- Developing measures for the implementation of strategies
- Gathering ideas while considering feedback from different parties
- Investigating the optimisation potential of processes and procedures
- Processing new ideas, concepts or procedures in preparation for their implementation
- Developing follow-up measures
- Important side-effect: promotion of exchange within and between different groups

If you would like to use the World Café concept, an **impulse lecture** is recommended to get all participants in the mood for the desired topic. During this lecture, the participants are presented with relevant background information on the subject area. Various questions are then derived from the content presented, which are then discussed in **small groups**. Ideally, these groups should have no more than 8–10 participants. Larger groups should be divided into this number per group. If you divide the total number of participants of an event by 8–10, you will know how many questions you need to prepare, and how many moderators or hosts are required.

Organising a **World Café** involves preparing **round tables** in the room. Each round table is dedicated to a specific theme. Usually, two to four metaplan boards, possibly accompanied by a flipchart, are provided to help work on a problem. Other supplies include post-its, metaplan cards, push pins and plenty of (working) board markers.

At the start, the participants distribute themselves evenly around the prepared round tables. There is a **moderator** at each table. These people should have experience in group moderation because they play a very important role. These could be people from the HR department. If the moderators are from the represented departments or even the responsible managers, biased results are possible. Furthermore, group tensions may become visible in the discussion rounds, especially when the moderator must act a little more authoritatively to steer the group dynamics.

Each moderator briefly introduces the question at hand on and moderates the group discussion. The moderator writes the participants' comments on post-its or metaplan cards and pins them on the board. He or she also can motivate the participants to write themselves. If the participants themselves are writing, more content can be developed. The moderator can also encourage the participants to express their creativity by drawing or sketching.

Depending on the complexity of the topic, approx. **20–30 min of discussion time** should be planned per topic table. When the time is up, all groups are asked to move to the next round table at the same time. In total, a World Café should not last longer than 2–3 h, because then the participants can run out of creativity. To avoid "running out" of creativity, one World Café can take place in the morning and another in the afternoon.

The participants can **rotate** between the theme tables in a clockwise direction. It is important that you give very clear instructions and show how they should rotate. This prevents confusion among participants, who are (ideally) deeply immersed in a question and sometimes difficult to motivate to continue. It is important that you plan in the rotation time, especially if not all the round tables are in the same room.

If the topic has already been worked on by one or more groups, the moderator will briefly present what progress has been made after each rotation. Therefore, the moderators remain at the same round table all the time. The **short summary of the results achieved** ensures that the "newcomers" can build on the ideas and suggestions that have already been developed by previous group(s) and do not have to start from scratch again. This enables participants to be **creatively stimulated automatically by the previously developed content**.

Ideally, sufficient **seating** should be available so that the participants can "plump down" creatively. Using bar stools and tables, where you can also write, have proven successful. Those who want to sit, can sit. Those who prefer to stand can also do so. Just like with a good espresso, in this type of **creative atmosphere**, ideas can flow freely. It is important that there is an intensive exchange not only with the moderator but above all between the participants. To encourage this, the moderator can keep asking more questions, formulate provocative assumptions or point out contradictions between the various statements.

At the same time, the moderator should also ask the more **reserved participants** for their contributions. Often these are very good and deep thinkers, who first consider their answers thoroughly, and are therefore initially rather reserved with contributions. The moderator must give them enough room, because their statements are often more valuable and deep than those of the **chatterboxes**, who are generally quick to react.

> **Remember Box**
> The main goal of the World Café concept is to facilitate an intensive discussion within the individual groups. It is the moderator's job to always keep this discussion going. Simultaneously, he or she documents the results on the presentation boards, so that everyone can see them.

The World Café concept is ideal when you wish to develop **different perspectives on selected topics** or **solutions for defined tasks** in larger groups. The goals of a certain procedure, possible starting points to achieve goals, as well as drivers and barriers of desired procedures can be determined.

The way the **questions are formulated** is very important. These should be formulated as simply as possible, so that all participants want to participate in a discussion. When dealing with change processes, it can be helpful to have questions formulated by those affected to ensure that the questions address the core of the changes. An **introductory question** can be formulated more openly because this enables lots of information and ideas to be gathered about a topic at first.

Depending on the topic, it may also be useful to seek concrete answers to the question, "What must be done?" This kind of **call to action** at the end of the discussion rounds is particularly important if you not only want to have ideas developed but also actually want to initiate change processes. The answer to the "What must be done?" question provides initial starting points to implement the solution.

> **Remember Box**
> By working on the same topics in several groups, all participants can gain more knowledge. They see what other participants have already worked on and can contribute their own ideas and evaluations. Thus, a proper knowledge networking takes place, especially if the participants come from very different areas of the company.

The **group discussions** in a World Café almost automatically also ensure that all participants listen closely to the contributions of others and let them finish their sentences. Ideas, suggestions and fears of others become apparent and can be discussed. The moderator should try to repeatedly bring in the "problem-solving questions" to break down possible resistance and blockades (cf. Sect. 1.4). This fosters a cooperative spirit in the group and a constructive atmosphere.

> **Remember Box**
> If the World Café is carried out in a respectful, constructive and cooperative atmosphere while simultaneously bringing together employees from very different areas of the company, it can also make an important contribution to cultural change in the company.

Once all the participants have made their way around all the round tables or when the time allotted for group work is up, all the participants are called back into the **plenum**, if there are many participants. At this stage, the moderators must present the overall results of the various rounds of participants. The participants can then ask questions and, if necessary, make further comments. However, this "audience participation" should not get out of hand, because everyone has usually already worked on each topic. Nevertheless, if there are fewer participants, a **vernissage** can take place. In this case, the moderators invite all participants to look at the overall results, which the moderator summarises in his or her own words again.

If the different teams have developed ideas or concepts for certain managers or departments, the moderators can present the results to them. The "recipients" can then comment on the results and, if necessary, indicate the next steps to start the transfer process.

The results achieved can be recorded in a **photo protocol** and forwarded to all participants after the event. This can also promote the implementation of desired changes.

▶ **Implementation Tips**

- When it comes to developing new ideas, solutions, concepts, etc., the World Café concept is an ideal addition to conferences and other corporate gatherings.
- You should prepare the World Café very carefully, since a good atmosphere, convincing moderators and well-formulated questions largely impact the success of the method.
- Allow enough time for individual questions, as well as rotating between the round tables.
- Ensure that there is intensive discussion between the participants.
- Have the moderators present the results in a plenary session or at a vernissage so that everyone gets an overall picture of the results.
- A photo protocol can contribute to a successful follow-up.

References

Brown, J., & Isaacs, D. (2005). *The World Café: Shaping our futures through conversations that matter*. San Francisco: Berrett-Koehler.

Lewrick, M., Link, P., & Leifer, L. (2018). *Das design-thinking playbook: Mit traditionellen, aktuellen und zukünftigen Erfolgsfaktoren* (2nd ed.). Munich: Vahlen.

Mootee, I. (2013). *Design-thinking for strategic innovation: What they can't teach you at business or design school*. Hoboken, NJ: Wiley.

Müller, H. (2013). *Mind mapping* (4th ed.). Freiburg: haufe.

Osborn, A. (1963). *Applied imagination* (3rd ed.). New York: Charles Scribner's Sons.

Poguntke, S. (2018). *Design-thinking*. Accessed March 22, 2018, from https://wirtschaftslexikon.gabler.de/definition/design-thinking-54120

Quade, S., & Schlüter, O. (2017). *DesignAgility – Toolbox media prototyping, Medienprodukte mit design-thinking agil entwickeln*. Stuttgart: Schäffer-Poeschel Verlag für Wirtschaft Steuern Recht GmbH.

Schallmo, D. (2017). Design-Thinking erfolgreich anwenden, So entwickeln Sie in 7 Phasen kundenorientierte Produkte und Dienstleistungen, Wiesbaden.

Stickdorn, M., & Schneider, J. (2010). *This is service design-thinking – Basics, tools, cases*. Amsterdam: BIS.

Uebernickel, F., Brenner, W., Naef, T., Pukall, B., & Schindlholzer, B. (2015). *Design-thinking: Das Handbuch*. Frankfurt: Frankfurter Allgemeine Buch.

Vahs, D., & Brem, A. (2015). *Innovations management, Von der Produktidee zur erfolgreichen Vermarktung* (5th ed.). Stuttgart: Schäffer-Poeschel.

Innovative Project Management Tools 8

You are certainly familiar with the **classic project management tools**. After all, they have been taught and largely used in the same way for decades. This classic approach is now being supplemented or replaced by new methods to cope with the increasing speed of change that challenges must be mastered. I would like to present the most important ones to you.

The methods described below belong to a range of topics of **agile project management**. Figure 8.1 shows how this differs from classic project management.

The agile methods consider the dramatically changed framework conditions with which companies are confronted today. These changes must also be reflected in the competence map of your company. The changes you that should aim for are shown in Fig. 8.2. The "competencies required nowadays" that are described form the basis for the further explanations (cf. also Müller 2017, pp. 27–36).

8.1 Scrum

Your toolbox for agile project management should always include the **Scrum** method (cf. Preußig 2015). The term "scrum" means "crowd" in rugby. This term intends to express that by compressing this method aims to achieve a higher speed, fighting power, mobility and at the same time good results. It is essential to have a highly qualified and passionate team that works together closely, adapts quickly to changing game situations and organises itself. However, this itself requires a largely **empowered team**. Meanwhile, just like in rugby, there are a few **precise rules**!

This specific process model was initially used primarily for agile software development. Scrum is used for numerous large tasks nowadays, not necessarily relating to IT. Scrum is also used in marketing, in sales and, e.g. in the joint development of platform concepts. While products are generally mentioned from this point on, note that this can refer to either a software or a different kind of solution.

Classic project management	Agile project management
▪ Requirements are, apparently, known from the start. ▪ Changes in requirements during the project are not planned. ▪ Changes in requirements (change requests) are associated with high additional costs. ▪ Requirements are primarily described as "technical" ("domain of the technicians"). ▪ The development process is sequential. ▪ The project management process follows clear and unchangeable rules and standards. ▪ The customer only sees the final result, not intermediate results. ▪ If there is a problem during the project, defined milestones are shifted. ▪ Large teams with a strict hierarchical structure are used (tasks are assigned from above). ▪ The members of the development team are proven specialists. ▪ The team members are physically separated and work on different projects at the same time. ▪ Communication takes place via extensive project documentation and during long meetings with extensive to-do lists. ▪ The cost estimation is made by the project manager or experts.	▪ Requirements are blurred at the beginning, and they are treated accordingly. ▪ Changes in requirements during the project are planned and welcome. ▪ Later changes in requirements are planned from the start and only cause low additional costs. ▪ Requirements are consistently described from the user perspective ("user stories"). ▪ The development process is iterative and incremental. ▪ The project management process is continuously optimised based on experiences. ▪ The results are continuously presented to the customer to obtain feedback. ▪ If difficulties arise, the focus is increased and a problem solution is sought immediately. ▪ Small teams are used, which organise themselves to a large extent (tasks are taken independently). ▪ In addition to expert knowledge, the team members also have general knowledge ("T-format"). ▪ The team sits in one room and focuses on one project. ▪ There is a high degree of informal communication; stand-up meetings are held. ▪ The cost estimation is carried out consensually in the team.

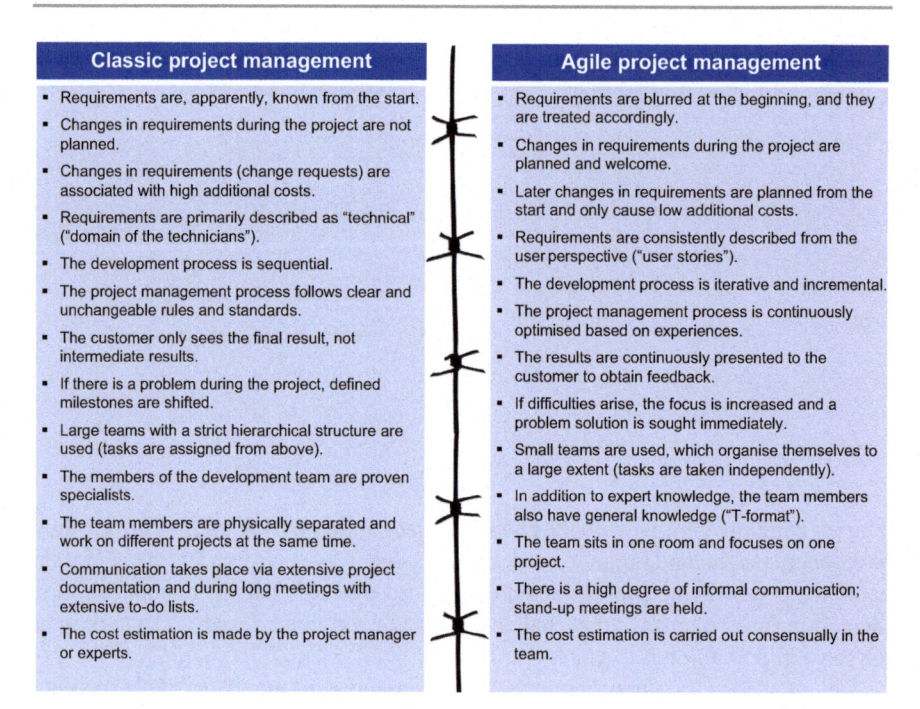

Fig. 8.1 Differences between classic and agile project management. Source: Adapted from Preußig (2015, pp. 41f)

Previously dominant competencies	Competencies required nowadays
▪ Extrapolative procedure in the sense of "more of the same". ▪ Perfection before speed – focus on time to market ▪ Hierarchical organisation – transactional leadership ▪ Tight management over goals ▪ Preserving the already established	▪ Disruptive thinking and acting – stepping out of one's own comfort zone ▪ Speed before perfection – focus on time to value ▪ More intensive work through networks – transformational leadership ▪ Leadership stronger through vision and "sense" (focus on purpose) ▪ Courage to change and to "constant change"

Fig. 8.2 Significant changes in the competence map. Author's own figure

The underlying procedure below is based on the values of the so-called **manifesto for agile software development** (cf. Beck et al. 2018):

- Individuals and interactions are more important than processes and tools.
- Functioning software is more important than comprehensive documentation.
- Intensive cooperation with the customer is more important than contract negotiations.
- Responding to change is much more important than simply following a plan once it has been developed.

8.1 Scrum

> **Remember Box**
> Scrum is the alternative to overwhelmingly hierarchical concepts that give employees precise work instructions to achieve goals (keyword micromanagement). In contrast, with Scrum you rely on highly qualified, interdisciplinary development teams, which strive for a precisely formulated goal.

The employees are free to choose their path to this goal. This enables you to use their knowledge and creativity potential during the entire development process. It is important that there are no specialists in the development team whose absence cannot be compensated directly in the team itself. Otherwise the entire process would come to a (temporary) standstill.

The limits of the classic approach to project management (waterfall concept) were determined quite early when it came to big IT projects. The programming work to implement the originally defined requirements and specifications often took too many months or even years. When the software was ready to use, it often turned out that the use cases or the relevant business transactions had changed so dramatically that a (partial) reprogramming became necessary to complete the version. However, the reprogramming measures were also in the same danger of becoming obsolete during the programming process!

To avoid these dangers, the **Scrum procedure model** was developed. It is based on the described experience that many projects are far too complex and their field of application far too dynamic to define and plan requirements comprehensively at the beginning of the development process. The reason being that many requirements and possible solutions are unknown or cannot be known when starting a project.

Therefore, it is important to achieve **resilient intermediate results** as early as possible during the development process to overcome this shortcoming. These intermediate results make it much easier to overcome ambiguities regarding the requirements than in a purely abstract clarification process that is defined before the project starts. Additionally, it is easier to develop solution approaches if the solution has already been specified.

> **Remember Box**
> More precisely, this means that when using the Scrum methodology, you not only develop the solution but also its planning incrementally and iteratively. "Incremental" means that you break down the entire process into smaller steps. "Iterative"—as in "repetitive"—indicates that you may go through certain work steps several times to find a persuading solution.

As a result, the long-term plan (known as the **product backlog**) not only becomes increasingly refined over time but is also improved with experience. The term "backlog" stands for the "backlog of work" to be processed. The detailed plan (the **sprint backlog**) is only created for the next short cycle. These cycles are called **sprints**. The use of Scrum is designed for teams of three to nine developers. If

Fig. 8.3 Scrum team and other players. Author's own figure

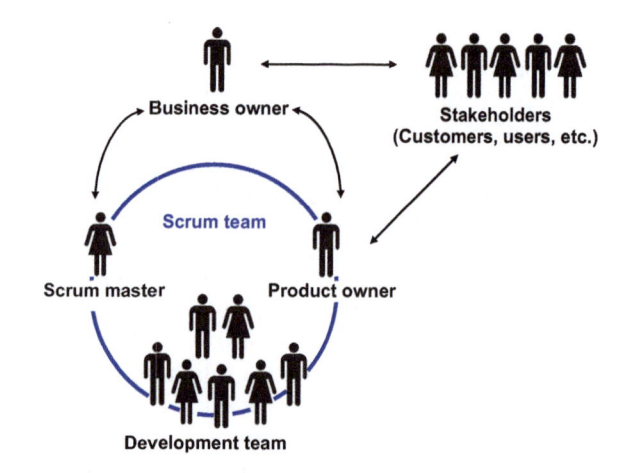

projects require further development, it is necessary to coordinate different teams. This is ensured by a so-called **Scaled Agile Framework**.

In Scrum different parties are distinguished with specific names. The **Scrum team** is at the centre of the Scrum process (see Fig. 8.3). It consists of a **product owner** (the actual customer), a **Scrum master** and several people who form the **development team**. The **business owner** is responsible for the overall organisation of the Scrum team. **Stakeholders** are above all the people for whom a solution is developed. This mainly refers to the customers and especially the users of the future solution. The roles are defined below.

> **Remember Box**
> The Scrum team consists of the product owner (the internal client), the Scrum master (as coach and consultant) and the development team.

Below is a detailed description of the **Scrum team members'** roles:

- **Product Owner**

   The product owner is responsible for the overall project, both in terms of the actual solution and its economic success. He/she presents the internal client, so to speak. This task involves defining and prioritising the desired product characteristics during the development process (the so-called product backlog). Working with the development team and stakeholders, the product owner brings together the product requirements. It is important that the product owner understands the wishes and requirements of the stakeholders in depth and brings them together to form a consistent target image.

   To ensure the desired agility of the process, the product owner should be equipped with the necessary competencies to be able to make all necessary decisions independently and quickly. In business, this is not always the case in practice, which adversely affects the achievable speed. If the waiting time for decisions of relevant stakeholders is too long, the Scrum process can come to a (temporary) standstill because the next sprints cannot be planned. You must avoid this.

- **Scrum Master**

    The Scrum master is responsible for the success of the Scrum process. Therefore, even though the Scrum master is usually not part of the development team, he/she works intensively with them. The main task of the Scrum master is establishing the Scrum rules and ensuring that they are being followed. He/she is also the contact person to overcome disturbances of the Scrum process. Such disruptions can result from insufficient communication within the development team, or between the development team and the product owner. Furthermore, it is his/her role to prevent the development team from being disturbed by other departments, so that the ongoing process is not disrupted.

    The Scrum master thus assumes the role of a coach for the development team, who provides support in critical situations. This includes unwanted competitive behaviour or a silo mentality when it comes to passing important information within the team. The Scrum master does not delegate tasks or give instructions to team members.

    Whether a full-time position is needed for the role of a Scrum master depends on several factors. A full-time position might be necessary if the coach is to support many Scrum processes running at the same time. Moreover, if the company does not have much experience with Scrum and requires important support and training to understand the roles and follow the rules of the game, the Scrum master role will be very demanding. In this case, to be able to make the right interventions, the Scrum master should have a lot of experience in using Scrum.

- **Development Team**

    The development team must deliver the product functionalities that are to be achieved in the sprint phases. The team must take the agreed upon quality standards into consideration. A key task of the development team is also to make an estimation of the effort required. To do so, the team uses the entries in the product backlog, or rather the product backlog refinement. The development team organises itself. The team does not have to let itself be told how to implement the backlog entries but can act relatively freely. This means it is necessary to empower the team.

    The development team must therefore be able to achieve the respective sprint goals without major external dependencies. Therefore, it is important that this development team is interdisciplinary. For instance, the team should include designers, developers, testers, quality managers, documentation and research specialists, etc. "Ideal" team members should be **specialists in a specific field** but at the same time have **holistic perspective**. As already indicated, the development team should consist of three to nine people. A certain size is necessary to be able to cover the necessary specialist disciplines.

    An important prerequisite for the success of Scrum is that the team members are willing to meet requirements that lie beyond their own field of expertise. This means a designer should also be prepared to carry out tests. At the same time, a programmer must be able and willing to think his/her way through design and quality tasks. The willingness to think and act in a consistently networked manner during development can increase the quality of the work, because "one-track specialists" and a silo mentality are not accepted. Much more can be achieved when all team members gain knowledge outside of their own field of expertise.

These different roles make up the **Scrum team**, which encounters the previously mentioned stakeholders. These stakeholders are outside Scrum (see Fig. 8.3). Stakeholders include the following groups:

- **Customers**

  Customers are the people for whom the product is developed. Customers can be in the own company itself if, for example, something is developed for a department. However, most often customers are outside the company. A key task of the product owner is being in close contact with the customers, so that their requirements and wishes can be incorporated into the development process. Therefore, it is essential that the product owner knows exactly what the customer wants. During the development process, the results of the sprints must be continuously presented to the customer to ensure that the expectations and achievements match. The product owner brings the feedback back into the development process.

- **Users**

  Users differ from customers since they are the ones who in fact use the product (cf. Fig. 8.3). A user can be a customer as well but does not have to be. An external marketing department can be the customer. Nevertheless, the employees recording information at the customer touchpoints and entering it into a system are the users. Furthermore, *Audi* can be the customer of an app development, while the actual users are the *Audi* drivers.

  Contrary to the customer, the users are particularly important, because they will actually use the product in their daily lives. Therefore, it is very important to get their view "of things". That is why the product owner should ensure that both parties are involved in the sprint review when users are not customers. The results, wishes and, if necessary, new requirements obtained in this way must be included in the product backlog refinement (cf. Fig. 8.4).

- **Business Owner/Management**

  The business owner is responsible for ensuring that the right conditions exist to implement Scrum, especially that the necessary resources are available. Firstly, this includes the provision of the necessary employees (product owner, Scrum master and development team), who must be able to work undisturbed. Additionally, the necessary premises and working materials must be provided. It is also essential that there is a "mental support" from the management, especially when the Scrum methodology is used for the first time. It is possible that "old" project managers will resist this method. Therefore, it might be necessary that the business owner clearly supports the Scrum master and/or the product owner.

Scrum terminology defines **three artefacts**, which are presented below. The term "artefact" comes from the Latin terms "art/-artis" for "handicraft" and "factum" for "what is made". Consequently, artefact stands for objects created or modified by humans. In the context of Scrum, there are the following artefacts:

- **Product Backlog**

  The product backlog is a structured list of the requirements for the product to be developed or the desired solution (see Fig. 8.4). These are not technical requirements but describe what is to be achieved from a technical and user perspective. User stories can express this perspective very well.

  The product backlog is not static, but instead continuously developed during the ongoing process. The product backlog is the starting point of the development team's work. It is a **work in progress**, and therefore never complete. Defined requirements can be amended, specified or removed. Moreover, it is possible to add new requirements. These requirements can be discovered during sprints and/or through information exchanges with stakeholders. The priorities of the respective entries can also be changed during the process. They are defined by the product owner, who is oriented by criteria such as economic benefit, user relevance, risk, etc. Entries with the highest priority are worked on the first sprints. Risks can arise from dependencies with other requirements. Such dependencies are referred to as **requirements traceability**.

  The product owner is responsible for developing the product backlog. The product owner must also continually update, improve and, if necessary, restructure the product backlog. The fundamental process for this is called **product backlog refinement** (see Fig. 8.4).

- **Sprint Backlog**

  The results of the sprint planning form the sprint backlog (see Fig. 8.4). This is the plan of the tasks to be performed in a sprint. It is created by selecting entries the product backlog for a sprint and breaking them down into individual work steps (tasks). For example, these tasks include development, testing and documentation. The members of the development team update the sprint backlog continuously once they have completed individual tasks. This results in a continuous overview of the current processing status. A task board is often used to visualise this.

- **Product Increment**

  The product increment is the sum of all product backlog entries created during a current sprint, as well as all previous sprints (see Fig. 8.4). At the end of each sprint, a finished partial product is delivered. This partial product is included in the product increment. This partial service should be designed in such a way that it can or could be delivered to the customer (keyword: **potentially shippable product**). Therefore, this partial service must be available in a usable state and thus correspond to the definition of done (what was supposed to be achieved).

Fig. 8.4 Overall flow of Scrum process. Author's own figure

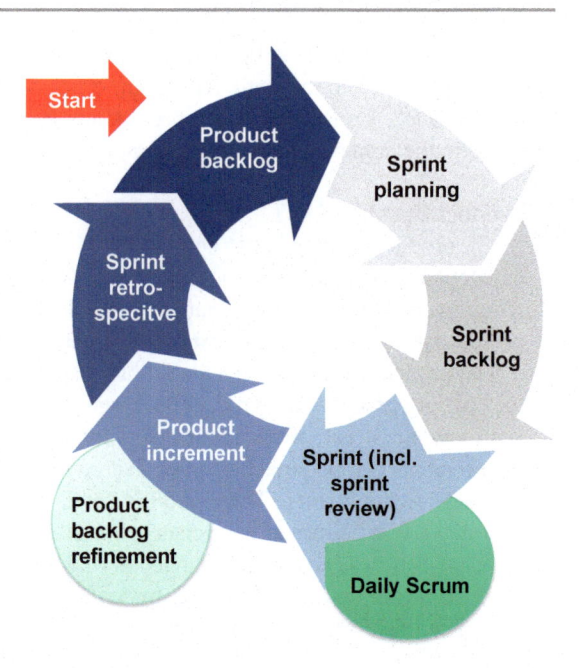

Figure 8.4 shows an overview of the **overall flow of Scrum process**. The starting point of each process is the product backlog. The contents of the following phases will be discussed later.

The **iterative and incremental approach** described above allows for essential improvements during the process. Working step by step helps to ensure that the project's progress and possible obstacles are recognised early and are always visible for all participants. This significantly increases **transparency** in the overall project regarding the possibilities and limits of feasibility within and outside of the Scrum team, as well as within the development team itself.

A so-called **burndown chart** is often used to visualise the progress, thereby increasing the transparency. It shows the work that has already been done and the work that must be completed, thus providing a perfect overview of the status of the project (see Fig. 8.5). The horizontal axis represents the sprints and the number of tasks still to be completed after each sprint is noted on the vertical axis. The line of the unfinished tasks of a sprint should hit the zero line at the end of the sprint at the latest. In Fig. 8.5, this is already the case after the ninth sprint. This chart makes it easy to see which **Scrum goals were achieved** during a sprint. In the daily Scrum, the development team can regularly update the burndown chart.

> **Remember Box**
> The burndown chart makes the progress of the project visible to everyone.

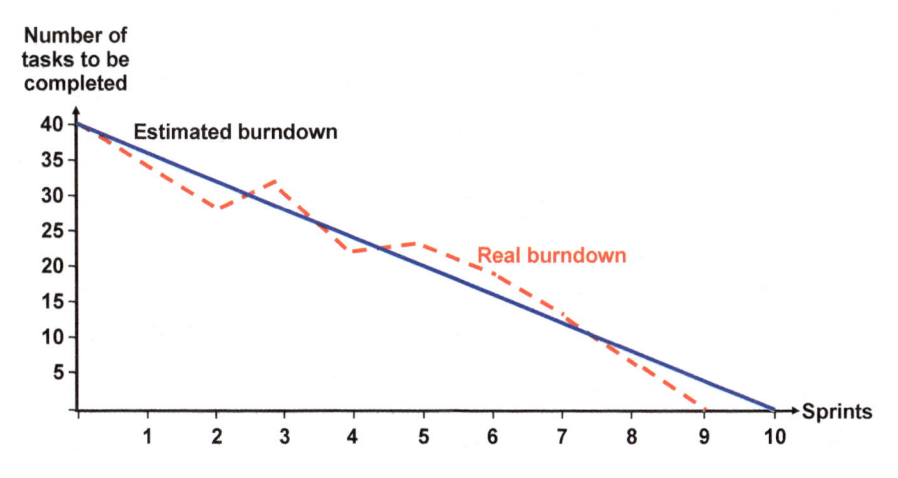

Fig. 8.5 Scrum burndown chart. Author's own figure

Alternatively, the estimated effort for each individual task can be displayed instead of the number of tasks. This is done by continuously estimating the effort that must still be put into all tasks. The higher creation effort leads to an even higher transparency of the project progress.

By documenting these **reviews in short intervals**, you can determine whether the project goals have been achieved and the previous procedure has been successful. Based on these findings, necessary **adjustments** can be made promptly. These can relate to the product, the underlying plans (including targets), as well as to the process itself.

In the Scrum process, the term "meeting" is replaced by **events** or **activities**. This should make it clear that it is not only about communicating but concretely working on the project, which is often not the case in meetings. It is necessary to define concrete time frames for all Scrum activities, which should not be exceeded. These time frames are called **timeboxes**.

> **Remember Box**
> Scrum enables you to manage the overall complexity of a task more easily and quickly, since you split the tasks into smaller, less complex components, and work on them in progressive stages. Thus, Scrum eliminates the need for the initial creation of the most detailed requirements and functional specifications possible.

The **procedure model of Scrum** is based on specific rules. These rules describe the following five activities:

- **Sprint Planning**

    Sprint planning is a key task of the development team (see Fig. 8.4). The product requirements defined in the product backlog are implemented incrementally, step by step, by the development team at intervals of 1–4 weeks. These intervals are called **sprints**. A sprint is therefore a work stage in which part of a product's functionality is developed. Ideally, all sprints should have the same duration, so that the project has a predictable rhythm.

    During sprint planning, the product backlog entries that are selected for a sprint are broken down into individual work steps called **tasks**. In this planning process, the incremental procedure becomes particularly visible. A task should not take more than 1 day. The result of this planning phase is the **sprint backlog**. It defines which steps are to be performed during a sprint (see Fig. 8.4).

    The sprint starts with a planning step (**sprint planning**) and ends with a review of what has been achieved (**sprint retrospective**; see Fig. 8.4). The sprints take place one after another. It is not possible to extend a sprint. When a sprint is over, it is over. Then a new sprint starts. Changes that could endanger the achievement of the sprint goal are not permitted during the sprint itself.

    If it seems obvious that the defined goals of a sprint can no longer be achieved, the product owner can cancel the sprint. This may be necessary if the development team has misjudged the effort required to achieve the goal. A running sprint can also be stopped if the requirements, and thus the goals of the sprint, have changed significantly. In these cases, the running sprint is first ended with a sprint retrospective. Then a new sprint starts with a new sprint planning process as usual.

    During the **sprint planning process**, two central questions must be answered:
- **What?-question**

    What is to be developed in the upcoming sprint, i.e. which goals are to be achieved?
- **How?-question**

    How should the work in the upcoming sprint be organised?

It should not take more than 2 h to plan each weekly sprint during this planning process. The planning process is, however, often split into two parts. Thus, if a sprint is scheduled for 4 weeks, the planning should not take more than 8 h.

It is the job of the product owner to **answer the What?-question** by presenting the desired product properties defined in the product backlog with the assigned priorities to the development team. Therefore, it is important that the product backlog has been prepared in the previously completed sprint in the so-called product backlog refinement (see Fig. 8.4). More concretely, this means that the prioritised product properties were put in order, and the entries for the next sprint were estimated. Based on this information, the entire Scrum team, meaning the product owner, Scrum master and development team, first develops a common understanding of the work that must be done. During this process, the desired characteristics and acceptance criteria for the desired solution are defined. Additionally, it involves defining the requirements or criteria, to use at the end of the sprint to assess whether the desired functionality has in fact been achieved. This is also referred to as the definition of done.

Definition of done is commonly understood by the entire Scrum team as work that is finished. It is determined by certain quality criteria and other mostly non-functional requirements, which are described in the definition of done at the beginning of a sprint. The definition of done written at the beginning of a project can be refined during the process.

The declared goal is to **complete a deliverable product** during a sprint. This is a product part (also called **product increment**; cf. Fig. 8.4) that has not only been sufficiently tested but is also integrated into the overall solution to such an extent that it could be given to the user.

In the next step of the planning process, the development team estimates the number of product backlog entries it can process in the next sprint. The team is responsible to estimate this effort. The order in which entries are processed is defined by the product owner. By combining these two perspectives, the Scrum team defines the **sprint goal** together.

The **How?-question is addressed** in the next step by the development team. The team determines which individual tasks must be achieved to reach the sprint goal, thus delivering the promised product backlog entries. The development team is responsible for planning this. If necessary, the product owner can be consulted during this phase to clarify open questions.

The result of the sprint planning process is the **sprint backlog** (see Fig. 8.4). It represents a detailed plan for the next sprint. This includes the planned product backlog entries, as well as the tasks so they can be implemented. It is often visualised with a task board. This provides an overview of the current tasks.

- **Daily Scrum**

    An integral part of Scrum is to have the development team meet regularly at the beginning of each working day of a running sprint. This is called **daily Scrum** or **daily standup** (see Fig. 8.4). It should not take more than 15 min. The product owner and Scrum master play a supporting role in this activity. Essentially, it is about directly exchanging information, especially within the development team. Through this regular exchange, **osmotic communication** can be achieved. This means that all members of the Scrum team have the same amount of information.

    Therefore, the daily Scrum is primarily about getting an overview of the work that has been completed. The daily Scrum is not intended to provide solutions to problems. Using a **task board**, each member of the development team can show what has been achieved since the last daily Scrum, what lies ahead until the next daily Scrum and what obstacles may have to be overcome in the process. The daily Scrum also focuses on **work in progress limits** (WIP limits). This means ensuring that not too many tasks are being worked on at once. Productivity could suffer as a result.

    This regular exchange of information quickly makes it apparent if the effort planning for a task was incorrect and will take longer than planned. A procedure to be worked out in the daily Scrum could consist of splitting the corresponding task into smaller tasks and distributing them to other members of the development team. There are two options if problems that arise within the daily Scrum cannot be solved within the tight time frame. First, they are only documented and handed over to the Scrum master for processing. Or the tasks are moved to a later activity that often occurs on the same day.

- **Sprint Review**

  The sprint review is an important part of the sprint that takes place at the end (see Fig. 8.4). It takes no longer than 1 h per sprint week. This activity involves the entire Scrum team, as well as the stakeholders, reviewing achieved result (product increment). This means the development team presents its results. These are compared with the defined sprint targets. The next steps are discussed based on the insights gained.

  The first task of the product owner is to analyse the functionalities developed by the team. This involves checking whether the defined acceptance criteria have been fulfilled. If the functionality is only partially finished, or if it has not yet been tested, these acceptance criteria have not been met. It is necessary to read such not yet finalised user stories (descriptions of the requirements from the customer's point of view) in the product backlog. They must be prioritised again for the next sprint. However, this formal check is only one aspect of the sprint review. This check often already takes place during the sprint. Nonetheless, acceptance is not the primary purpose of the sprint review, which is primarily concerned with feedback from stakeholders. The acceptance of the functionalities of the product increment is therefore often implemented within the framework of the sprint.

  However, rather than a purely formal review, it is much more important that customers and users are involved in the sprint review. After all, the entire Scrum process is oriented around their wishes and expectations. The sprint review that takes place after each sprint is used to obtain feedback from these important stakeholders throughout the entire process. This can result in new requirements from customers and users. It is also possible that a functionality fulfils all previously defined acceptance criteria according to the Scrum team but that customers or users don't see this the same way. This happens if an implemented functionality hinders the user's workflow and is therefore not practicable.

  The product owner notes the stakeholder's feedback during the sprint review. Based on these results, the product backlog must be adjusted or supplemented in the next product backlog refinement. This acquired knowledge is used to plan the next sprint.

> **Remember Box**
> After each sprint, the developed solution is put to acid test by the users. This type of "real use" test does not only take place after the entire process has been completed!

- **Sprint Retrospective**

  The sprint retrospective takes place at the end of each sprint. It should not last more than 45 min per sprint week. For a 4-week sprint, this activity should take about 3 h. During this time, the entire Scrum team checks its own procedures to identify weak points and implement optimisations in the next Scrum. The Scrum master supports the development team and can ideally contribute his/her experience from a variety of similar processes.

This **analysis on a meta-level** consists of an open and constructive discussion. This is also the time to discuss personal thoughts that need to be cleared up before the next sprint. Therefore, it is necessary to have a protected area without external disturbances. Stakeholders can only participate if explicitly invited.

A **five-phase concept** has proven useful to **carry out the sprint retrospective**:

Phase 1
The basis of a successful sprint retrospective is an **atmosphere of mutual appreciation**. The moderator must ensure that a **constructive language** is used based on the communication rules in Chap. 1. If problems have arisen within a sprint, more **problem-solving questions** should be asked which can lead to new solutions (see Sect. 1.4). The entire activity must take place in such a climate. This ensures that an openness is achieved, which is needed to overcome the difficulties that have come up. It is good if all the participants come with the mindset that all team members have done the best they could.

Phase 2
Based on this basic consensus, the relevant points are first brought together on an unrated **open issue list**. This kind of list with the defined obstacles is also called an **impediment backlog**. This involves looking back at the last sprint and pinpointing both what went well and not so well. Critical points from earlier sprints should not come up, since it would mean previous sprint retrospectives could not clarify all relevant points. If, however, such points come up, they must now be clarified according to the motto "disturbances come first".

Phase 3
Now it's time to get to the bottom of the points collected on the open issue list. This is done using concepts of **root cause analysis**. This involves identifying the actual causes of errors or problems in the previous sprint. It should ensure that not only symptoms but also the actual causes are identified and eliminated accordingly. This phase provides important insights for the quality management of the entire Scrum approach.

Phase 4
After a comprehensive root cause analysis, **action items** are now defined. Within the development team, a concrete decision is made about how to act in the future. It means making and documenting appropriate agreements on concrete measures with all participants, which will be used or considered in the next sprint.

Phase 5
The sprint retrospective should be concluded on a positive note that is oriented towards solutions. There should be a positive motivation to tackle the next sprint.

- **Product Backlog Refinement**

    The product backlog refinement (sometimes also referred to as backlog grooming; grooming stands for "maintenance") is an ongoing process. In this process, the product owner continuously develops the product backlog together with the development team. This plays an essential role in the Scrum concept, because this process does not revolve around requirements and target specifications that were defined at one point for many months.

    On the contrary, new findings, experiences and requirements from customers and users can be continuously integrated throughout the entire development process and used as a basis for further work. Stakeholders play a particularly important role in product backlog refinement because the desired functionalities must pass the test as being useful in the daily lives of customers and users. Thus, the product backlog refinement activities often take place with selected stakeholders.

The following steps are part of the **product backlog refinement process** (see Fig. 8.4):

- Reorganising the existing entries in the product backlog
- Eliminating entries that are no longer relevant
- Adding new entries in the product backlog
- Making existing entries more concrete
- Merging or splitting of different entries (e.g. based on the findings of a sprint review)
- Estimating the effort of entries
- Planning possible releases

The following **techniques**, some of which have already been mentioned, are frequently used within the **Scrum framework**:

- **User Story**

    A user story is a specific technique used to compile the requirements for a product from the user's perspective. In general, the everyday language of the user is used. These user stories are used to describe the product features a user wants in the product backlog. These user stories are often expressed as follows: "As a user of X, I expect the function Y or the property Z to achieve the benefit A". For a coupon management app, the following could be a user story: "As a user of the app of my customer retention programme, I would like to activate all relevant coupons that are still valid today by clicking just one button. I want only coupons from shops in my proximity to be activated".

    Part of the product backlog refinement task consists of the product owner and development team clearly understanding these user stories and using them to determine acceptance criteria for the definition of done. Furthermore, it is necessary to clarify whether such a user story should be worked on within a sprint or be broken down into smaller stories. The insights gained must be documented in the product backlog.

- **Task Board**

  The task board is an important tool for the Scrum team that is used to visualise the sprint backlog. It documents which product backlog entries have been selected for a sprint. Additionally, it is possible to identify which tasks must be processed and what their status is. This is often doing with a **Kanban board** (see Fig. 8.6).

  Often the task board consists of the four columns shown in Fig. 8.6. The first column defines the requirements from the product backlog that the development team has selected for each sprint. As illustrated by Fig. 8.6, the other columns contain the status of the tasks that need to be completed.

  Using this task board, each member of the development team can explain which tasks have been performed on the previous day, and whether they have been completed. Tasks that could not be completed in 1 day or where problems occurred are marked separately. Overcoming these problems can result in new tasks on the task board. This also helps to increase transparency, because obstacles and necessary measures to remove them become visible.

- **Planning Poker**

  Methods used to estimate the effort required for the various tasks are very important in Scrum. This process is designed as a **dynamic procedure**. In the first step, the members of the development team make initial estimates independently and uninfluenced. The so-called **planning poker** is used to accelerate this process.

  First, each participant receives a set of playing cards. This contains **cards with levels of difficulty** (from trivial to simple, medium, difficult to very difficult or extremely difficult) or **cards with numbers and characters**. The number "0" stands for a task that is too small to be processed in isolation. Numbers from "1" to, e.g. "40" stand for a concrete estimated effort. This is rarely expressed in hours and instead in working days (0, 1, 2, 4, 8, 20, 40, 80). The sign "∞" indicates that the whole task is considered too large and complex to be estimated. It must be broken down into subtasks. A "?" means that the task is not outlined precisely enough to be planned.

  Here is a description of the planning poker process. First, the product owner presents the user story, which must be estimated in terms of effort. The participants can exchange ideas and ask the product owner questions to understand this user story. Each member of the development team then chooses a card that best matches the perceived level of difficulty. All selected cards are revealed at the same time to avoid the effects of group pressure. Next, the members with extreme values (lowest and highest) explain their reasons for the rating. This process is repeated until a consensus is reached, and this is also called iteration. This overall process is carried out for all user stories.

  To prevent these estimates from getting out of hand when there are many user stories, you can make time specifications for estimating the individual stories. If no consensus is reached within the defined time span, it could be an indication that the user story is imprecise. It is then necessary to create a new and more precise user story.

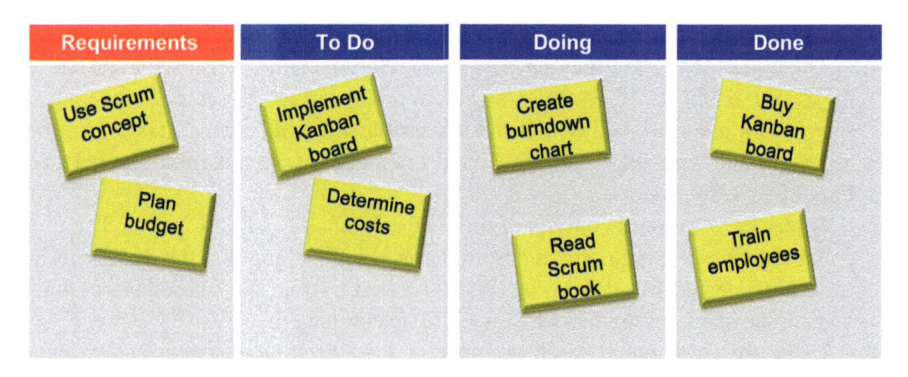

Fig. 8.6 Scrum Kanban board. Author's own figure

- **Impediment Backlog**

    The Scrum master uses this to collect the observed work obstacles for all to see. The impediment backlog often does not only contain the obstacles that have been found but can also show tasks for their solution to solve them and their status. Obstructions can also be noted directly on the task board and thus made visible to everyone.

By consistently implementing this procedure, you can make your projects significantly more agile.

▶ **Implementation Tips**

- The powerfulness of this tool is shown by the complexity of the Scrum approach with its many technical terms and precise process steps. Therefore, you should optimally prepare its implementation in your company.
- When using it for the first time, there are two possibilities. First, you can train one of your managers as a Scrum specialist to build up the know-how in your own company. Such a Scrum specialist can take on the role of the Scrum master.
- Otherwise, you can rely on external Scrum specialists to prove the efficiency of this concept in your company for the first time. This procedure also makes sense if you are unsure whether Scrum will be used permanently in your company.
- Since many internal resistances must be overcome when using Scrum for the first time, external support is usually the first choice. This increases the method's chance of success.
- If your company is constantly faced with comprehensive development tasks, you should, however, build up your own Scrum competence. Rather sooner than later!

- Remember that good Scrum teams need time to develop, because they require a different kind of cooperation in content and spirit.
- Lastly, an indispensable prerequisite for the success of Scrum is that the Scrum team is comprehensively empowered.
- And don't forget to figure out in which situations Scrum is the better appropriate solution in comparison with the traditional waterfall concept.

8.2 Lean Startup

The **lean startup** development concept is based on similar considerations to the Scrum approach presented in Sect. 8.1. It aims to bring solutions to the market more quickly that are highly relevant there because there is a convincing supply/demand fit. By using lean startup, you can make an important contribution to ensuring this **supply-demand fit**, which is decisive for success, through a specific procedure (see also Lennarz 2017, pp. 63–72).

> **Remember Box**
> The core idea of lean startup is as simple as it is obvious and yet often not consistently implemented. It's about developing a product or service very close to the market and incorporating continuous feedback from potential customers during the development process.

In doing so, you consistently leave the ivory tower of product development and face the criticism of your target group early and relatively unprotected. However, it is better to do so early and relatively unprotected than after completing the development work, when all budgets for development and market launch have already been used.

The necessity to act much closer to the market results from the content of the **analysis grid for innovations**. Figure 8.7 shows you which type of innovation is likely to be accepted in the market. If a product is changed very comprehensively and thus shows a high degree of innovation, it has a higher potential for success. However, the behavioural changes on the part of the customers and thus the resistance to innovation are also significantly greater. Consequently, product launches will be accompanied by a long **dry spell**, as was the case with the CD (compact disc) introduced in 1982 (cf. Fig. 8.7).

On the other hand, streaming offers quickly became **bestsellers** because they offered decisive convenience advantages. Products that make only minor changes to established products but represent a significant change in behaviour will **certainly fail**. **Easy selling**, on the other hand, can be accompanied by innovations that result in minimal behavioural changes. However, from the customer's point of view, it is questionable why a product change should take place at all.

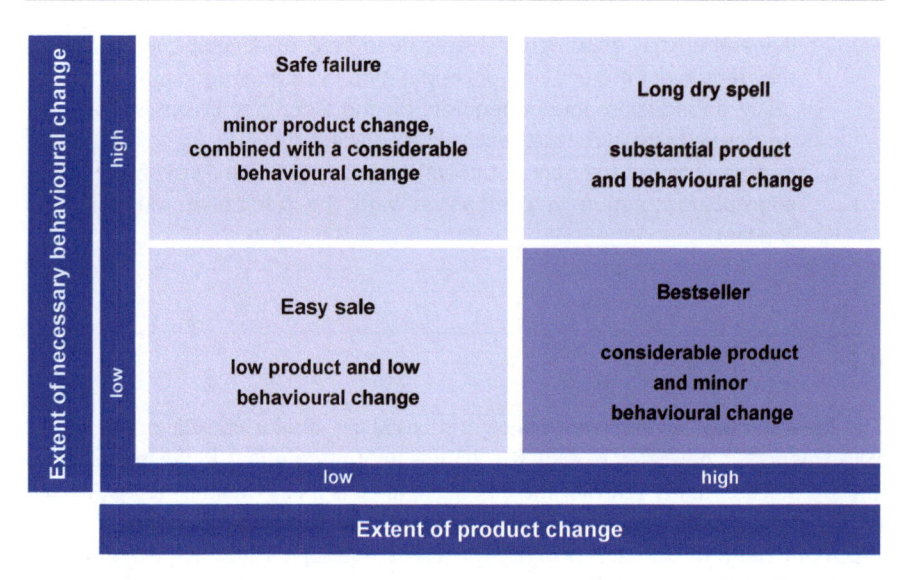

Fig. 8.7 Analysis grid for innovations. Source: Adapted from Gourville (2006, p. 54)

[Grid described:
- Y-axis: Extent of necessary behavioural change (low/high)
- X-axis: Extent of product change (low/high)
- High behavioural / Low product: **Safe failure** – minor product change, combined with a considerable behavioural change
- High behavioural / High product: **Long dry spell** – substantial product and behavioural change
- Low behavioural / Low product: **Easy sale** – low product and low behavioural change
- Low behavioural / High product: **Bestseller** – considerable product and minor behavioural change]

It is precisely in this area of conflict that lean startup is applied to help company founders develop market-relevant innovations. This is because particularly startups are often better able to develop **ground-breaking innovations** than established companies, which (too) often concentrate on product variations (see Sect. 3.5 for more details). At the same time, the aim is to significantly shorten the **time span between product development and market launch** (cf. Kreutzer 2018).

However, nowadays, many companies still align their behaviour with the **time to market**. The time to market is measured in days, weeks, months and/or years and indicates the lead time between a product/service idea and its launch on the market. During this time, the phases of product/service development and, if necessary, market tests are carried out. Since there is no productive deployment during this period and thus no "test" in actual deployment, this entails risks of aberration. At the same time, costs for market research, prototype construction, communication, market research, etc. are incurred. On the other hand, sales are generally not yet generated. A value for the customer is achieved through product/service innovation only after the development and test phase has been completed and consequently after the launch of the product or service innovation (see Fig. 8.8).

However, you should try to place innovations on the market as quickly as possible to beat competitive offers and take advantage of the so-called innovators and early adopters that are generally willing to pay more (cf. on the diffusion process for new products Kreutzer 2017, pp. 231–233). The time to market of many companies is still often too long. This means that a lot of time passes before a marketable product or service innovation is available. A delayed market launch pays off especially for products and services with a very short life cycle, especially if a lot of time must still be invested in development. The faster an offer is replaced by a

8.2 Lean Startup

Fig. 8.8 Time to market. Author's own figure

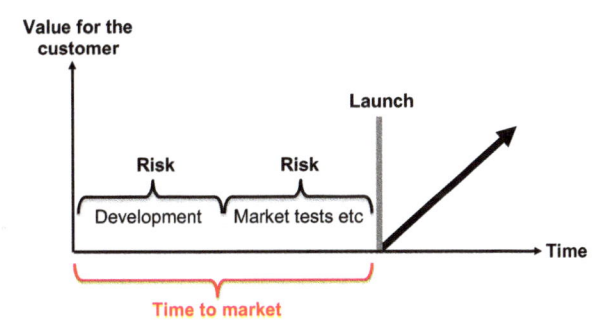

revised one, the more unsuccessful the companies will be who have not geared their development processes to speed.

> **Remember Box**
> An orientation towards the time to market is becoming less and less appropriate to today's requirements for the speed of innovation processes.

To achieve speed, you should therefore concentrate more on **time to value**. The time to value is also measured in days, weeks, months and/or years and indicates the lead time between a product/service idea and its first customer benefit. Consequently, there is no waiting for a perfect product or service innovation to be introduced to the market.

> **Remember Box**
> The challenge today is focusing on time to value!

Firstly, **rapid prototyping** can contribute to shortening time. This involves generating "tangible" products and services from the product/service idea as quickly as possible to test their suitability. Additionally, the market launch can already begin once a stable product or a functioning service innovation is available that can generate value for the customer. This is called a **prelaunch**. It marks a very early introduction into the market with an initial functional product or service. For products, this is referred to as a **minimum viable product** (MVP). It refers to a product or service that meets the minimum requirements to be used by customers (see Fig. 8.9).

Fig. 8.9 Theory of the minimum viable product (MVP). Author's own figure

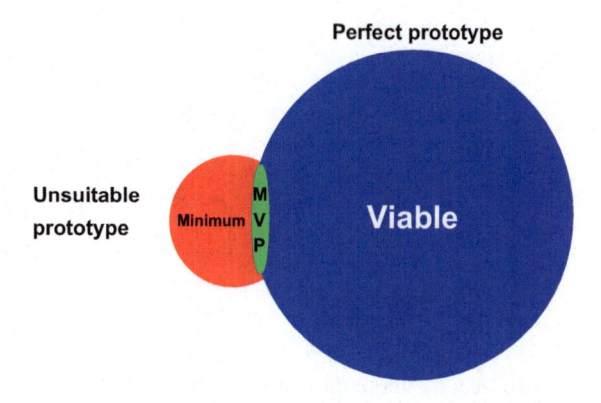

Remember Box

Companies such as *airbnb*, *Amazon*, *Dropbox* and *Zappos* have driven their original business ideas forward through the lean startup approach.

You should examine whether this concept, which is discussed in the context of lean startups, especially in software development, is also useful in your company (cf. Ries 2017).

Compared to the time to market approach, the prelaunch mentioned above enables you to achieve a **benefit for the customer** much earlier. At the same time, you will learn what you need to optimise, and which features urgently need to be developed while working together with real customers. This continuous development goes hand in hand with an early **creation of value for the customer**. You can launch the "final" product or service later. Often a smooth transition from the prelaunch phase to the launch phase is the best option, with continuous value creation for the user (cf. Fig. 8.10).

Fig. 8.10 Time to value. Author's own figure

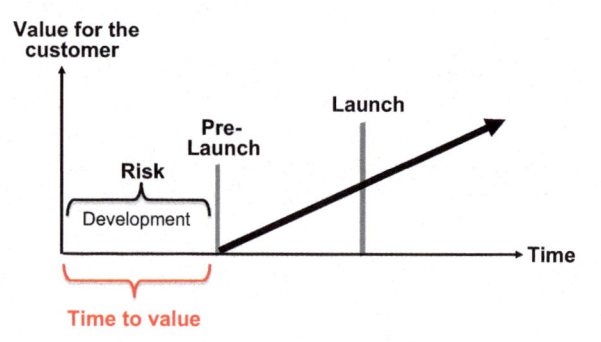

8.2 Lean Startup

> **Remember Box**
> Don't mix the time to value concept with the banana approach. The first concept delivers value for the customer from the very beginning. The banana approach goes like this: The unfinished product matures at the customer—therefore he/she has to suffer a lot! This is not the idea of time to value—because it doesn't create value for the customer!

As soon as an operational product or a functioning service innovation is available, you can offer it to a (limited) circle of users ("**prelaunch phase**"). Based on the ideas of agile management, this enables you to gain ideas to further develop and optimise the offer in cooperation with "real" users and take them into account in the currently unfinished innovation process (cf. Edelman and Singer 2015). The actual **launch** then occurs somewhat later (cf. Fig. 8.10).

> **Remember Box**
> By focusing on the time to value, you can achieve several goals:
>
> - On the one hand, your company can penetrate the market earlier with its own offers.
> - Secondly, you can fine-tune a product or service in a real market environment as well as identify and stop undesirable developments at an early stage.
> - Thirdly, you may already be able to achieve your first (reduced) profits by offering a 70/80% solution. This allows you to at least partially cover the costs incurred in the innovation process for market research, prototype construction, communication, etc.

The **lean startup method** is based on the following considerations and offers a market-oriented procedure model in three stages (cf. fundamentally Ries 2017):

- Build
- Measure
- Learn

Based on the idea of time to value, the goal of this approach is to bring a product, a service or a complete business idea to market as quickly as possible. To make it relevant for the target group, comprehensive feedback should be obtained as early as possible. This should provide impulses and ideas for further development and, if necessary, for a reorientation of the innovation. Through this consistent market orientation, you can save both time and money.

Fig. 8.11 Lean startup model. Author's own figure

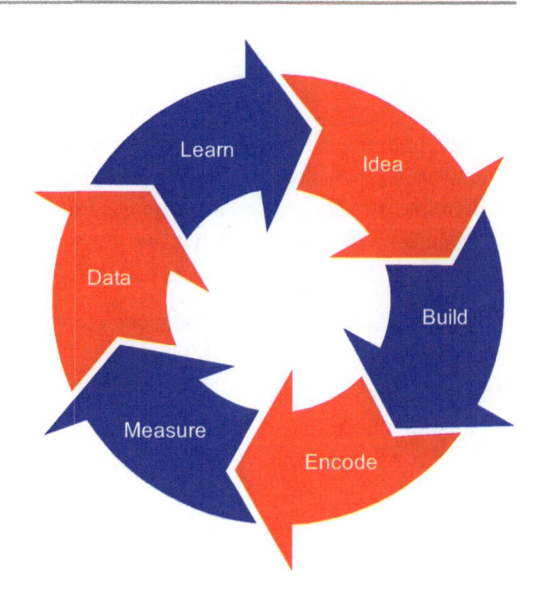

For this purpose, iterative tests of important performance features of the product or the service itself are carried out. However, you can also "test" pricing, distribution concepts, positioning ideas and elements of brand management on the market during the ongoing development process. Since this process is constantly repeated, there is a **cycle of building, measuring and learning** shown in Fig. 8.11 results. In this way, you consistently align your performance with the requirements of the market. You repeat this cycle in a lean startup until the solution is accepted by the market.

Here is a description of the phases of the **building, measuring and learning cycle**.

Phase 1: Building—Lean Product Development Based on a Starting Hypothesis
The starting point of the cycle of building, measuring and learning is an **idea** in the form of a market problem which is to be solved. The start of the product, service and/or business model development is based on different hypotheses, which must be tested on the market during the process and, if necessary, adapted or rejected.

The concept of the business model canvas presented in Sect. 3.3 can be used for **building** and thus for the process of developing a new solution. A comprehensive business plan is not yet necessary in this early phase, since the solution idea can still change several times, possibly dramatically, during the iterative approach.

Based on the results of the canvas, a first prototype of the solution can be created, possibly using design thinking (see Sect. 7.3). This prototype should initially only contain the central functions and/or properties of the intended solution to reduce complexity. Products can be mapped with their core services in the prototype, without the need for beauty and design. With services, the process steps in the prototype can be limited to the central features.

Once the concept has been created, thought through and found to be conclusive, the next step is to create the product or a corresponding prototype. This alone should already offer added value but should be reduced to the most essential functions and properties. You can put less emphasis on appearance and disregard unnecessary additional features. For services, the individual process steps are simplified as much as possible. As already mentioned, this "miniature output" of the final performance is referred to as the **minimum viable product** (MVP; see Fig. 8.9).

Phase 2: Measuring—Gaining Comprehensive Feedback from Potential Customers
Once the activity referred to as **encoding** in Fig. 8.11 has led to a minimum viable product, the **measurement** phase starts. The aim is to check the relevance and functionality of the solution found in the market. You present the prototype or minimum viable product to the target customers and obtain feedback. In addition to focus groups and surveys, workshops can also be held with the target groups.

> **Remember Box**
> We should not use the results of market research like a drunk would use a lamppost, namely, to hold on to them. Rather, we should use the results to enlighten ourselves.
>
> Market research should not make decisions for us but contribute to new findings.

The special feature of this type of market research is that potential customers can already buy the prototype, be it a product or a service. You can only determine the relevance of a service in the market if there is a concrete demand and thus money is used. Focusing solely on the prospective (future) purchasing behaviour by simply asking for a possible purchase intention is not sufficient. Different price strategies can also be checked in the individual repetitions of the cycle of building, measuring and learning. You can check which of the price differentiation strategies shown in Fig. 8.12 are to be used.

As already indicated, the same applies to sales channels, positioning, branding, etc. Thus you can check which sales form is to be used, based on Fig. 8.13.

Moreover, based on Fig. 8.14, you can determine which market development tasks can be used for business.

To make these measuring phases as lean as possible, existing solutions should be used as far as possible for measuring. The spectrum ranges from simple shop concepts (for testing the online shop) to building kits for developing the corporate website to testing advertising formats (e.g. via *Google AdWords*). Such a lean procedure also saves time and money in the measurement phase.

Reference plane	Term	Implementation
Person	Personal price differentiation	Free current account for students, student-subscription for newspapers and magazines, senior citizens´rates in museums
Region	Regional price differentiation	Price differences for identical cars or medicines in different EU countries
Timeframe	Temporal price differentiation	Low prices in the early and late seasons, high prices in the high season; air fares according to time of flight/early booking discounts; happy hour offers in clubs
Service	Performance-related price differentiation	Various prices for 1st and 2nd class travel with the train, or in Lufthansa´s First, Business and Economy Class
Quantity	Quantity-based price differentiation	Granting volume discounts to important customers
Distribution channel	Distribution channel-related price differentiation	Different conditions for online and offline bookings; different rates for online and offline services (brokerage, banking); discounter vs. department store
Demand mix	Price bundeling, bundling, coupled offer	Customers who purchase several products at the same time pay a lower price

Fig. 8.12 Types of price differentiation as input for the lean startup process. Author's own figure

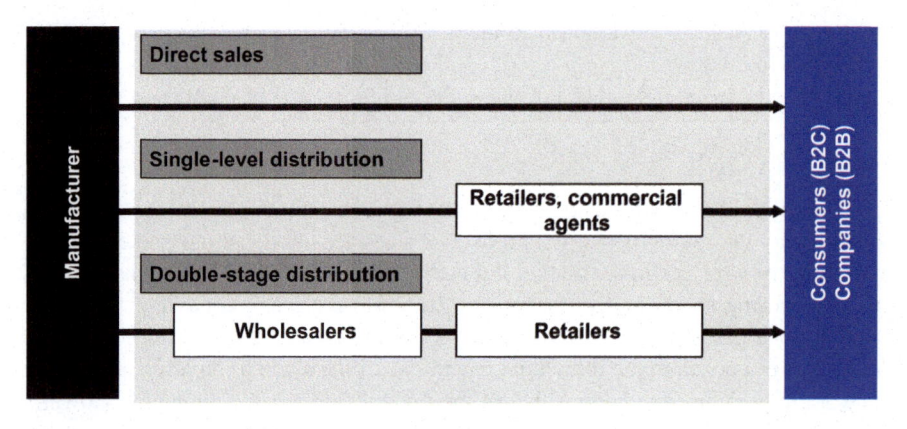

Fig. 8.13 Basic forms of distribution. Author's own figure

Phase 3: Learning—Analysis of Feedback and Development of New Hypotheses
Based on the **data** obtained during the measurement phase, the necessary **learning** takes place. For this purpose, the knowledge gained must be comprehensively evaluated to test the validity of the original hypotheses of the recently completed building, measuring and learning cycle. After the initial run of this cycle, the following questions can be answered:

8.2 Lean Startup

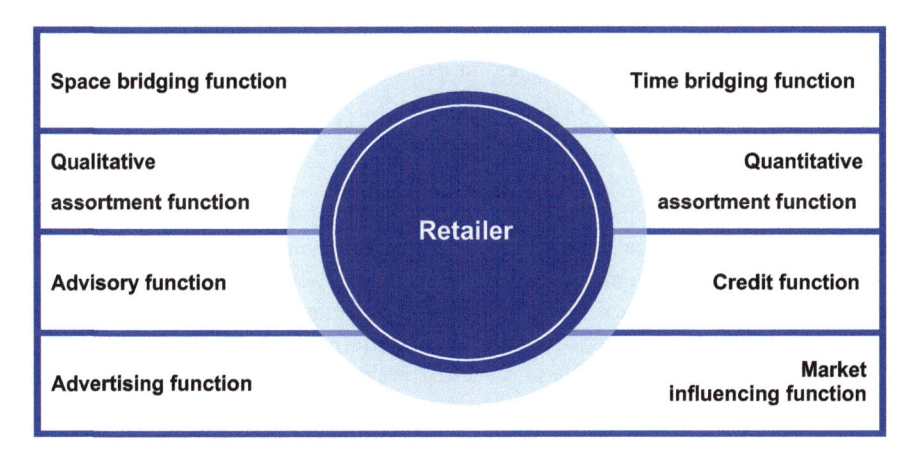

Retailer

- Space bridging function
- Qualitative assortment function
- Advisory function
- Advertising function
- Time bridging function
- Quantitative assortment function
- Credit function
- Market influencing function

Fig. 8.14 Tasks that business partners can take on. Author's own figure

- Does the problem on which the first cycle was based exist at all, or do (alternative) solutions already exist?
- Are people at all interested in solving a problem?
- Is there a willingness to pay an "appropriate" (from your point of view "profitable") price for the intended problem solution?
- Was the development based on the right target group?
- Is the intended distribution channel suitable for the target group?
- Is the desired positioning understood?
- Does the brand concept convey the core idea of the service?

You may find that some of the initial hypotheses were certainly incorrect. You should be pleased that this became clear so early during this process!

> **Remember Box**
> If you fail, fail fast, fail cheap and fail early!

Based on the knowledge gained, you can formulate new hypotheses for the next cycle of building, measuring and learning. Then you start the next cycle. It is important in all measuring and learning phases that you base your findings on sufficiently large amounts of data. Otherwise you may be led in the wrong direction by a small amount of data.

> **Remember Box**
> Do not use the NOMS method, the "national one-man sample", during the measurement phase. Just because a person, be it the husband or wife, the son or

(continued)

> daughter or even the boss, thinks the world is one way or another, don't believe it.
> It is better to ask your real target group, and not too few people!

After the learning comes the next idea, the next building, the next encoding, measuring, learning! Based on the knowledge you gain, you will be able to orient not only your hypotheses but also the solutions more and more comprehensively to the market. The building, measuring and learning cycle comes to an end when you have the impression that the market is "hot" for your offer.

Based on the findings of these so-called prelaunch phases, the launch phase follows, i.e. the comprehensive market launch (see Fig. 8.10). By running the cycle several times, your risk of failure has been significantly reduced, with little use of time and resources.

▶ **Implementation Tips**

- The lean startup concept is intuitive for you. It is a prime example of customer-oriented corporate management.
- Its use does not require any special knowledge that goes beyond the ability to conduct professional market research (cf. Chap. 4).
- This means that you can approach this concept without any major external support.
- In any case, it is important that you make it clear to the employees involved what is to be achieved through this concept.

References

Beck, K., Beedle, M., van Bennekum, A., Cockburn, A., Cunningham, W., Fowler, M., et al. (2018). *Manifest für Agile Softwareentwicklung*. Accessed March 26, 2018, from http://agilemanifesto.org/iso/de/manifesto.html

Edelman, D. C., & Singer, M. (2015, November). Competing on customer journeys. *Harvard Business Review*. Accessed March 27, 2018, from https://hbr.org/2015/11/competing-on-customer-journeys

Gourville, T. (2006). Wann Kunden neue Produkte kaufen. *Harvard Business Manager, 8*, 44–57.

Kreutzer, R. (2017). *Praxisorientiertes Marketing, Grundlagen – Instrumente – Fallbeispiele* (5th ed.). Wiesbaden: Springer.

Kreutzer, R. (2018). *Praxisorientiertes Online-Marketing, Konzepte – Instrumente – Checklisten* (3rd ed.). Wiesbaden: Springer.

Lennarz, H. (2017). *Growth Hacking mit Strategie, Wie erfolgreiche Startups und Unternehmen mit Growth Hacking ihr Wachstum beschleunigen*. Wiesbaden: Springer.

Müller, H.-E. (2017). *Unternehmensführung, Strategie – Management – Praxis* (3rd ed.). Munich: De Gruyter.

Preußig, J. (2015). *Agiles Projektmanagement*. Freiburg: Scrum, Use Cases, Task Boards.

Ries, E. (2017). *The lean startup: How today's entrepreneurs use continuous innovation to create radically successful businesses*. London: Penguin Books.

9 Budgeting Concepts

The **budgeting process** determines the means to be used to achieve different objectives. This chapter presents various concepts developed for communication policy tasks. The **communication budget** includes all costs related to the design, production and distribution of the means of communication. Due to the specific importance of advertising as a core area of communication policy, the following description of budgeting is based on this communication instrument.

9.1 Percentage of Sales Method

When **deriving the advertising budget from specific reference values**, you base budgeting on the planned or past sales **turnover**. In concrete terms, this can mean that a company decides to invest 10% of its annual turnover in advertising. This concept is called the **percentage of sales method**. Similarly, the expected or past **profit** can also represent the basis for assessment. The derivation could be that 5% of the previous year's profit is invested in advertising.

This approach, however, causes **procyclical advertising behaviour**. If a company generates high turnover or profits, advertising investments increase. In the opposite case, they decrease and possibly intensify a downward movement. This cannot be in your interest, because it would turn the causal principle upside down.

9.2 Competitive Parity Method

With the **competitive parity method**, you base your budgeting on the **advertising budget of competitors**. The central parameters for this are SoA and SoV. **SoA** (**share of advertising**) describes the percentage of the advertising expenses of a brand or a product in relation to the total advertising expenses of the defined competitive environment. **SoV** (**share of voice**) indicates the percentage of the advertising contacts of a brand or a product in the total contacts of the defined environment.

Depending on the position achieved or targeted, the budget can be set higher, lower or equal in relation to the competitor. It should be noted that only the input (i.e. the amount of the budget used) is considered, but not the efficiency and effectiveness with which a budget is used. You should therefore refrain from using such a budgeting method.

9.3 All You Can Afford Method

The **all you can afford method** is a similarly inappropriate approach. This involves checking within the company which budgets are "left over" for advertising. It becomes clear that this is a simple procedure but that it neglects any connection between goals and effects and does not recognise that advertising is a central tool for generating turnover and especially profit. It should not be misinterpreted as an instrument for the use of funds. Consequently, you should also not use this method.

9.4 Objective Task Method

The procedures described above are pragmatic and relatively easy to implement. However, they do not consider the objectives that advertising is intended to achieve. The goal-oriented methods try to overcome this disadvantage (**objective task method**). These methods **derive the advertising budget from defined advertising goals**. An attempt is made to deduce the necessary budget from the advertising targets. This could be an increase of the unaided awareness from 45 to 49% or the acquisition of 250 new customers the next year in Spain.

Such an approach presupposes the existence of viable **hypotheses about the effects of advertising use**, which is often not the case. Even if such hypotheses exist, they are generally based on past experiences and are not necessarily valid for the future. The limited transferability may be due to changes in the overall economic development, the market entry of new competitors, the increase in media costs, a changed advertising behaviour or other preferences of the target group. Nevertheless, you should base every advertising plan on concrete hypotheses so that marketing can do justice to its role as a value creator and not as a value destroyer or cash burner.

Additionally, the **persuasiveness** and **conclusiveness of the argumentation** of the **marketing manager** "fighting" for the advertising budget still have a particularly high weight in the distribution of budgets. Moreover, as an experienced manager, you build enough "buffers" into your planning to be able to achieve the required communication results despite (foreseeable) cutbacks.

9.4 Objective Task Method

> **Remember Box**
> The only appropriate budgeting method consistently derives a necessary budget from the desired objectives. The necessary hypotheses will become more and more reliable over time. You must only start with this more elaborate procedure once.

▶ **Implementation Tips**

- Even if the percentage of sales, competitive parity and all you can afford methods have simplicity as an argument on their side, you should consistently refrain from using them.
- This recommendation applies not only to advertising budgeting but also to other budgeting issues (such as R&D budgets, the definition of personnel budgets, etc.).
- The only sensible approach is to derive the necessary budgets from the goals to be achieved. In this way, you can achieve or force a goal-oriented approach, even in the budgeting approach itself.
- This procedure is much more complex than the methods mentioned above. However, it forces you to consistently think about the relationship between means and effects and to formulate hypotheses.
- In this way you promote the effective use of the budget.
- Therefore, you should always derive budgets from the objectives, even if this is very labour-intensive and therefore time-consuming, especially at the beginning.
- However, this is the only way you can gain the relevant experience to make your budgeting more and more successful.

10 Strategic and Operational Marketing Plan

To develop a closed marketing concept, you must combine the decisions made at the various levels into a single plan. This must be done at both strategic and operational levels.

10.1 Creating a Strategic Marketing Plan

Figure 10.1 shows the characteristics of a typical **strategic marketing plan** (see also Meffert et al. 2015, pp. 217–341; Tomczak et al. 2015). First, you will find the strategic definitions from the target setting phase (cf. Chaps. 2 and 3). Furthermore, the results and findings gained from the various strategic analysis instruments and forecasting methods are integrated here (cf. Chaps. 4 and 5).

Based on the knowledge gained from the various analysis instruments, the definitions are made in the marketing area (cf. Fig. 10.1). This includes the concretisation of **strategic marketing objectives** and the documentation of **marketing strategies** to be introduced, which are concretised in the strategic **offer portfolio**.

Moreover, it must be determined how marketing is to be organised. On the one hand, this includes the **structural organisation** of marketing, which determines the form in which marketing is anchored in the company organisation. This can take the form of a management board department, a divisional function or a subordinate service function. The hierarchical position of marketing, the number of employees working in this area and the budget available to marketing can be interpreted as an indicator of the **anchoring of marketing as a management concept** in the company. Additionally, it is necessary to determine how the relevant **marketing processes** will run. These relate specifically to the areas of planning, implementation and controlling.

Strategic marketing plan	
Business definition	**Strategic marketing targets**
Strategic corporate targets – business mission • Sales, profit • Market share • EBITDA	**Marketing strategies** • Market field strategy • Market stimulation strategy • Market segmentation strategy • Market area strategy
Assessment of the company's success as well as the contribution of SBUs to the success in the past • Entire company • SBU 1, ..., n	**Strategic offer – portfolio** • Product/service portfolio • Technology portfolio

Prognosis for the long-term development of the company's relevant environment
• Microenvironment (customers, suppliers, investors, competitors)
• Macroenvironment (political/juridical environment, socio-cultural environment, economic and technological environment)
	Marketing organization
	• Organizational structure of marketing
	• Operational structure of marketing
	  • Planning processes
	  • Implementation processes
	  • Control processes

Fig. 10.1 Rough structure of a strategic marketing plan. Author's own figure

> **Remember Box**
> In the strategic marketing plan, you document the long-term goals, strategies and other specifications for the marketing area.

10.2 Creating an Operational Marketing Plan

The **operational marketing** plan (cf. Fig. 10.2) serves as the basis for the steps to be implemented within a fiscal year and thus represents a concretisation of the presented strategic marketing plan, which is usually oriented towards 3–5 years. In the operational marketing plan, the **relevant market is first concretised**. Based on the strategic specifications of the company, it defines for which offer the plan is valid and which target groups are addressed in which regions and/or countries. After this concretisation, the **opportunities and risks can be determined**, which particularly stand out for the year being planned.

- What changes will there be in competition?
- Which factors will have an additional impact on market development? The general economic situation can be expressed in the propensity to buy and invest but also in the development of unemployment.
- Are there any signs of technological and/or legal changes that require attention during the action period?
- What are the challenges associated with additional digitisation?

10.2 Creating an Operational Marketing Plan

Operational marketing plan	
Definition of the relevant market • Product/service • Core and peripheral target group • Regional target area (catchment area)	**Marketing targets** • Target definition for the planned acitivies • Establishment of a target pyramid or a balanced storecard (incl. all departments involved) • Documentation of roles and responsibilities
External conditions – opportunities and threats • Key competitors (today and in the future) • Market development (incl. major influencing factors) • Technological and juridical change	**Marketing strategies** • Settlement of the selected strategic options • Concretization of the strategic design of the activities planned
Internal conditions – strengths and weaknesses • Performance of sales force • Quality level of products/services • Marketing department's level of qualification and motivation	**Marketing instruments** • Design of the marketing diamond • Integration of different activities
Implementation and control • Clear contentual responsibilities for implementation and control • Clear procedural responsibilities for implementation and control	**Marketing budget** • Size of budget • Distribution of budget among activities planned

Fig. 10.2 Rough structure of an operational marketing plan. Author's own figure

The results of the analyses and forecasting methods presented are also incorporated into the design of the operational marketing plan. The results of customer value analyses must also be considered here (see Chap. 6).

While **concretising the strengths and weaknesses** of the company, it is important to work out the results of a comparative analysis in the competitive environment. These can show the strength of the company's own sales team or how the company's own range of services can be evaluated in comparison with competitors. The level of qualification and identification of marketing employees in general is also to be recorded here (cf. Sect. 4.3). Moreover, it must be noted who is responsible for **implementing all marketing activities**:

- Which internal company networks must be considered when different functional areas must take over marketing tasks?
- Who is responsible for controlling marketing activities?

These questions must be answered both in terms of content (i.e. "What should be done?") and process (i.e. "How should something be done?").

In addition to fixing these framework conditions, the **marketing goals** must also be documented in concrete terms (cf. Chap. 2). A pyramid of objectives or a balanced scorecard must be designed, and existing conflicts of objectives addressed. The **marketing strategies** derived from this should be concretised as guidelines for operative marketing and broken down into the **design of marketing tools**. You must pay attention to the integration of the marketing tasks that may be processed by different functional areas. The parenthesis around all these activities represents the **marketing budget**, in which not only the amount is determined but also the

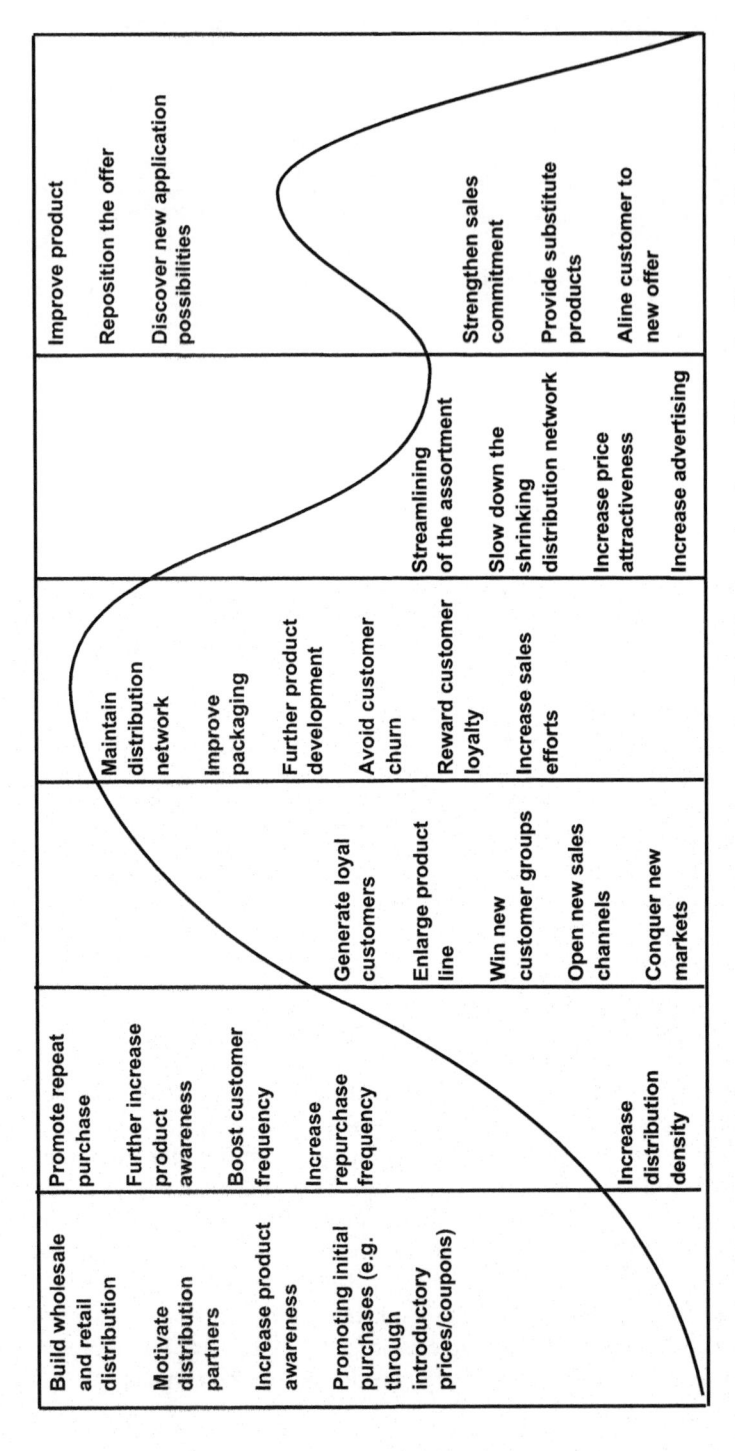

Introduction	Growth	Maturity	Saturation	Decline
Build wholesale and retail distribution	Promote repeat purchase			Improve product
Motivate distribution partners	Further increase product awareness			Reposition the offer
Increase product awareness	Boost customer frequency			Discover new application possibilities
Promoting initial purchases (e.g. through introductory prices/coupons)	Increase repurchase frequency	Maintain distribution network		
		Improve packaging		
	Generate loyal customers	Further product development		
	Enlarge product line	Avoid customer churn	Streamlining of the assortment	
	Win new customer groups	Reward customer loyalty	Slow down the shrinking distribution network	Strengthen sales commitment
	Open new sales channels	Increase sales efforts	Increase price attractiveness	Provide substitute products
Increase distribution density	Conquer new markets		Increase advertising	Aline customer to new offer

Fig. 10.3 Ideal-typical assignment of action modules of a marketing plan as a function of the respective phases of the product life cycle achieved. Author's own figure

allocation to different action areas and priorities is carried out. The results of the budgeting concepts discussed must be considered (see Chap. 9).

> **Remember Box**
> In the operational marketing plan, you define which goals you want to achieve in 1 year, which measures are to be implemented for them and how they are to be implemented in terms of organisation and budget.

Based on an operational marketing plan, you can start actions that are oriented to the **phases of the product life cycle**. Figure 10.3 provides an ideal-typical assignment. Depending on the concrete marketing goals and strategies (e.g. regarding positioning), such an assignment can also be different. Figure 10.3 serves here only as an approach for your possible activities.

▶ **Implementation Tips**

- Developing a strategic and operational marketing plan is essential.
- In the marketing plan, you consolidate all short- and long-term action-relevant information.
- The strategic marketing plan comprises the long-term strategic specifications that have been made for marketing.
- In the operational marketing plan, you express which goals are to be achieved and how the marketing strategies are to be implemented in the current year using individual tools.
- Based on this, you can assign individual tools to different activities in the individual phases of the product life cycle.
- You continually check the validity of the marketing plans and make any necessary adjustments.

References

Meffert, H., Burmann, C., & Kirchgeorg, M. (2015). *Grundlagen marktorientierter Unternehmensführung, Konzepte – Instrumente – Praxisbeispiele* (12th ed.). Wiesbaden: Springer.
Tomczak, T., Kuß, A., & Reinecke, S. (2015). *Marketingplanung, Einführung in die marktorientierte Unternehmens- und Geschäftsfeldplanung* (7th ed.). Wiesbaden: Springer.

Change Management Tools 11

11.1 Designing the Change Management Process

Through **change management**, you can achieve the goal-oriented, comprehensive, often cross-departmental transformation of structures, processes, business areas and entire companies. Change management can ensure a comprehensive alignment to new requirements of the external environment. If you initiate such a change process, you should define in advance exactly what kind of changes in leadership and organisation are necessary in your company:

- **Change management at the level of organisational structures**
  In this case, the organisational structure of a company, which is reflected in the organisational chart, is further developed. This is often referred to as reorganisation.
- **Change management at the process level**
  The concepts for accelerating internal processes are located on the process level, which refer to innovative concepts of project management (cf. Chap. 8).
- **Change management at the business unit level**
  Change management in this area of the horizon 2 and horizon 3 business models can be accompanied by the sale of entire business units or divisions that no longer fit with the corporate strategy that has developed. This category also includes the entry into new business areas that become necessary to achieve a new corporate strategy. The leading developments can emerge from the innovation engine (cf. Sect. 3.5).
- **Change management at the level of the entire company**
  At this level, the entire company is realigned. This may become necessary if the existing performance engine is to be replaced by concepts developed in the innovation engine (cf. Chap. 3).

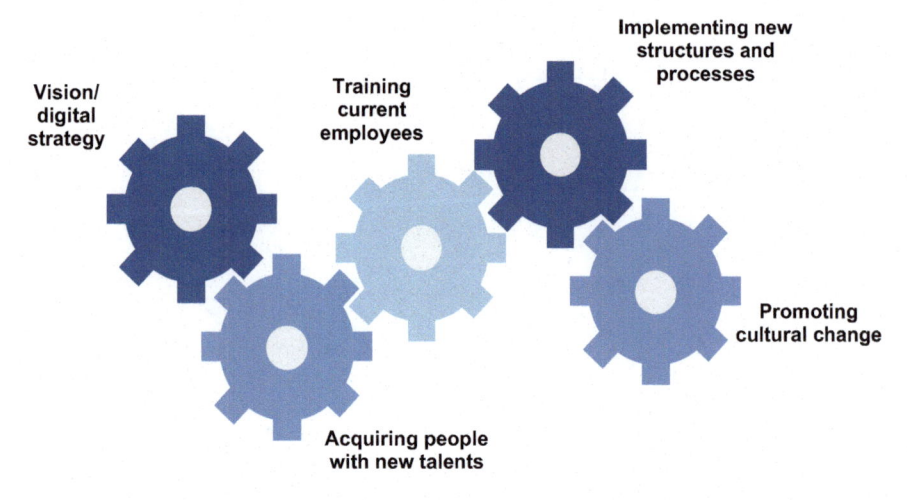

Fig. 11.1 Change management steps. Author's own figure

> **Remember Box**
> The worst organisation quickly becomes the best if you want to change something, at least from the perspective of the people directly affected.
> This sentence applies to changes of the prevailing working time model, the existing remuneration system, the installed customer relationship management software, the sales force organisation and much more. It always fits!

Figure 11.1 shows you the **change management steps** that are necessary to further develop leadership and organisation. At the start of the change process, there must first be a convincing vision, the realisation of which is consistently worked towards in subsequent years. You may need to acquire people with new talents to do so. At the same time, it is also necessary to train current employees to prepare them for future tasks in the best possible way. Furthermore, new structures and processes need to be implemented. Whether such a change process ultimately leads to success depends above all on the result of promoting the necessary cultural change.

> **Remember Box**
>
> Culture eats strategy for breakfast!
> Peter Drucker

Without a thorough cultural development, you cannot enter second or third horizon business models (see Sect. 3.5; also Kreutzer 2018). For without a cultural

11.1 Designing the Change Management Process

transformation, the classic "rejection reactions" that also occur in organ transplantations begin, namely, the rejection of foreign cells!

> **Remember Box**
> Digitisation is not a question of process or technology, but a question of culture!

With this knowledge, the extent to which employees are affected by the change process must be determined. You can analyse the respective extent using the **matrix of effect** in Fig. 11.2. On one hand, a distinction is made between the two axes "extent of change in thinking and behaviour patterns" and on the other the "extent of threat". This matrix enables a typology of the perceived changes. At the same time, typical behavioural patterns are identified that can be expected as a reaction to the emerging changes. From this, the tasks for change management and the managers entrusted with it are derived.

If the extent of the changes and the personal threat are classified as low, there will be a **lack of interest** in the consequences. If the extent of the change is considered small, but the personal threat is considered high, **fear** and a **sense of powerlessness** are the reactions that are often observed. On the other hand, if the extent of the changes is high, while the personal threat is low, it can result in a **lack of interest** or **reactance** in the sense of a rejection of the changes. However, if the extent of the changes and the personal threat are highly pronounced, **fear** and **reactance** combine to form an explosive mixture.

You should carry out the analysis based on the matrix of effect from the perspective of each individual employee. This is because the same changes can be interpreted and evaluated very differently against the background of the individual experiences of each individual employee. Young, adventurous employees can see

Fig. 11.2 Matrix of effect: typology of perceived changes. Author's own figure

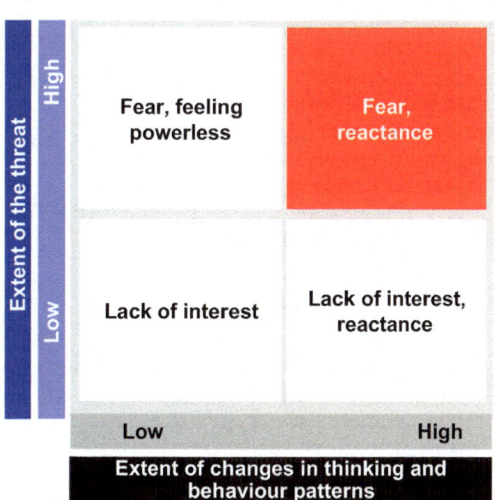

Fig. 11.3 Classification of different change triggers in the matrix of effect. Author's own figure

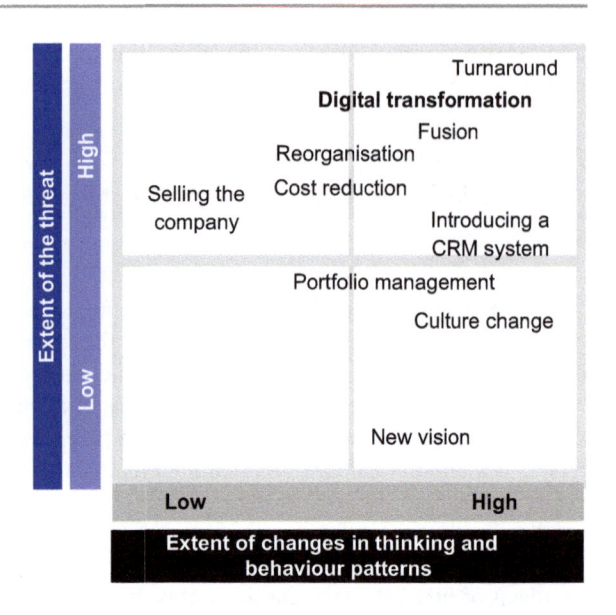

	Low	High
High (Extent of the threat)	Selling the company	Turnaround / **Digital transformation** / Fusion / Reorganisation / Cost reduction / Introducing a CRM system
Low		Portfolio management / Culture change / New vision

Extent of changes in thinking and behaviour patterns

such changes as career opportunities, while established and often older employees fear for their acquired vested rights. Figure 11.3 shows which reactions can "typically" be expected in certain change processes. The assessment made here can diverge considerably between the employees concerned. However, most of the various triggers of the change processes can be classified in this way in terms of the expected reactions.

> **Remember Box**
>
> Who always only does what he already can, always remains only what he already is.
> Henry Ford

11.2 Phases and Tools of the Change Management Process

When designing the change management process, you should distinguish between the following phases (see Lewin 1947):

- **Unfreezing phase**
  The starting point for any kind of change process is the realisation that the entrepreneurial status quo, at the various levels discussed, no longer meets the requirements of the markets and/or the corporate strategy. The necessity of change processes is becoming more and more apparent to the people concerned. To make changes possible, you must **"thaw" the existing state**. Only in this way can the willingness to change be achieved. However, because the company is

often in a state of equilibrium before the change process is initiated, many forces are released to maintain this state. To overcome these persevering forces, the desired direction of the change process must be worked out in this phase, so that it becomes comprehensible why change is necessary.
- **Moving phase**
  In this phase, the task is to initiate necessary changes in line with the change objectives. It is a matter of saying goodbye to what has become "loved" and breaking new ground in many areas. The frequently balanced state in the company is left behind to create space for new structures, processes, business areas and corporate strategies. The aim is to **define a new state of equilibrium** and to strive for and achieve it.
- **Refreezing phase**
  In the third phase, an attempt is made to **anchor the new state of equilibrium**. For this it is crucial that flanking processes are used to anchor this new state (e.g. through incentive systems for employees adapted to the new strategy). Otherwise, inertia in companies can lead to a quick return to the "old routine", and the change process fails. The refreezing of the new target state in the company is a prerequisite for the changes to be sustainable.

Often the desired goal of a new state of equilibrium is not achieved, not comprehensively and/or not within the planned time corridor. What causes can be responsible for this? Experience with change management processes shows that there are seven important **obstacles to successful change management**. You should avoid these in any case. The following obstacles must be overcome successfully during the above-mentioned process:

- The **lack of insight into the necessity of the change process** among managers and employees often represents the biggest hurdle in the implementation of changes.
- The **lack of a leading figure for the change process** at the top management level undermines the acceptance of the required changes.
- A **lack of experience with change processes** among managers and employees makes successful implementation more difficult.
- **Insufficient know-how** to cope with new tasks slows down the transformation process.
- **Trench warfare** between different people, levels and departments ties up important energy on secondary war scenes.
- The **lack of a corresponding remuneration system** geared to the new requirements can be misunderstood as management's insufficient approval of the change process.
- The **inability or unwillingness to change** parts of the management as well as the employees is also a major obstacle.

If the incentive system is not aligned with the new strategic target line, there will be conflicts between managers and employees. Should the behaviour be aligned with the new goals if the "old" behaviour is rewarded at the same time? In such a situation, it is not surprising that managers and employees follow the monetary incentives. After all, this can also be interpreted as meaning that the company's corporate management itself is not yet convinced by the new strategic orientation; otherwise, the incentive system would already have been adjusted accordingly.

How strongly your own incentive system is already geared to new requirements, in the direction of agility, innovative strength and thinking and acting in networks, can be determined using the following litmus test. For this purpose, you should self-critically analyse what employees and managers in your company are rewarded for:

- For achieving precisely defined goals in their own area?
- For network thinking beyond their own area of responsibility?
- For going off the beaten track?
- For questioning processes and procedures that have been tried and tested for many years?
- For the boldest ideas that cannibalise the existing business?
- For "lending" the best employees in virtual teams?

You can analyse the different **employee types in change processes** using Fig. 11.4. Whether managers and employees are positive or negative about change depends on the extent of the perceived personal risks. When managing the change process, it can be assumed that, especially at the start, a small **team of promoters** is faced with many people having a negative attitude. This includes **sceptics** who do not believe in the success of the process. The **resisters**, and above all those who put the brakes on, consciously oppose the changes. They delay decisions and consistently boycott their implementation. If people with such resistance potential are not

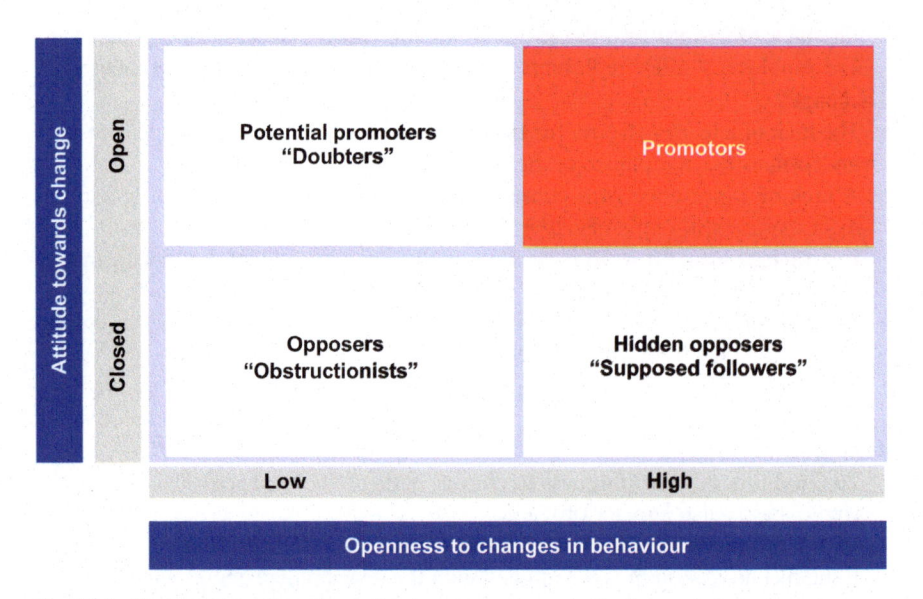

Fig. 11.4 Segmentation of employees in change processes. Author's own figure

11.2 Phases and Tools of the Change Management Process

won over to the cause during the change process or leave the company, the change process will fail.

> **Remember Box**
>
> You can only change yourself, but you can always change yourself!
> Elisabeth Lukas

> **Remember Box**
> Therefore, consider the important guiding principle for your business of "turning those affected into participants". Ideally, you will even succeed in turning managers and employees not into "fulfillers" during the change process but into "fulfilled".

Therefore, it is precisely those who put the brakes on, the resisters and sceptics who should consistently be involved in the change process with corresponding tasks. You should make sure that individual teams do not consist only of people who are sceptical or put the brakes on. The promoters are particularly challenged in all teams. These promoters must be trained and installed as **change managers**, because they represent the central resource for the successful design of the change process.

If you are responsible for the successful design of a change management process, you should know the typical **behaviour patterns within a change process**. These are shown in Fig. 11.5 based on the time axis and perceived personal competence. If

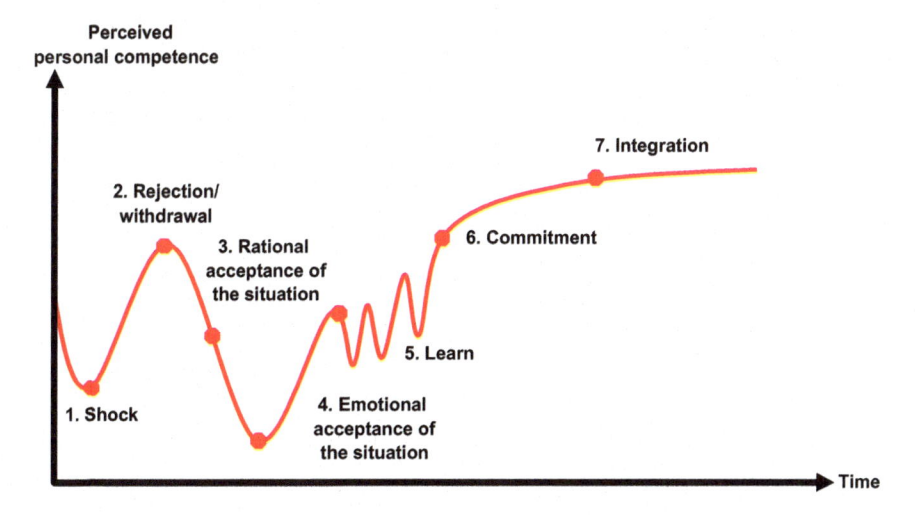

Fig. 11.5 Classic course of a change management process. Author's own figure

managers and employees are offered the prospect of a profound change, this often triggers a **shock reaction**. The perceived own competence sinks, because the person concerned does not yet know exactly how to react and master the new challenges. When the body and mind have recovered from the shock, many of those affected exhibit behaviours of **rejection** or **withdrawal**. The perceived competence rises again, because now a solution seems to exist, namely, resistance. For managers, this behaviour of the team members often occurs unexpectedly and therefore surprisingly. Every manager who is confronted with such a behaviour pattern should bear in mind that this defence corresponds to normal human behaviour during a change process.

Ideally, when provided with information, the rejection phase is followed by **rational acceptance** of the situation. The affected person rationally accepts his or her destiny but has not yet dealt with it emotionally. Then, ideally, the person **emotionally accepts** of the situation. It is the task of the change manager to ensure that these phases are in fact achieved. Next, there should be **learning phases**, so that high-level personnel and co-workers can prepare themselves for the new tasks and challenges. This involves offering training courses and coaching throughout the change process, because this learning does not occur on its own. After several learning phases, a **commitment**, a rational and emotional YES for change can finally be achieved. This is the prerequisite for reaching the phase of integration of the new challenges. Depending on the extent of the change, this process can take many months or even years!

The classic course of a change process shown in Fig. 11.5 can be analysed in more detail using the **four-room model**. It becomes clear in which form the already discussed burdens of the change process become concrete. Based on the insights gained, you can take appropriate countermeasures (see Fig. 11.6).

- **Room 1: Satisfaction**

    Room 1 is dominated by employee satisfaction (cf. Fig. 11.6). Ideally, everyone here would like to keep what they have achieved and not leave their comfort zone. From the respective subjective perspective, there is no need to leave the comfort zone. Everyone makes the best of the existing situation, again subjectively speaking, and is satisfied with it. A need for change is not seen. Most employees often have this kind of attitude before a change process starts.

    By the way, the relaxation room is very close to the room of satisfaction. This is where one is welcome to rest. Service according to regulations is possible!

- **Room 2: Renouncement**

    The calmness described in room 2 is gone, because the change process has already started (see Fig. 11.6). However, the employees in this room do not yet want to admit that (unpleasant) change is already taking place. The classic reaction to this is that of the three monkeys: hear nothing, see nothing, say nothing! One pretends as if everything is in order but knowing that the attitude is wrong and does not do justice to reality.

11.2 Phases and Tools of the Change Management Process

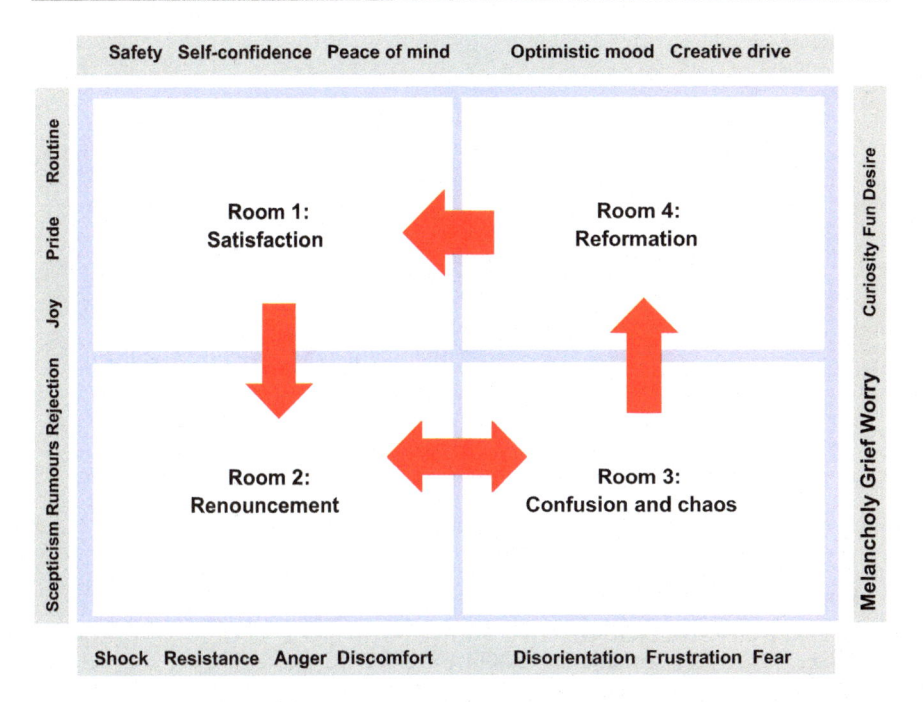

Fig. 11.6 Four-room concept of change management. Source: Adapted from Human Change (2018)

This behaviour leads to a feeling of unease, insecurity and discomfort among the employees. The response to impulses for action is resistance and defiance (see also Fig. 11.5).

- **Room 3: Confusion and chaos**

    With every change process, whether it is initiated internally or externally, the time comes when everyone must realise that there can be no such thing as "continuing on" in the same way (cf. Fig. 11.6). Frustration, worry, helplessness, powerlessness and fear are the consequences, because one is not prepared for the necessary changes. The employees feel like they are standing on quicksand and, again from a subjective perspective, have not yet found any anchor points for the reorientation: the existing is melting away (phase 1); the new has not yet taken on any concrete form (phase 3; cf. Fig. 11.7). In between, a large neutral zone opens in phase 2, which must be shaped creatively and energetically.

    To ease the employees' rigid shock, it is necessary to have a powerful vision, which at least gives a rough orientation of where the journey should go (cf. Chap. 2). Only this will motivate the residents of room 3 to regain their courage and start walking again.

    At this point, the emotional turning point can and must be reached (cf. Fig. 11.5). Now, at least the majority of those affected must accept the vision, the goals of the transformation and then also the emerging changes. This acceptance is necessary on both the emotional and the rational level. Then phase 2 in Fig. 11.7 is also actively shaped.

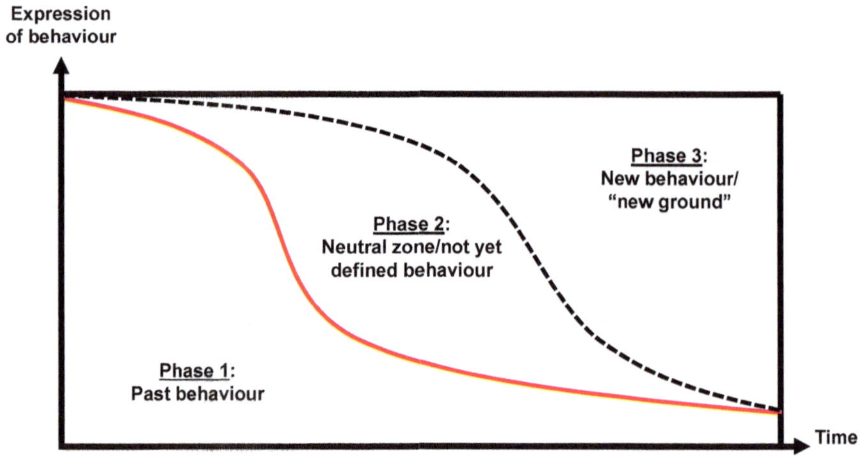
Expression
of behaviour
Phase 3:
New behaviour/
"new ground"
Phase 2:
Neutral zone/not yet
defined behaviour
Phase 1:
Past behaviour
Time

Fig. 11.7 Challenge in the change process. Source: Adopted from Lewin (1947, p. 28)

- **Room 4: Reformation**
  During the change process, all employees should gradually arrive in room 4 (see Fig. 11.6). At this stage, the transition to phase 3 from Fig. 11.7 is completed. New experiences were gained, and setbacks regarding the defined objectives were dealt with and accepted as a learning opportunity. At the end of phase 3 in Fig. 11.7, certainty reappears because the "new behaviour" gradually becomes the "normal behaviour". Fears are overcome, and new tasks can be accepted powerfully until the next comprehensive change process!

This four-room model draws your attention once again to the various emotional phases that employees go through in a change process.

> **Remember Box**
> It is a non-delegable task for the responsible managers not only to endure these emotional phases but also to actively shape them in a goal-oriented manner.

To identify the effort and resources required for the change management process in the company, you should systematically record the **intensity of the change** for the affected areas and departments. Two dimensions can be considered here:

- **Extent of the threat—from the point of view of each individual employee**
  Keep in mind that the greater the extent of the perceived threat, the greater the need for orientation throughout the entire organisation.
- **Scope of necessary changes in thinking and behaviour patterns—related to each individual employee**

11.2 Phases and Tools of the Change Management Process

This means that the more extensive these changes are, the more unwillingness and resistance can be expected, and the stronger the defence reactions will be.

It is important that you and all involved change managers are aware of the **influencing factors of the change process**. Thus, it is helpful to look at the **iceberg model** in Fig. 11.8. Rather rationally controlled managers focus on the visible **level of "fact and figures"** during a change process, but not only then. However, no change process can be successfully designed at this level alone. The invisible **elements on the psychological level** are of much greater importance. These must be considered comprehensively throughout the change process, because this is where acceptance or resistance to change manifests itself (cf. Schein 2003).

In addition to these factors, it should be made clear that the biggest obstacle for a change process is (previous) success! The refusal to recognise the need for action and the negative attitude towards innovations must be overcome by the management (see Christensen 2016).

> **Remember Box**
> Every kind of leadership always begins with the leadership of oneself.

Therefore, this task cannot be delegated by top and middle management to the level of employees. The other employees will largely orient themselves with their

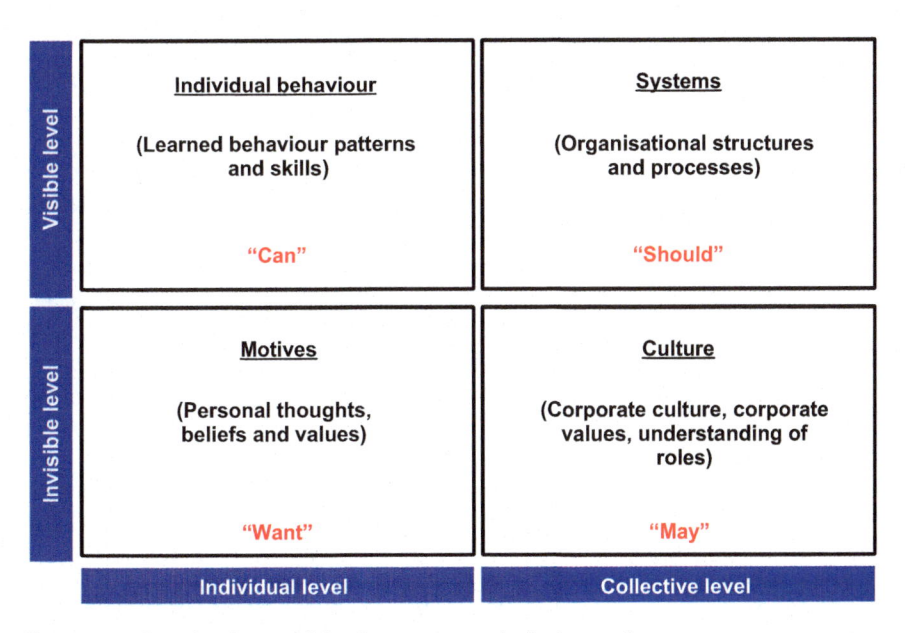

	Individual level	Collective level
Visible level	**Individual behaviour** (Learned behaviour patterns and skills) "Can"	**Systems** (Organisational structures and processes) "Should"
Invisible level	**Motives** (Personal thoughts, beliefs and values) "Want"	**Culture** (Corporate culture, corporate values, understanding of roles) "May"

Fig. 11.8 Influencing factors of the change process. Author's own figure

behaviour and willingness to say "yes" to the necessary changes, because "model learning" also takes place continuously.

In many companies, the initial situation of change management is often as follows. **Middle management** is the most stubborn in opposing the necessary changes. Why? Since the managers operating there have the most to lose, such as their status, income, personal assistance, large team, influence, company car, etc. Often these people, in comparison to younger employees, do not have the necessary qualifications to actively shape the change themselves. Therefore, we often talk about the **strategic clay layer**, or also the paralysing layer, which interrupts the flow of information from "top to bottom" and from "bottom to top". Many ideas and suggestions from the lower management level and the market are lost because they are not passed on from middle management to top management but are sunk into stuck hierarchical structures.

Top management, on the other hand, is often much more receptive to change, since this is what top management is paid to do. On the one hand, members of top management have often already reached the zenith of their professional development. On the other hand, they themselves are "gilded" by "golden handshakes" and other things in the truest sense of the word when they fail and leave the organisation. In these positions it is much easier to be courageous. And it is courage, willingness to innovate and creative power that are required at the top of the company, but they are still not always sufficiently available.

Lower management, on the other hand, has little to lose because these employees are only at the beginning of their careers or are satisfied with such a position. On the other hand, it is changes in the company that offer the opportunity to prove one's own efficiency and willingness to perform. Moreover, positions are often created during a change process, and positions previously filled by other people become vacant! This encourages "attacks" and committed work during the change process.

To successfully design a **change process**, various prerequisites must be fulfilled (cf. Fig. 11.9). First and foremost, a convincing **vision** must be conveyed and the **skills** necessary to implement it built up in the company. Furthermore, **coordination** is required to harmonise and network the individual implementation steps. Moreover, as already mentioned, the financial, personnel and time **resources** necessary for the change process must be made available. To ensure coordinated and goal-oriented action, an **action plan** with concrete milestones is required, which must be communicated comprehensively. After all, a commitment is required, from top management to the "last" employee. If all elements are considered equally, the desired **change** can be achieved. Even if just one element is ignored, failure is inevitable in different ways.

If there is no corporate vision, **confusion** arises (cf. Fig. 11.9). All or many move, but not towards a common goal, because this has not been communicated. **Fear** arises when the affected employees lack the necessary skills to implement the reorientation and no opportunity is created to acquire them. And fear is always a bad advisor! **Anger**, as well as rage, is the result, if the individual steps are not coordinated with each other, and therefore many things are a "waste of time".

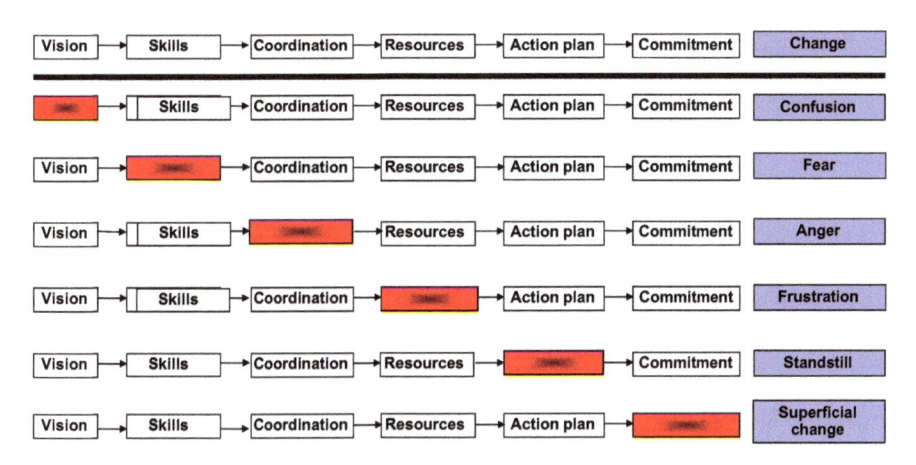

11.2 Phases and Tools of the Change Management Process

Fig. 11.9 Prerequisites for successful change management. Author's own figure

Frustration builds up when the resources for the necessary steps of change are missing and employees get upset. If an **action plan** is missing, there is a risk of standstill, because nobody wants to move in the wrong direction. Finally, if there is no **commitment**, only superficial change is achieved. The company only seems to be picking up speed, but below the surface, everything remains the same, and many remain in their comfort zone! Once again it becomes clear how comprehensively the task of change management must be understood.

Every change process also affects the involved teams. The **team development clock** (also called **team clock**; cf. Tuckman 1965) can also be used when smaller change processes affect only one team. First, the team development clock helps you to analyse the status quo of your team, especially if it does not "work" properly. You can also use this concept when an employee leaves your team or new team members join. These are times when the team's system, which is usually balanced, is disrupted and all members must realign themselves. This is also necessary if your team is given completely new tasks that force it to realign itself. When forming new teams, you should also use the team development clock. In all these cases, the team will go through the four phases defined in Fig. 11.10. It is your task is to make this phase active and goal-oriented.

- **Forming phase**

    Team building begins with the forming phase (see Fig. 11.10). At this point it is paramount that all team members **first get to know each other**. Everyone mingles, getting to know each other in a polite way. In this phase, none of the team members are aware of the goals nor processes (such as team meetings, task coordination, audit processes). Even the generally "acceptable" rules of conduct in the team are still unclear. These team rules can include punctuality, reliability and the extent of private joint activities.

Phase 4: Performing

Goal-oriented cooperation based on defined roles, communication channels, etc.

Phase 1: Forming

Getting to know each other, "scanning", polite approach

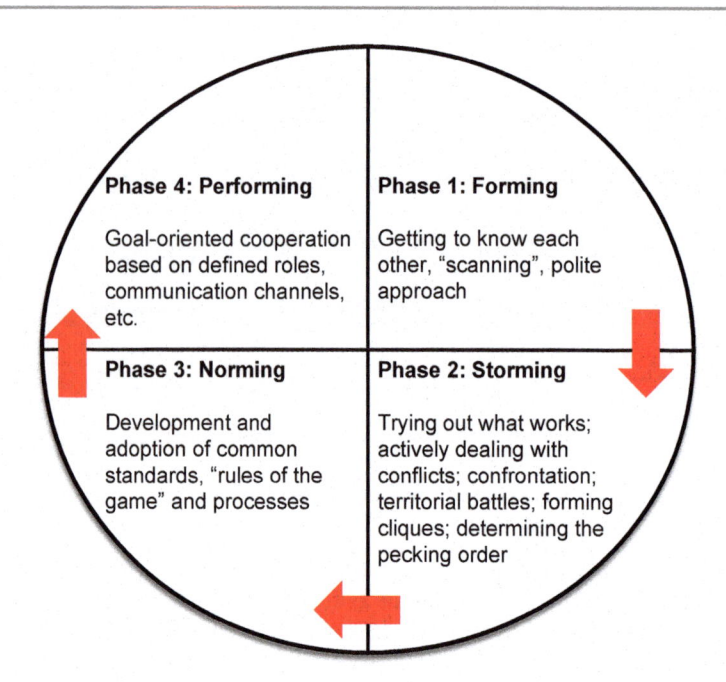

Phase 3: Norming

Development and adoption of common standards, "rules of the game" and processes

Phase 2: Storming

Trying out what works; actively dealing with conflicts; confrontation; territorial battles; forming cliques; determining the pecking order

Fig. 11.10 Team development clock. Author's own figure

As a manager you must make "clear announcements", inform and be available to communicate with the team members. Missing information will otherwise be replaced by suspicions and rumours in this phase!

The efficiency of your team in this phase is rather low, because you are still too busy with yourself. That is why you have the non-delegable task of actively promoting the process of getting to know each other, just like a host. You can do this through welcome meetings, mentoring, rounds of introductions, etc. In addition, you must proactively provide important information about working together. It has often been shown that a well-managed entry of team members pays off over many years through good cooperation.

> **Remember Box**
> You must actively shape the forming phase and keep it as short as possible.

- **Storming phase**

    The term "storming" already makes it clear that this phase is no longer calm (cf. Fig. 11.10). All team members are aware that "the cake" is now being distributed. Each team member has slowly gained an impression of the other members. **Sympathy** and **antipathy** are emerging; first cliques are formed. The first **conflicts** and **tensions** arise, which are also actively carried out. You try out what works and what is accepted in this team.

In this phase, the so-called **pecking order** is also formed. This defines who stands in which position in the **team hierarchy**. Who is the (perhaps only informal) leader, who belongs to the inner circle, who is more of a supporter and who is an outsider? Studies repeatedly show that teams are only productive when this pecking order has been determined. During this process, intense **territorial battles** often occur, whose causes are more personal than objective (cf. von Rosenstiel and Nerdinger 2011, pp. 280–356).

Moreover, in this phase a lot of energy is used for the team dynamics, which is not available to do the actual tasks. Therefore, you must actively shape the team and not leave it to the team itself. It is your job to set limits by sanctioning certain behaviour patterns. However, you also act as a mediator, moderator and coach to steer the group dynamics on a constructive path. This also includes openly addressing conflicts and not escalating them (Chap. 1 provides many hints about how to do this). This also includes helping introverted team members to be heard and ensuring that no psychological injuries occur during the conflicts.

> **Remember Box**
> You will only be able to progress to the next phase if you actively shape and direct this storming phase. At the same time, you will demonstrate your ability as a true leader and earn the respect of your team.
>
> Don't forget that respect must be earned! It is not awarded with a hierarchical position.

- **Norming phase**

    In this phase, based on the results of the storming phase, standards, rules and processes to work together in the future are defined (cf. Fig. 11.10). This consolidation will not take place without prior "storming". Now the team has (ideally) reached a higher level of maturity and knows how to deal constructively with conflicts and how to achieve solutions to problems in an appreciative way. Rules of the game have been defined that are acceptable (to all).

    In this phase you should work towards positioning yourself as an emotional contact. If leaders, out of incompetence, unwillingness and/or ignorance, do not fulfil the role of emotional leader, this important role will be filled by another team member or even by a person outside the team. This then becomes the so-called mother of the company and is the sought-after contact person for emotional questions and no longer the "appointed" leader.

> **Remember Box**
> One thing that especially male executives should remember is that arguments (to avoid the martial term "battles") are usually not won with objective

(continued)

arguments (alone), even if these are often advanced with decisions. The truth is that our decisions, even professional ones, are often more than 90% emotionally dominated!

At the end of the norming phase, you have distributed the tasks and roles within the team. Everyone (ideally) knows what is expected of them. This clarifies the "how" of the cooperation. It fulfils the prerequisite for working together in a goal- and solution-oriented way.

Remember Box
In the norming phase, you will also be challenged as a consultant and coach. However, you don't have to intervene as frequently and energetically as before. The bigger challenge is fulfilling your role as a professional authority that discusses the upcoming tasks with the team. Therefore, the forming phase should not take too long.

- **Performing phase**

    A team has only reached its highest level of productivity with the performing phase (cf. Fig. 11.10). The group conflicts are solved, so that now (ideally) everyone can fully concentrate on the tasks. The necessary appreciative cooperation is achieved through the common rules and standards and remains so until the next disruption event allows the team development clock cycle to begin again with the forming phase.

Such an ideal-typical procedure requires an adequately trained leader, who also relies on appreciation, open and honest communication and fairness in the cooperation. However, this is not always the case in day-to-day business.

Remember Box
You should develop a deep understanding of the individual phases of the team development clock and the associated emotional and rational sensitivities. It is important that none of these phases are skipped when forming a team, even if the managers (sometimes) would like to do so.

However, it is also important that you, as a leader, speed up the first three phases, so that they can be completed cleanly but also quickly. Otherwise the team will never work together productively. Therefore, you should lead the team purposefully from phase to phase.

11.2 Phases and Tools of the Change Management Process

Based on this knowledge, the following **tools for successful change management** should be used consistently:

- The **starting signal for the change process** must be given by the CEO or the management of the company. It is important that their contributions to the overall process are continuously visible and that the goals and needed actions are concisely formulated. It is particularly important that the "words" are followed by appropriate "deeds" (see Danoesastro et al. 2017; Aiken and Keller 2007).
- A committed **mentor in the company management** accompanies the entire change process and continuously helps to overcome (new) obstacles.
- There must be a **continuous communication between those responsible for change and the company management** to involve the company management in the process and to secure their support on an ongoing basis. It is essential to check whether the defined milestones have been achieved and, if necessary, more measures must be initiated to achieve the objectives.
- After **kick-off meetings** for all employees, **departmental meetings on the topic of "change"** are to be held on an ongoing basis so that all employees at all levels can see what direction they are striving for and what is expected in terms of their own contributions. Transparency about the process thus creates the necessary orientation that is necessary for coordinated work.
- To promote motivation for the tasks, often performed in addition to day-to-day business, these **performance contributions** of the individual employees and the teams must be appropriately **recognised**. The managers have the important task of making successes visible to all and rewarding special performance contributions.
- During the change process, the new or additional **requirements placed on employees** and their **responsibilities** must be made more **precise** and transparent at an early stage. Then everyone in the organisation calms down, because they know who is responsible for which change.
- Consistent **use of the team development clock** in all teams that are affected by the changes.
- The individual **performance evaluations** must be aligned with the new objectives to reward the desired new behaviour patterns accordingly and anchor them in the long term. If the "old behaviour" is still rewarded, then people will not adapt new behaviour patterns.

To achieve sustainable changes, you should also install **change controlling**! A central prerequisite for this is the **formulation of precise change goals**. Change controlling forces precision in implementation and quickly makes (unwanted) deviations visible to everyone! Such deviations must be escalated promptly so that they can also be recognised at the top management level and counteracted accordingly. In addition, the installation of a change controlling underlines the seriousness and durability of the desired changes! Throughout the company it becomes clear that the defined change is in fact desired in the long term.

All described activities and processes are necessary to successfully design a change process. Nowadays, many companies face the challenge of designing a

```
┌─────────────────────────────────────────────────────────────────┐
│                     Digital Transformation                       │
├─────────────────────────┬──────────────────────┬────────────────┤
│ Product/service         │ Holistic brand       │ Enterprise 4.0 │
│ innovations             │ management           │ (Platform concepts,│
│ (Internet of Everything,│ (Customer experience │ value chain,   │
│ Big Data, development   │ management,          │ agile management,│
│ of ecosystems etc.)     │ omnichannel strategy │ IT security etc.)│
│                         │ etc.)                │                │
└─────────────────────────┴──────────────────────┴────────────────┘
```

Development of a company-wide digital strategy – embedded in the corporate strategy
- Development of concrete digital targets to be achieved through the digital strategy
- Definition of responsibilities and budgets (incl. organisational anchoring, training)
- Development of a controlling system to monitor the digital transformation

Critical analysis of the status quo – internal and external
- **Internal:** perceived pressure to act, employees' willingness to act, extent of data and process silos, networking with (digital) cooperation partners, existence of a (digital) vision and strategy, allocation of budgets to classic/digital projects, IT digital readiness
- **External – competition:** challenge from (new) competitors, establishment of competing business models (e.g. sharing economy), access to relevant data streams, design of a digital/holistic brand management
- **External – customers:** determination of (digitally driven) interests, habits and expectations of one's own target groups, evaluation of "digital performance" by interested parties and customers

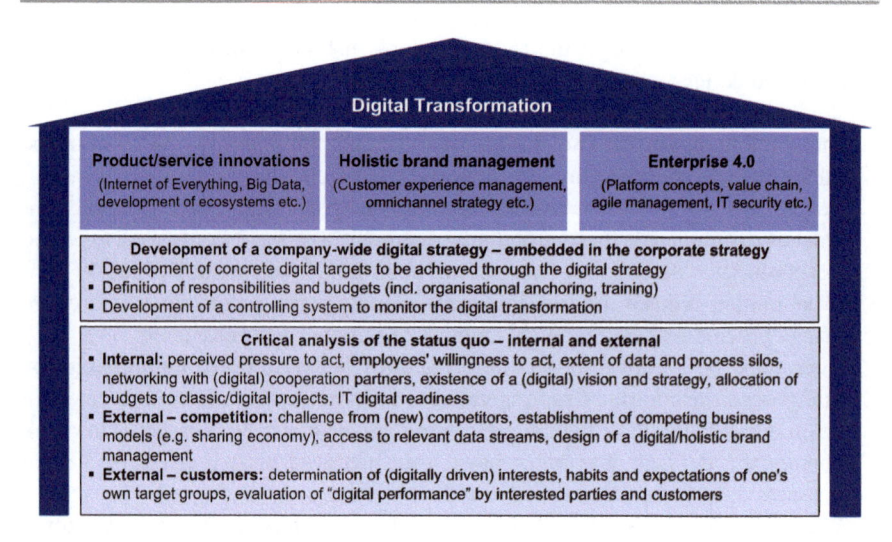

Fig. 11.11 House of digital transformation. Author's own figure

digital transformation (cf. Schallmo and Rusnjak 2017, pp. 1–31; Meffert and Meffert 2017). The associated challenges are presented in Fig. 11.11. Just like with any strategy process, digital transformation should begin with a **critical analysis of the status quo**. Consequently, this step forms the ground floor of the **house of digital transformation**. The company should be equally internally and externally analysed. **Within the company**, it is about recognising the experienced pressure to act and the willingness of your employees to change. Moreover, the extent to which data and process silos do not make full use of values must be determined. Furthermore, you must examine how comprehensively or not your company has a network with (digital) cooperation partners (cf. the value chain analysis in Sect. 4.7).

Additionally, you should check whether your company already has a (digital) vision and/or a digital strategy, or whether they still need to be developed. Moreover, you can determine how large the budget share is that is already attributable to digital projects. How "fit" is your IT to cope with the associated challenges (keyword digital maturity; see Sect. 4.10)? This involves the question of how professionally you already access the data available in your company about leads, customers, products/services and the value-added process (**small data**). These can be used to determine customer values, predict customer behaviour or optimise manufacturing processes (**predictive analytics**). Furthermore, you can determine to what extent additional **Big Data** can be accessed to refine these calculations and gain additional insights.

In terms of **external relations of your company**, two analysis directions are particularly important, namely, the **competitors** and **customers**. Which challenges do (new) competitors already present? Have business models already been established in your industry that adapt better to challenges than your own? What access does your company have to relevant data streams, compared to other providers? To what extent do you already implement holistic brand management, also in comparison to important competitors?

The external analysis also includes the extent to which the (digitally driven) interests, habits and expectations of your prospects and customers have changed. How do these people evaluate your "digital performance" in general and in the light of relevant competitors? What action is necessary for your company, from the point of view of **prospects and customers**?

Based on the insights gained, it is possible to **develop a company-wide digital strategy**, which is embedded in the corporate strategy (see Chap. 3). This involves not only developing concrete digital goals but also defining responsibilities and providing budgets. Moreover, controlling should be geared to monitoring the digital transformation. Within the digital strategy, it necessary to define the targeted **product and service innovations**, which, for example, are based on the Internet of Everything and/or Big Data. Alternatively, you can also define the development of ecosystems as a goal (cf. Kreutzer and Land 2015).

Based on your strategic definitions, you must aim to implement a **holistic brand management**, which focuses on customer experience management or the implementation of an omnichannel strategy (cf. Kreutzer and Land 2017). To underpin such processes organisationally, the development goes in the direction of **Enterprise 4.0**. This means it is necessary to establish the platform concepts, value chain systems and powerful IT systems mentioned above as enablers. It also includes establishing an agile management that makes use of innovative project management instruments (cf. Chap. 8).

> **Remember Box**
> Digital transformation is not a project, but a process.
> This process starts once, but it will never end due to further exponential and disruptive developments.

▶ **Implementation Tips**

- If you are personally responsible for the successful implementation of a change management process, you should use the tools presented in this section.
- It is important that you have the support of the top management throughout the entire process; otherwise, even the best tools will be useless.
- At the beginning, create an understanding for the necessity of the change process among all managers involved.
- Furthermore, you should prepare all managers to deal with the fact that emotions will be running high among the affected employees during the change process.

- These emotional outbursts must first be accepted. If they are not accepted, the emotions cannot be managed.
- Then it is necessary to align the energy associated with emotionality with the common (new) goal.
- Celebrate (smaller) successfully completed milestones with the affected employees. For most employees, the change process means one thing above all: more work in addition to the day-to-day business that still needs to be completed.
- Plan sufficient time for the management of the change process. You will need much more time than you think at the beginning.
- And don't forget the three most important success factors of change management: communication, communication and communication.
- The house of digital transformation provides guidance when designing a change process to establish your company in the digital age.

One last food for thought:

Even those who don't make up their minds have made up their minds a long time ago!

References

Aiken, C. B., & Keller, S. P. (2007) *The CEO's role in leading transformation*. Accessed March 28, 2018, from https://www.mckinsey.com/business-functions/organization/our-insights/the-ceos-role-in-leading-transformation

Christensen, C. M. (2016). *The innovator's Dilemma: When new technologies cause great firms to fail*. Boston: Harvard Business School Press.

Danoesastro, M., Freeland, G., & Reichert, T. (2017). *A CEO's guide to leading digital transformation*. Accessed March 20, 2018, from https://www.bcg.com/de-de/publications/2017/digital-transformation-digital-organization-ceo-guide-to-digital-transformation.aspx

Human Change. (2018). *Das 4-Zimmer-Modell oder die vier Phasen von Veränderungsprozessen*. Accessed March 29, 2018, from http://human-change.de/agb/54-das-4-zimmer-modell-oder-die-vier-phasen-von-veraenderungsprozessen.html

Kreutzer, R. (2018). Customer experience management – wie man Kunden begeistern kann. In A. Rusnjak & D. R. A. Schallmo (Hrsg.), *Customer experience im Zeitalter des Kunden, best practices, lessons learned und Forschungsergebnisse* (pp. 95–119). Wiesbaden: Springer.

Kreutzer, R., & Land, K.-H. (2015). *Digital Darwinism, branding and business models in Jeopardy*. New York: Springer.

Kreutzer, R., & Land, K.-H. (2017). *Digital Branding – Konzeption einer holistischen Markenführung*. Wiesbaden: Springer.

Lewin, K. (1947). Frontiers in group dynamics, concept, method and reality in social science; social equilibria and social change. *Human Relations, 1*(1), 5–41.

Meffert, J., & Meffert, H. (2017). *Eins oder null, Wie Sie Ihr Unternehmen mit Digital@Scale in die Zukunft führen*. Berlin: Ullstein.

Schallmo, D., & Rusnjak, A. (2017). Roadmap zur Digitalen Transformation von Geschäftsmodellen. In D. Schallmo, et al. (Hrsg.), *Digitale Transformation von Geschäftsmodellen* (pp. 1–31). Wiesbaden: Springer.

Schein, E. (2003). *Organisationskultur*. Bergisch Gladbach: EHP.

Tuckman, B. W. (1965). Developmental sequence in small groups. *Psychology Bulletin, 63*(6), 384–399.
von Rosenstiel, L., & Nerdinger, F. W. (2011). *Grundlagen der Organisationspsychologie, Basiswissen und Anwendungsbeispiele* (7th ed.). Stuttgart: Schäffer-Poeschel.

Index

A
A/A test, 154
ABC analysis, 161
A/B/n testing, 155
Absolute market share, 41
A/B testing, 152–155
Acquisition, 67
Acquisition-oriented segmentation, 57
Action-directing role, 34
Action items, 207
Advantages of speaking in a negative way, 28
Advocates, 168
After-sales services, 85
Agile project management, 195
All you can afford method, 222
Alternative facts, 22
Ambidexterity, 76
Analogy, 147
Analogy forecast, 147–148
Analyse, 98
Analyse the strengths and weaknesses, 101
Analysis grid for innovations, 211
Analysis grid to determine digital maturity, 140, 141
Analysis of strengths and weaknesses, 103
Analytical-creative search procedure, 186
Animations, 17
Ansoff Matrix, 50, 51, 63
Artefacts, 201
As a foundation, 60
Assessing target markets, 114
Assumptions, 10
Attribute listing, 176, 177

B
Backlog grooming, 208
Backup pages, 15
Balanced scorecard, 44–48
Balanced scorecard in marketing, 47
Bargaining power, 110
Basic concept, 109
Basic concept of A/B testing, 154
Basic concept of a customer journey map, 136
Basic concept of a value chain, 128
Basic concept of BCG portfolio analysis, 118
Basic concept of the balanced scorecard, 45
Basic concept of the SWOT analysis, 100
Basic requirements, 72
BCG portfolio analysis, 118, 119
Behaviour patterns within a change process, 237
Benchmarking, 123–127
Benchmarks, 123
Benefit associations, 80
Best-in-class company, 124
Best-of-breed, 124
Big picture, 15
Bivariate data analysis, 96
Blind area, 103
Blind area of your own company, 104
Body language, 7
Boston Consulting Group (BCG) portfolio, 117
Brainstorming, 175
Brainstorming guidelines, 175
Brainwriting, 176
Brand and product line innovations, 84
Brand attributes, 80
Brand awareness, 80
Brand behaviour, 80
Brand expectations, 80
Brand extension, 83
Brand identity, 79, 80
Brand identity approach, 80, 81
Brand image, 80, 81
Brand lovers, 168
Brand management, 79
Brand management concepts, 79–85
Brand-product lines matrix, 83

Brand scorecards, 47
Brand user experience, 82
Brand value proposition, 80
BtB customer survey, 93
Budgeting concepts, 221–223
Budgeting process, 221
Building blocks of the canvas model, 69
Building, measuring and learning cycle, 216
Burndown chart, 202, 203
Business model canvas, 68
Business model innovations, 70, 75
Business owner, 198, 200
Buying power, 111

C
Canvas, 68
Canvas concepts, 68–72
Carry out the sprint retrospective, 207
Cash cows, 117
Causal study, 91
Challenge in the change process, 240
Change controlling, 247
Change management, 231
Change management steps, 232
Change management tools, 231–250
Characteristics, 115
Characteristics and principles of design thinking, 178
Choosing employees, 115
Choosing media, 114
Churn prevention, 65
Cite studies, 13
Classic 5 Forces analysis, 108
Classic project management tools, 195
Collection of information, 64
Comfort zone, 2
Communication budget, 221
Company-driven support costs, 165
Company mission, 35
Company vision, 33
Comparisons, 11
Competence map, 196
Competence pyramid for determining customer value, 168
Competitive forces, 108
Competitive parity method, 221
Competitive position, 109
Component of the model culture, 139
Component of the model governance, 140
Component of the model leadership, 138
Component of the model operations, 139
Component of the model people, 140
Component of the model products, 139

Component of the model strategy, 138
Component of the model technology, 140
Concentrated marketing, 57
Concept for determining customer value, 168
Concept for services development, 84
Concept of customer-oriented strategies, 49–68
Concept of the net promoter score, 171
Concepts for the development of strategies, 49–85
Concepts to determine customer value, 167
Concluding part of a presentation, 7
Conclusion, 6
Conclusion using an analogy, 148
Confidence in various forms of advertising, 166
Consumer survey, 93
Content for the customer journey map, 135
Content of a goal, 38–39
Contract production, 67
Control, 37
Control cockpit, 44
Convergence, 182
Core processes, 128
Core values, 33
Corporate core values, 35
Corporate purpose, 35
Corporate values, 35
Cost-benefit analysis, 114
Course of a change management process, 237
Cover image, 13
Creating an operational marketing plan, 226–229
Creating a persona, 59
Creating a strategic marketing plan, 225
Criteria for market segmentation in the BtC market, 58
Criteria of market segmentation in the BtB market, 59
Criteria to determine customer value, 164
Cross-industry benchmarking, 125
Cross-selling, 63
Customer-brand relationship, 80
Customer-driven support costs, 165
Customer journey map, 134–137
Customer lifetime value (CLV), 158, 165
Customer perspective, 46
Customer reference value (CRV), 159, 165, 168
Customer relationship life cycle, 60, 62
Customer relationship management (CRM), 63, 157
Customer retention/customer development management phase, 62
Customer value determination, 157, 160
Customer value models, 157–172
Customer win-back management, 65
Cycle of building, measuring and learning, 216

D

Daily Scrum, 205
Daily standup, 205
Dale Carnegie, 3–4
Data analysis phase, 96
Data collection phase, 92
Data protection, 65
Decide, 183
Decision fields of the market area strategy, 66
Define, 182
Defining a target group, 58
Defining customer value, 114
Definition of done, 205
Definition of goals, 36–42
Definition phase, 89
Delphi method, 148–150
Delphi study, 148
Delphi survey, 148
Depth of digitalisation of the value-added processes, 139
Deriving the advertising budget from specific reference values, 221
Descriptive analytics, 150
Descriptive study, 91
Design challenge, 182
Design for an A/B website test, 153
Designing the change management process, 231–234
Design of the customer journey map, 134
Design phase, 91
Design thinking, 177–184
Desk research, 91
Determine customer value, 163
Determining the creditworthiness of potential customers, 114
Determining the customer value, 157
Determining the space and time of a design thinking process, 179–180
Detractors, 170
Development of vision and mission, 33–36
Development team, 198, 199
Differences between classic and agile project management, 196
Differentiated marketing, 57
Digital (information) value chain, 131
Digital maturity analysis, 137–141
Digital maturity model, 137, 138
Digital opinion leaders, 159
Digital transformation, 71, 247
Digitisation of the value chain, 139
Direct activities, 128
Direct investments, 67
Disadvantages of speaking in a negative way, 29

Discrepancy between one's own image and that of others, 103
Divergence, 182
Divergence phases, 178
Diversification strategy, 52
Document, 60
Documentation phase, 96
Downstream integration, 52
Drivers of customer value, 164
Dualism, 77
Dualism in the transformation process, 78
Dual or hybrid organisation, 78

E

Earnings before interest and tax (EBIT), 41
Earnings before interest, tax, depreciation and amortisation (EBITDA), 41
Earnings before tax (EBT), 41
Ecological factors, 97
Economic factors, 97
Economy strategy, 54
Effectiveness, 38
Efficiency, 38
Elements on the psychological level, 241
Emotional account, 24
Emotional map, 23, 25
Empathise, 184–186
Empathy maps, 180, 181
Employee perspective, 46
Employee types in change processes, 236
Enthusiasm requirements, 73
Error sources in the customer management, 162
Exaggerations, 10
Exhaustive survey, 95
Experiments, 94
Expert survey, 93
Explorative study, 90
Exporting, 66
Extended product life cycle, 106
Extent of a goal, 39
External benchmarking, 124
Eye contact, 8

F

Facial expression, 8
Features to describe your prospects and customers in the BtC market, 64
Field research, 92
Financial perspective, 46
5D concept of marketing research, 89, 90
Five-phase concept, 207

5 Forces analysis, 108
Forecasting methods, BNF–155
Foreign direct investments, 67
Forming phase, 243–244
Formulating the goals, 37
Formulation of precise change goals, 247
Formula to calculate the NPS, 170
Forward integration, 52
Four-room concept of change management, 239
Four-room model, 238
Franchising, 67
Future scenarios, 145

G
Gap analysis, 133–134
Gestures, 8
Goal cockpit, 45
Goal competition, 43
Goal complementarity, 43
Goal conflicts, 43
Goal harmony, 43
Goal indifference, 44
Goal neutrality, 44
Goals, 36
Golden circle, 34
Golden nugget list, 12
Group interviews, 93
Group presentations, 19
Growth areas, 2
Growth pains, 2

H
Hidden agenda, 14
Hidden area, 103
Hierarchical target system, 35
Holistic brand management, 82
Horizon 1 business models, 74
Horizon 2 business models, 75
Horizon 3 business models, 75
3 Horizons framework, 74, 75
Horizontal diversification, 52
House of digital transformation, 248

I
Iceberg model, 241
Idea killing, 175
Ideate, 182
Identification role, 34
Identify corporate strengths and weaknesses, 102
Identity role, 34

Identify the relevant competitors, 100
Immunisation effect, 29
Impediment backlog, 207, 210
Indirect activities, 128
Individual interviews, 93
Industry-specific benchmarking, 125
Industry structure analysis, 108
Influencing factors of the change process, 241
Infographics, 18
Innovation centre, 77
Innovation engine, 77, 78
Intensity of the change, 240
Interactions of third parties with your brand, 82
Internal benchmarking, 124
Introduction, 6
Iterative cycles, 179

J
Johari Window, 103
Johari Window for self- and company analysis, 104
Joint venture, 67

K
Kanban board, 210
Kano model, 72
Key values of a company, 35

L
Lateral diversification, 52
Leading questions, 10
Lead management, 62
Lean change canvas, 71, 72
Lean startup, 211–220
Lean startup method, 215
Lean startup model, 216
Legal factors, 97
Lego serious play, 184–186
Level of "fact and figures", 241
Licencing, 66
The limits of the classic approach to project management, 197
Line extension, 83

M
Machine learning, 151
Macro- and microenvironment, 98
Macro criteria, 58
Macroenvironment, 98

Management-oriented market segmentation, 56
Manifesto for agile software development, 196
Market area strategy, 50, 66
Market attractiveness, 120
Market attractiveness-competitive advantage portfolio, 120
Market capitalisation (market cap), 42
Market development strategy, 51
Market field strategy, 50–53
Marketing diamond, 57, 80
Marketing scorecard, 47
Marketing tool audit, 105
Market layer model, 53
Market penetration strategy, 50
Market segmentation strategy, 50, 56–66
Market share, 41
Market share market growth portfolio, 117
Market stimulation strategy, 50, 53–56
Mass market strategy, 57
Matrix of effect, 233, 234
Maximisation goals, 39
Mechanism of speech, 24
Medium, 4
Medium-value strategy, 54
Merger, 67
Metaphors, 11
Method 6-3-5, 176
Methods of data collection, 92
Methods to create new products, services and business models, 175–192
Micro criteria, 58
Microenvironment, 98
Middle-purpose relationship, 43
Milestones, 40
Mind map, 186–188
Mind map concept, 187
Minimisation goals, 39
Minimum viable product (MVP), 213
Mission, 33
Mission statements, 35
Mobilisation role, 34
Model for determining the (customer-) reference value, 169
Moderator, 190
Mono-casual explanations, 15
More-selling, 63
Motivation, 37
Moving phase, 235
Multibranding, 84
Multivariate data analysis, 96

N
Negations, 21
Negative statements, 22

Net promoter score (NPS), 170–172
Next Best Offer, 151
Norming phase, 245

O
Objective task method, 222
Objectivity, 95
Observation, 94
Obstacles to successful change management, 235
One-sided reasoning, 29
Open area, 103
Open issue list, 207
Operational goals, 39
Operational marketing audit, 104
Operational marketing plan, 226
Opportunities and threats of the industry, 107
Orientation and guidance, 36
Overall flow of Scrum process, 202

P
Page numbers, 18
Panic zone, 2
Paralysing layer, 242
Partial sample survey, 95
Passives, 170
Pecking order, 245
Percentage of sales method, 221
Performance engine, 77
Performance requirements, 72
Performing phase, 246–250
Persona concept, 59
Persona foundation document, 61
Personal dialogue assessment, 27, 28
Personal interview, 93
Personas, 59
PEST/PESTEL analysis, 97–99
Phase 1: building, 216–217
Phase 2: measuring, 217
Phase 3: learning, 218–220
Phases and tools of the change management process, 234–250
Phases of convergence, 178
Phases of the design thinking process, 180
Phases of the product life cycle, 229
Phenomenon of social desirability, 94
Physical and digital value chain, 132
Pictures, 11
Pitch, 9
Planning poker, 209
Planning the implementation of analytical tools, 89–96
Platform canvas, 70, 71
Platform concepts, 70

Pointing out mistakes, 18
Point-of-view, 182
Point rating model, 114
Political factors, 97
Poor dogs, 118
Portfolio analysis, 117
Positioning gaps, 55
Positioning models, 54, 55
Posture, 7
Potentially shippable product, 201
Predictive analytics, 150–152
Predictive maintenance, 151
Prelaunch, 213
Prelaunch phase, 215
Premium strategy, 54
Preparation of the presentation content, 21
Preparation of the presentation style, 20
Preparation of the presenter, 20
Prerequisites for successful change management, 243
Pre-sales services, 84
Prescriptive analytics, 150
Presentations, 1–30
Primacy effect, 7
Primary research, 92
Problem-focused questions, 24
Problem-solving conversation, 28
Problem-solving questions, 25
Procedure model of Scrum, 203
Procedure of a design thinking process, 178–179
Process benchmarking, 124
Process of design thinking, 179
Process perspective, 46
Pro domo effect, 13
Product backlog, 197, 201
Product backlog refinement process, 208
Product development strategy, 51
Product increment, 201, 205, 206
Production site, 67
Production value, 165
Product life cycle, 105
Product/market matrix, 50, 51
Product owner, 198
Product/service benchmarking, 124
Profit, 41
Project management tools, 195–220
Promoters, 170
Prospective customer survey, 93
Prototype, 182
Provider-oriented approach, 101
Pyramid of goals, 43–44

Q
Qualitative research, 91
Quality assurance, 128
Quality criteria, 94
Quantitative research, 91
Quantitative surveys, 93
Question marks, 118
Questions about problems, 24

R
Rapid prototyping, 179, 182, 213
Recency effect, 7
Reference value, 159, 165
Refreezing phase, 235
Relative competitive advantages, 120
Relative market share, 41
Relevant market can be defined, 100
Relevant set, 100
Reliability, 95
Report about solutions and accomplishments, 26
Representative, 14
Representativeness, 95
Requirements, 37
Requirements traceability, 201
Research goals
Resolution of an organisational dilemma, 77
Return on capital employed (ROCE), 42
Return on investment (ROI), 42
Return on marketing investment (ROMI), 158
Return on sales (ROS), 42
Reverse mentoring, 140
RFMR method, 166
Rivalry between companies, 108
Rivalry of the manufacturers active on the market, 111
Roles goals play, 36
Room 1: satisfaction, 238
Room 2: renouncement, 238
Room 3: confusion and chaos, 239
Room 4: reformation, 240
Root cause analysis, 207
Rough structure of an operational marketing plan, 227
Rough structure of a strategic marketing plan, 226
Round tables, 190

S
Sales, 41
Sales services, 85
Sample size, 14

Index

Satisfaction goals, 39
Scenario analysis, 145–146
Scenario funnel, 145, 146
Scope of a goal, 40
Scoring model, 114–116
Scoring model for evaluating a new product, 116
Scrum, 195–211
Scrum framework, 208
Scrum master, 198, 199
Scrum procedure model, 197
Scrum team, 198, 200
Scrum team members' roles, 198
Secondary research, 91, 92
Secondary sources, 92
Segmentation of employees in change processes, 236
Segmenting the market, 56
Selecting distribution channels, 115
Selecting of production sites, 114
Sentiment analysis, 169
Serial-position effect, 7
Service strategies, 84
Share of advertising (SoA), 221
Share of voice (SoV), 221
SMART goals, 40
Social factors, 97
Social influencer scores, 169
Social scoring services, 169
Sprint backlog, 197, 201, 204, 205
Sprint goal, 205
Sprint planning process, 204–205
Sprint retrospective, 204, 206–207
Sprint review, 206
Sprints, 197
Stakeholders, 198, 200
Standard strategies, 117
Stars, 117
Start to a presentation, 6
Statistical significance, 153
Step-by-step concept of benchmarking, 125
Storming phase, 244–245
Storytelling, 11
Strain on the eyes, 15
Strategic alliances, 67
Strategic business unit (SBUs), 118
Strategic clay layer, 242
Strategic goals, 39
Strategic group, 101
Strategic marketing audit, 104
Strategic marketing plan, 225
Strategies, 50
Strategies for international expansion, 67

Strength-weakness analysis, 103
Subsidiary, 67
Success factors of presentation content, 13–21
Success factors of presentation styles, 4–13
Success factors of respectful communication, 21–30
Suitable animation, 18
Suppliers, 110
Supplier survey, 93
Supply-demand fit, 211
Supporting processes, 128
Survey, 93
SWOT analysis, 99–114
SWOT matrix, 112
SWOT synthesis from the consumer goods market, 113
Synthesis of internal and external perspectives, 112
Synthesis of the external and internal perspectives within the SWOT analysis, 112
System of goals, 43
System of value chains, 128

T

Targeting, 57
Task board, 205, 209
Tasks, 204
Taxonomic market segmentation, 56
Team clock, 243
Team development clock, 243, 244
Team for design thinking, 178
Team hierarchy, 245
Technical terms, 11
Technological attractiveness, 121
Technological factors, 97
Technological resource strength, 122
Technology, 12
Technology portfolio, 121–123
Termination, 65
Territorial battles, 245
Test, 183
Testing method, 153
Theory of the minimum viable product (MVP), 214
Threat of new entrants, 109
Threats from substitute products, 110
Timeboxes, 203
Time frame of a goal, 39, 40
Time to market, 212, 213
Time to value, 213, 214
Timing, 19

Tool audit, 105
Tools for successful change management, 247
Tools for the strategic analysis, 89–141
Topicality, 14
Touch points of a customer journey, 135
TOWS analysis, 99
Transaction-oriented segmentation, 60, 63
Transformation roadmap, 138
Trend extrapolation, 143–144
Triad of customer service, 63
Triple jump, 34
T-shape personalities, 178
Turnover, 41
Two-sided reasoning, 29
Types of market segmentation, 57

U
Uncomfortable truths, 11
Undifferentiated marketing, 57
Unfreezing phase, 234
Univariate data analysis, 96
Unknown area, 103
Unspoken questions, 5
Up-selling, 63
Use of majuscules, 16
User-generated content, 82
User story, 208

V
Validity, 94
Value-added chain, 127
Value chain, 127, 128
Value chain analysis, 127–132
Value creation network, 129
Value-oriented customer management, 159
Vertical diversification, 52
Video training sessions, 12
Vision, 33
Voice modulation, 9

W
Way it is presented, 4
The way you start the discussion, 26
Weighting, 115
When presenting, 7, 8
Work in progress limits, 205
Workshops, 93
World Café, 189–192
World Café concept, 189
Writing their speech out, 9
Written survey, 93

Z
Zero measurement of your company, 171

Printed by Printforce, the Netherlands